Command at Sea

Command at Sea

Great Fighting Admirals from Hawke to Nimitz

OLIVER WARNER

CASSELL
LONDON

CASSELL & COMPANY LIMITED
35 Red Lion Square, London WC1R 4SG
and at Sydney, Auckland, Toronto, Johannesburg,
an affiliate of
Macmillan Publishing Co., Inc.,
New York

First published 1976

ISBN 0 304 29667 8

Printed in Great Britain by
Richard Clay (The Chaucer Press), Ltd.,
Bungay, Suffolk

F176

TO
VICTORIA HOWARD-VYSE
(née Collingwood)

Contents

	Prologue: The Quality of Command	xi
1	The Great Lord Hawke	1
2	Admiral Saunders and the Capture of Quebec	17
3	Louis-Antoine de Bougainville	33
4	Suffren's Great Adventure	45
5	Lord Howe and the Relief of Gibraltar	59
6	Children of the Service: the Gardners	67
7	Children of the Service: the Rowleys	79
8	Nelson's Collingwood	89
9	Lord de Saumarez	103
10	Farragut: the American Paragon	125
11	Beatty of the 'Lion'	143
12	The Greatest Command of All: Nimitz	169
	Epilogue: 'Valour and Sufferance'	186
	Notes on Sources	189
	Index	191

Illustrations

following page 36

Admiral Hawke: a print by J. McArdell after a lost portrait by George Knapton (1698–1778). *National Maritime Museum, London*

Admiral Saunders, by Richard Brompton (1734–83). *National Maritime Museum, London*

Bougainville; marble bust by F. J. Bosio (1769–1845). *Musée de la Marine, Paris*

Suffren: bust by Jean-Antoine Houdon (1741–1828). *Musée de la Marine, Paris*

Lord Howe: wax profile by John Flaxman (1755–1826). *National Portrait Gallery, London*

Admiral Lord Gardner, by Karl Anton Hickel (1745–98). *National Maritime Museum, London*

Alan, 2nd Lord Gardner: print by H. R. Cook after a drawing by Henry Edridge. *National Maritime Museum, London*

Admiral Sir Joshua Rowley, by George Romney (1734–1802). *National Maritime Museum, London*

Sir Charles Rowley as a young officer: portrait, hitherto unpublished, by Daniel Gardner (1750–1805). *Sir Charles Rowley, Bt.*

Admiral Lord Collingwood: posthumous portrait by Henry Howard (1769–1847). *National Portrait Gallery, London*

Admiral Saumarez, by Samuel Lane (1780–1859). *National Maritime Museum, London*

Danish privateer, frigate *Cort Adeler* of Copenhagen, attacked by British forces on 20 August 1808. Drawing by C. W. Eckersberg (1763–1853). *Maritime Museum, Kronborg Castle, Denmark*

Admiral Farragut in 1865. *Naval Historical Section, Washington Navy Yard*

USS *Hartford* running past New Orleans forts during Farragut's attack, 1862. *Naval Historical Centre, Washington Navy Yard*

Farragut's flagship, the *Hartford*, still afloat, 1901. *Naval Historical Centre, Washington Navy Yard*

Admiral Beatty, By Sir Arthur Cope (1857–1940). *National Maritime Museum, London*

The battle Cruiser *Lion* flying Beatty's flag during the First World War. *National Maritime Museum, London*

Admiral Nimitz in 1939. *Naval Historical Centre, Washington Navy Yard*

Admiral Nimitz signing the Japanese Surrender, 1945. *Naval Historical Centre, Washington Navy Yard*

Prologue:
The Quality of Command

The characters herein, drawn from the Navies of Britain, France and the United States, had in common the quality of command. The attribute is easier to state than to define, and can be exercised in many ways. Sometimes it arises from pride in the commander on the part of those commanded; sometimes from affection; sometimes from fear. Always it takes for granted that the leader knows his business from top to bottom, and will not throw lives away. Men trust him. As a result, they give their best, sometimes in greater measure than they knew they possessed.

One particular circumstance distinguishes the sea commander from his equals in most other spheres. He stands the same chance of death, mutilation or capture as the least experienced sailor in his fleet. What affects others will affect him personally. This fact 'concentrates the mind wonderfully', as Dr Johnson remarked of a man who was to be hanged in a fortnight.

The greater number of the portraits are concerned with the age of sail, with a society closely knit by professional ties; by friendship; sometimes by kinship; by shared dangers and experiences. Such a condition was once assumed as normal. When steam became a dominant factor in sea warfare matters grew more complex and no direct links occur between, for instance, Farragut, Beatty and Nimitz. What remained was the quality of command, which was more than ever necessary to face successfully a series of problems and decisions outside the range of their predecessors.

Napoleon, in his recorded thoughts on war, stated that the first quality of a commander was personal knowledge of campaigning, since 'a captain is not born, but made'. He should be imperturbable, have an open mind, show no change of expression under stress, so that he 'gives orders in battle with as much coolness as when perfectly at ease'. He should 'exhort the timid, in order to increase the small number of the brave'. Finally, he should add to other talents one for employing men 'each at the post to which his character calls him'.

The Emperor had generals in mind, though some of his remarks are of wider application. Admiral Sir William James, writing of his own profession, once said what 'aces' he thought should be in the hand of the ideal sea commander. They were three: first, the ability to inspire loyal, wholehearted service, which was the transcendent gift: next, a fertile imagination and a creative brain, as in the ability to plan battles: finally, eagerness to make use of the ideas of others, and to take them into his confidence.

It is clear that Sir William remembered Nelson when he suggested what fitted the model admiral. Few of those included in the present selection had all his 'aces', the least common being the third, which, although possible at the pace of, and under some of the conditions of, sail, could not often be so at a later period. Even the second was not nearly so widely distributed, or so vital as other qualities possessed by such men as Hawke, Saunders and Suffren. These were the ability to squeeze every possible advantage out of any situation, good or bad, and the resolution to follow up success, if necessary to the point of exhaustion.

Another characteristic, present pre-eminently in Suffren and Saumarez, but shared by others, is that of being unruffled by adversity, however sharp or protracted, or by mistaken decisions, or by the shortcomings of subordinates, together with the will to persist until any given task is concluded.

War being in its nature what Wolfe once called it, an 'option of difficulties', the element of sustained thought, described by Rodney as a 'painful' business, is essential to their solution. Again, there is the element of luck, so often stressed by Napoleon—not only the ability to seize Wolfe's 'lucky moment' in a campaign or battle, but luck as a personal attribute of the commander. Finally, the paragon must be ever-hopeful. 'Shoot pessimists at sight!' Lord Fisher once exclaimed, and the history of conflict makes clear that a great commander will turn in wrath upon anyone who saps his own or his men's confidence in victory.

Beginning the series no earlier than the time of Hawke, in the high eighteenth century, is in itself an indication of the range of possibilities from which to choose. It has been the aim of the selection to blend the famous with the less well known. A summary of achievement in a concluding section will, it is hoped, suggest why all these subjects deserve remembrance.

O.W.

1

The Great Lord Hawke

⚓   ⚓   ⚓

In London, indeed in Britain generally, the year 1781 was dismal. For once, sea-power had failed the army. In October, a force under General Cornwallis surrendered to the Americans at Yorktown, for the simple reason that during the course of the previous month, Admiral Graves had neither beaten his French opponent de Grasse, whose fleet was aiding the Colonists, nor tempted him to leave his anchorage in the Chesapeake more than temporarily. 'Under all circumstances,' wrote Washington, 'a decisive naval superiority is to be considered the basis upon which every hope of success must ultimately depend.' De Grasse had achieved 'superiority' without defeating Graves in battle. As a result, victory for the Colonists in their war against the Mother Country became certain, though campaigning would continue through some final stages.

Within a day or two of Cornwallis's humiliation, Admiral Lord Hawke died at his home at Sunbury. He had had an exceptional record of active service, and had risen to be political head of the Admiralty as well as senior admiral. Yet, such is the transitory nature of celebrity, that his passing caused no stir, Horace Walpole merely remarking that he did not seem to have bequeathed his mantle to anyone. He was buried neither in Westminster Abbey nor St Paul's, but in the quiet Hampshire church of St Nicholas at North Stoneham. Already, set into the floor of the nave, there were slabs commemorating Lady Hawke and one of her children, who had both died long before. But the chief living representative of the family was determined that there should be some visible record of the stature of the admiral. Martin Bladen, the second Lord Hawke, who had been trained in law, commissioned the sculptor John Francis Moore to erect a fitting monument, Moore having already created the memorial to Field-Marshal Lord Ligonier in the Abbey. The work was to be part heraldic, part graphic, and there must be an inscription worthy of the man.

The College of Arms had already done well by the admiral. Above the motto *Strike*—an apt allusion to the culminating act in hawking—the peer's crest showed, in terms of heraldry 'a hawk rising erminois, beaked, belled, and charged on the breast with a fleur de lys'. His coat of arms consisted of 'a chevron erminois between three boatswains' whistles purpure'. It is unlikely that a more appropriate armorial achievement for naval services was ever devised, although the sculptor omitted to show the crest, and took some liberties with the rest.

As for the inscription, the words chiselled by the mason ran:

D. O. M.*

This Monument is Sacred to the Memory of

Edward Hawke, Lord Hawke, Baron of Towton in the County of
York, Knight of the Bath, Admiral and Commander in Chief of
the Fleet, Vice-Admiral of Great Britain &c, who died October
the 17th 1781 Aged 76.

The Bravery of his Soul was equal to the Dangers he encountered;

The Cautious Intrepidity of his Deliberations, superior even to the
Conquests he obtained;

The Annals of his Life compose a period of Naval Glory unparalleled
in later Times;

For wherever he Sailed Victory attended him.

A Prince, unsolicited conferred on him Dignities which he Disdained
to ask.

Samuel Johnson, whose work Hawke added to his library, remarked
that in lapidary inscriptions a man was not upon oath. For this reason
memorials are apt to include nonsense. But Martin Hawke, if it was
he who composed the words still so clear today, was dignified, economical, perceptive and exact. In only one detail, that of the unfailing
attendance of Victory, could some qualification have been admitted.
In his heyday, Hawke had had charge of the naval side of a combined
operation whose aim was to attack Rochefort. From that affair few
had emerged with credit, though the expedition had at least been
spared a direct repulse.

As an embellishment to the memorial, Hawke's heir caused a battle
to be depicted which had occurred some twenty-two years earlier.
During its course, the admiral, pursuing the French among the rocks
and shoals of Quiberon Bay, had achieved one of the more spectacular
feats in the history of sea warfare. The sculptor rose to the subject with
distinction. He showed, as his centre-piece, Hawke's flagship, the
Royal George, going into action with the appropriate signals flying,
supported in close order by the rest of the fleet. And of all high points
in the admiral's life, the encounter of 20 November 1759, remembered
as one of a succession of triumphs by sea and land which had marked
the 'wonderful year', had rightly been chosen as the peak of a splendid
career.

Pilgrims to North Stoneham have been rare, but Hawke's monument was not superfluous, for within his own profession he had been
known as a prime example of the aggressive leader. Never content
with a passive role, he was a master of that dangerous and eroding

* *Deo optimo maximo*—to God, best and greatest.

4

operation of war, close blockade of a hostile coast. If his death caused little comment, his reputation did not diminish with time. Although the 'period of naval glory' which was coincident with his years afloat had indeed been 'unparalleled', and might have seemed to contemporaries to have been overshadowed by more recent events, the tide was soon to turn. The monument was not even in place before Rodney defeated de Grasse off the island of Dominica, captured his flagship and saved Jamaica from invasion.

The victory, although it came at the end of a humiliating campaign, was in fact a prelude to a succession of outstanding feats which were achieved when the country next engaged in warfare. Moreover, it would be men trained in Hawke's school who would take a leading part in that revival of fortune which would bring the sailing navy to the height of glory.

⚓   ⚓   ⚓

Hawke's father practised law, but died before his son entered the Navy. Edward Hawke did this at the age of fifteen under the patronage of his maternal uncle, Martin Bladen, M.P. This gentleman, of Yorkshire family, had himself served in arms as Aide-de-Camp to Massue de Ruvigny, who was created Earl of Galway for his services to William III. Bladen later became a supporter of Sir Robert Walpole, first Minister under the early Hanoverian kings. At least some patronage was almost essential to a rise in naval rank, and although Bladen, as Commissioner for Trade and Plantations, did what he could for his nephew, Hawke did not become a lieutenant until the age of twenty-four. Progress was then more rapid. He was made Master and Commander in 1733, and a post-captain the following year. This was due first to his own merit, and also to the fact that the most essential step—post-captain's rank—occurred through mortality on the West India station, where he was then serving. So unhealthy was the area at that time and later that it was a fruitful source of quick promotion.

Elevation to the flag list came through the iron rule of seniority. Here, Hawke was lucky. He held captain's rank for the not unduly long span of thirteen years. When he became a Rear-Admiral at the age of forty-two, he had already shown his exceptional capability in battle.

The war which continued between 1739 and 1748, known as the War of the Austrian Succession, first between Britain and Spain, and later between France and Spain together, was remarkable chiefly for the circumnavigation of the globe by George Anson and his exploits in the Pacific. It also established Hawke's reputation as a senior officer, for at a battle off Toulon, fought between Admiral Mathews and a combined Franco-Spanish fleet in February 1744, Hawke's 70-gun ship *Berwick* was the only vessel to gain much distinction. Having driven the Spanish *Poder* out of the line by superior gunnery, Hawke had the temerity to break the rigid formation which the Fighting Instructions enjoined and ensured the destruction of the Spaniard, even though mismanagement by others robbed him of her capture.

Hawke attained flag rank, as Rear-Admiral of the White, three years after Toulon. Admirals on the active list were known, until the middle of the nineteenth century, as belonging to the Blue, the White or the Red Squadrons, the Blue being junior. Hawke's promotion was partly the result of a desire by the Admiralty to promote certain captains, including Edward Boscawen, who were junior to Hawke on the list. Bladen had died the previous year and, lacking influential support, it was possible that Hawke might be superannuated or 'Yellowed', as it was called, there being no Yellow squadron. But George II, who valued a fighter, insisted that he be employed at once in his new rank. Within a few months he justified the trust in a significant way.

On 14 October 1747, when commanding a squadron of fifteen ships whose captains included such men as Rodney, Saunders and Philip Saumarez, Hawke came up with a convoy from La Rochelle, bound for the Antilles and escorted by a force under L'Etanduère. Hawke was in a position to chase the French admiral, who sent his merchantmen ahead. After a severe running fight he almost annihilated the enemy force, capturing six men-of-war. L'Etanduère, who saved his convoy, fought with great bravery. Gallantly supported by the Comte de Vaudreuil in the *Intrépide*, he got his shattered flagship back to France. Among the prisoners taken by Hawke was Lieutenant Suffren of the *Monarque*, who held that Vaudreuil's defence of his chief was one of the finest actions he ever saw.

Although Hawke missed taking many prizes from the merchantmen, he was able to send word of French movements to Pocock in the West Indies, and Pocock snapped up forty ships. The action set the seal not only on Hawke's reputation, but on his tactics. If possible, he would turn any action of which he was in charge into a chase, accepting the fact that his force must fight in a scattered fashion. He felt he could trust his captains to do their duty.

The Fighting Instructions, drawn up in the course of the previous century during wars with the Dutch, came into being because it was found that a strict line of battle was the best method by which ships could support one another and make full use of their broadsides. In action, signals were hard to see, owing to gun-smoke and general

6

confusion, besides which the signal vocabulary was limited. The simplest evolutions were, indeed, all that could be expected. Finally, keeping an orthodox line of battle was supposed to provide against what was euphemistically called 'shyness'. This meant not steering as close to the enemy as the admiral intended. It could also refer to running away. Officers' accounts of actions under sail abound in uncharitable slurs on their fellows.

Hawke's action, which became known as the second battle of Finisterre, took place five months after a victory by Anson over Admiral La Jonquière in the same area of sea. By this time, Anson had become established as the leading naval personality of his generation, and he had gained a peerage. He was six years older than Hawke, was immensely rich by reason of his capture of a Spanish treasure ship, and was at home in politics. Six of his ships took part in Hawke's engagement, four of them under the same captains. Hawke's future would depend largely on his relationship with Anson, whose nature was discreet, and whose loyalty to those who served him well was proverbial.

Hawke was back at home by the end of October, and Anson made the journey to Portsmouth to congratulate him. When summoned to London, Hawke was received in triumph. It had been a startling year, with promotion, independent command and success crowding hard upon one another. Now, by the King's favour, there was to be a star for his coat, and a red ribbon. Henceforward Sir Edward Hawke, Knight of the Bath, would be considered for command whenever there was a critical sea operation in prospect.

His wife, Catherine, *née* Brooke, whom he had married in 1737 when she was seventeen, lived for only nine years longer to enjoy her husband's title and renown, but there is evidence that she was happy. Her surviving children, three boys and a girl, were devoted to her, and Hawke wrote that she was 'the best wife, the best mother, and the best of friends—for truth, engaging tenderness and good nature she was the delight of all who knew her'. Although the requirements of the service took him from her side for long spells, in peacetime Hawke and his wife enjoyed country life together, and for some years lived at Swaythling near Southampton. Catherine died when the admiral was serving abroad, with the children still of tender years. A friend called Sarah Birt, who had been enlisted to help in the home, and who may have been a distant relation, became a second mother to them after their bereavement. Hawke did not remarry, and he and the children looked to 'Sally' for guidance for the rest of their lives.

Martin Hawke remembered his mother when commissioning the

monument for North Stoneham, adding at the bottom that it was equally 'Sacred' to her, 'the Beauty of whose Person was Excelled only by the accomplished Elegance of her Mind'. With a final filial courtesy, Martin concluded of his parents that: 'In the Conjugal, Parental and Social Duties of Private Life, They were equalled by few, excelled by none.'

⚓   ⚓   ⚓

The foundation of Britain's predominance at sea, shaken as it was at the time of the American war, was consolidated through the events of the Seven Years War (1756–62). This decided, among much else, the destiny of Canada and India, and it saw the establishment of a powerful state in the Prussia of Frederick the Great.

The main war at sea, which had begun with serious 'incidents' on both sides of the Atlantic, continued with tragedy, consequent on the appointment of Admiral Byng as commander of a fleet sent to relieve Minorca, which was then held by a British garrison and was under siege. Byng failed. Minorca fell; and by a gross perversion of justice, the admiral was shot, not for cowardice, but misjudgement. Voltaire's stinging comment that in England it is thought well to kill an admiral from time to time, *'pour encourager les autres'*, had in this instance a wry truth.

It fell to Hawke, with what he called a 'cargo of courage', to restore prestige in the Mediterranean. His second-in-command was Charles Saunders, who had recently attained flag rank. Both men were, however, to find other spheres than the Mediterranean in which to influence the war—Saunders in Canada, Hawke nearer home. Both men, and indeed all naval and military commanders, were soon to feel the stimulus of a great War Minister, William Pitt, whose belief it was that the best way to aid Britain's ally, Prussia, was by subsidy, by a series of combined operations which made the best use of the Navy and by blockade. 'Your country,' observed Frederick to the British Minister in Berlin, 'has been long in labour, and has suffered much, but at last she has produced a man.'

It was in battle and blockade that Hawke excelled. Little luck attended the only combined operation in which he was concerned. This was the attempt on Rochefort which took place in the summer of 1757. The fault lay in the disposition of the general, Mordaunt, a man of sixty who embarked in a mood of pessimism, one which was reflected in his much younger second, Conway. The expedition sailed, deliberated and returned, having done nothing. The generals felt that the difficulties were too great, and Hawke refused to press them. They

8

decided, wrote Wolfe, 'not to attack the place they were ordered to attack, and for reasons that no soldier will allow to be sufficient'.

Two rising men learnt something from the experience, Wolfe himself, and a sailor, Richard Howe, a pair Horace Walpole described as being like the union of cannon and gunpowder. Wolfe wrote: 'We have lost the lucky moment in war and are not able to recover it. The whole expedition has not cost the nation ten men; nor has any man been able to distinguish himself in the service of his country, except Mr Howe, who was an example to us all.'

Howe, captain of the *Magnanime*, won admiration by his fierce and successful attack on the fortified Ile d'Aix. Rodney, who was with the fleet, wrote that he 'gained the universal applause of both army and navy'. Wolfe made a reconnaissance with a naval party, and put forward a plan of assault of which no notice was taken.

Howe, who succeeded to a peerage by the death in action of his elder brother at Trout Brook, Lake George (now in New York State), was unwittingly the cause of Hawke's most serious tiff with the Admiralty, to whose Board Anson had already tried, but failed, to appoint him. Pitt decided that Howe was the man to conduct the naval side of an attack on St Malo the following year. He was made a commodore which, then as now, marked an appointment rather than a substantive rank in the Navy. He was sent to the fleet with directions to Hawke to afford him all the assistance in his power.

Hawke, who had not been made privy to the strategical scheme in hand, took this as a slight, struck his flag and hastened to London. He had nothing against Howe, whose ability he valued, but he felt that he had been by-passed, even though no slight had been intended. Their Lordships had been too secret.

The situation was resolved by Anson. Although he was then in office as First Lord, he decided that he would himself take charge of the fleet. Hawke volunteered to serve as his second, and the offer was accepted. It is some measure of the stature of the three men involved, who all, in due time, occupied the highest rank, that the difficulties were resolved without lasting harm to their personal relationships. Incidentally, according to a letter Wolfe wrote to his father, it was Hawke's gratuitous commendation, relayed by Anson to the King, which led to his promotion to the rank of full colonel—so that the Rochefort fiasco at least had the merit of bringing forward two younger officers who would make their mark in history. The generals were not pleased about Wolfe, who was considered mad, but once again it was the personal decision of George II which counted.

Hawke had resumed chief command in home waters by the year 1759, during the course of which so many of Pitt's schemes and hopes were fulfilled. From May until the following winter, thanks to ceaseless care and good organization, his fleet was engaged on blockade. Officers and men came to know the coastline, the islands and islets of Brittany as few have ever done except their own inhabitants: Ushant; the Passage du Four; Molène; the Black Rocks, so well named; St Mathieu Point; the Goulet, leading into Brest Road; Toulinquet Point; Douarnenez Bay; the Passage and Point du Raz; Penmarch— it was an area of sea whose rocks and shoals, whose tidal and wind conditions wore many a captain to a shadow, both in Hawke's own day and when his example was followed by successors. It accounted for not a few ships, but the price was worth while. The order 'well in with Ushant with an easterly wind' meant that the French could not get out of Brest in safety in weather conditions favouring a sortie. During the prevailing westerlies a more distant watch sufficed, but was never relaxed.

Even so, French military strength was formidable enough for the Paris government to plan an elaborate scheme of invasion which, so it was hoped, would deal a major blow at England, or Ireland, or both. A large army was assembled in Brittany, and it was intended that the Brest and Toulon fleets should unite to secure its passage.

Boscawen, who had made a name for himself the previous year for his part in the capture of Louisbourg, was then in charge in the Mediterranean, where he was watching de la Clue. An attack on the defences of Toulon failed, and de la Clue took advantage of the repulse to escape. He was pursued with vigour, and an arduous chase by Boscawen was rewarded in the bay of Lagos, on the southern coast of Portugal.

Disregarding Portuguese neutrality, Boscawen followed de la Clue close inshore and captured three French ships. Three more were burnt, and of the only two that escaped, one was badly damaged. When Hawke heard the news he wrote, with characteristic generosity, 'No man in England can be more pleased with your good fortune.'

Hawke's own reward, after a particularly heavy season of gales, came in November. It was late in the year for the transport of troops, but the French army was still assembled in the neighbourhood of Quiberon. On the fifth of the month the main English fleet was forced by weather to run for the shelter of Torbay, and Conflans, the French admiral, took the chance to put to sea. He had been reinforced not by de la Clue but by Bompart from the West Indies, and when the wind turned easterly on the fourteenth, the French commander-in-chief knew it to be his duty to take his ships to where they could cover the embarkation of the army of invasion.

The wind blew fair for friend and foe alike, and it enabled Hawke to leave Torbay the same day Conflans set out from Brest. As soon as Hawke reached his rendezvous off Ushant, he had word from a merchantman of French movements and he guessed Conflans's intention. He headed south, under press of sail. As his great flagship surged through the water, away in London a mob was burning him in effigy for not having brought the French to account!

On 19 November, Conflans sighted ships ahead of him and thought them to be those of Commodore Robert Duff, who was watching Quiberon. He was right. Duff's force promptly divided. Some ships went before the wind, others hauled up to southward. Conflans, with his main force, followed Duff's first division, that is, he held towards the coast. Then, early next day, ships in the rear of the French line signalled that there were vessels coming from the west. Look-outs on board the flagship *Soleil Royal* soon confirmed that there was indeed a fleet approaching in line abreast under a cloud of sail. It was the strength of England, bearing down for an attack.

Conflans found it hard to credit the speed at which Hawke had not only resumed his station but divined French intentions. He annulled his signals to pursue Duff, and tried to assess the capacity of Hawke's force as well as his possible tactics. Hawke had 23 ships of the line, including four three-deckers, which were by far the most powerful type of man-of-war then afloat. Conflans had 21, four of them of the largest size.

Taken by surprise as he was, Conflans's situation seemed far from desperate. He was nearing his own coast and had no lack of pilots. It was now blowing hard from west-north-west, and the ships were on a lee shore. Conflans had merely to lead in among the rocks and shoals of the Bay, and he should be safe. Hawke, so he reasoned, would never have the nerve to follow him close inshore. He did not know his man.

For Hawke, the day saw the justification of a lifetime of professional skill and knowledge. He had his blue flag flying from his mainmast, and the signals 'Form as you chase' was soon at the fore. Below it, another, signifying 'Every ship to use her utmost endeavour to engage the enemy as close as possible' meant that no one could mistake his intention. Hawke remarked to his retinue that he was 'for the old way of fighting, to make downright work with them'. He was not alone. His fleet, which contained three future First Lords—himself, Howe and Keppel—and a cluster of future commanders-in-chief, was animated with the same spirit. Howe, once again a captain, and in the famous *Magnanime*, was ordered to lead the line.

Soon the guns roared out amidst the thunder of the surf. As Conflans rounded the Cardinals, the group of rocks near the entrance to the Quiberon anchorage, broadsides were brought to bear on the French rear. Hawke was about to fight an action in a scene of Handelian grandeur in a way for which there was no precedent. No one but a seaman with utter confidence in his men would have aspired to achieve victory under the very cliffs of a hostile shore, every vantage point of which was crowded with hostile troops.

One of the first French ships to be closely engaged, the 74-gun *Thésée*, opened her lower deck ports to enable the heaviest guns to fire. In the state of the sea at the time this was rash, for waves swept in, and she sank, taking nearly all her company with her. Captain Keppel of the *Torbay*, at great risk and with expert seamanship, had boats hoisted out, and saved the only 24 men to be rescued out of a total of 650. The *Royal George* herself witnessed the surrender of the *Formidable*, the flagship of Saint-André du Verger. The *Héros* struck to Howe, but he could not take possession, and the Frenchman tried to get away. After the *Superbe* had been sunk with all hands by the massive power of the British flagship, the rest scattered. Seven escaped to the mouth of the little river Vilaine, into which all but one, the *Inflexible*, which was wrecked at the entrance, entered at the height of the tide, after jettisoning guns and stores. A few captains, disobeying orders, made their way to Rochefort and, of these, none had taken any serious part in the fighting.

Conflans's *Soleil Royal*, with her richly decorated stern galleries and her magnificent bronze cannon, rode out the night off Croisic. Next day, when the French admiral found himself uncomfortably close to Hawke, he ran his ship ashore, where she was burnt by her own crew, much to the disappointment of landing parties eager for loot and souvenirs. The same fate befell the *Héros*.

Hawke's dispatch was worthy of the occasion. 'Night was now come,' he wrote of the time when daylight was fading, 'and being on a part of the coast among islands and shoals, of which we were totally ignorant . . . and blowing hard upon a lee shore, I made the signal to anchor.' Not all his fleet heard the signal guns, and the night was made terrible by human cries and the sound of ships in distress. By morning, two of the British fleet were gone, the *Essex* and *Resolution*. They had run upon Four Shoal, but most of the crews were saved, and even some of the stores. Hawke altogether lost between three and four hundred men, and these two ships. The French loss was at least 2,500 men and a total of seven ships. As the crews were mostly Breton, the news was felt sorely in the neighbourhood of the battle.

Summing up his thoughts on one of the great moments in the history of the Navy, Hawke wrote: 'When I consider the season of the year, the hard gales on the day of action, a flying enemy, the shortness of the day, and the coast they were on, I can boldly affirm that all that could possibly have been done has been done. As to the loss we have sustained, let it be placed to the account of the necessity I was under of running all risks to break this strong force of the enemy. Had we had but two hours more daylight, the whole had been totally destroyed or taken; for we were almost up with their van when night overtook us.'

Hawke made the most of his predominance in the area by occupying some of the islets in the Bay, and on these his men grew vegetables. He and Boscawen afterwards took charge of the fleet alternately. To keep a hold on what had been won was an essential preliminary to the reduction of the island fortress of Belle Isle, which was captured two years later.

⚓   ⚓   ⚓

A hero's welcome should have marked Hawke's next appearance in London, if only to emphasize the irony of the earlier and ill-timed manifestation by the mob. He should also have had a peerage. Matters did not go that way, for although Hawke had sat for some years as an MP for Portsmouth, he had never been important in the corridors of power and was still without experience as a member of the Board of Admiralty. However, in the way of civilities he had nothing to complain of, and to the already handsome total of prize money which had accrued to him over the years, Parliament added a pension of £2,000 a year for two lives.

It was a bountiful enough treatment, if it is recalled that neither Boscawen nor Saunders had been given a peerage in recognition of their respective feats of arms. All three admirals did well for themselves pecuniarily, and Boscawen, ere his early death before the Seven Years War was over, built a mansion at Hatchlands in Surrey at the expense of the enemies of his country, as his monument duly recorded. It is an enduring reminder of an age of taste, and of the enlightened patronage of the young Robert Adam, who decorated the interior. It also emphasizes the fact that in the eighteenth century, granted early promotion, a measure of luck and a state of war, the Navy could be the means of fortune as well as providing the chance for honour and glory. Apart from his partiality for Johnson, and for the comedies of Plautus in translation, little remains to indicate Hawke's private enjoyments. He did, however, commission two competent portraitists to record his appearance—George Knapton soon after he had been knighted, and Francis Cotes after Quiberon.

The concluding stages of the war, during which Hawke continued to exercise command in home waters, were complicated by the addition of Spain to the country's enemies, and by the death of George II. Spain's participation at such a point merely led to an extension of British successes including, in the Caribbean, the capture of Havana and, in the Far East, the occupation of Manila. Among the aims of the new King were peace, prosperity and the pursuit of geographical discovery, and he had every right, at the time of his accession, to 'glory in the name of Britain', as he said in the course of his first speech from the Throne. The draft, in the royal handwriting, is extant, and those who believe that George III, Hanoverian by descent and Hereditary Elector of that country, stated that he gloried in the name of 'Briton' have a strange idea of his outlook.

After the peace treaty signed at Paris in 1763 Hawke, whose health had suffered from his long spells at sea, could have hoped for a period of ease. This he was granted, and it was sweetened by the honorific title of Vice-Admiral of Great Britain, an ancient post which carried a salary with it.

His resumption of activity came about unexpectedly, and was preceded by a gesture typical of his generosity. Pitt, now Earl of Chatham, in a rearrangement of government posts, invited Admiral Saunders to become First Lord. Saunders was only forty-six, and some years junior to Hawke. A few of the older flag officers, notably Pocock, protested that the appointment would 'occasion discontent and murmuring'. Pocock actually said as much to Hawke, thinking he would be the first to agree, only to be disconcerted by Hawke's exclamation of pleasure at the choice. He added that he was about to visit Saunders to congratulate him in person. The author of the biographical notice of Saunders in the *Naval Chronicle*, who was well informed, adds that hearing Hawke's view 'not only moderated Admiral Pocock's displeasure, but induced him to adopt a similar conduct'.

Saunders had had previous experience of administrative work. Ten years earlier he had held the post of Comptroller of the Navy. He did not find that guiding the Board of Admiralty was a bed of roses, and resigned after a few weeks. To Hawke's surprise, since Pitt had once described him as 'no Minister', Pitt wrote to say that he had nominated the admiral to succeed him, and that his choice had the approbation of the King. Hawke duly took first place on a Board to which he had hitherto been a stranger, a situation which was possibly unique. In the turmoil of exchanges, Lord Howe, who had previously been a junior Lord of the Admiralty, secured the lucrative but independent post of Treasurer of the Navy. This was considered a political rather than a service 'plum'.

Hawke was in office for just over four years, the later part of his tenure disturbed by ill health. He left no permanent mark on the structure or administration of the Navy, as did Anson. But for two appointments he deserved much credit. They concerned James Cook and Howe. In 1768, when it was agreed with the Royal Society that the Admiralty should supply a ship which could take scientists to observe the Transit of Venus across the sun from what was then known as the South Seas, Hawke insisted that a sea officer must have command of the vessel. Cook, then a warrant officer and the most competent surveyor in the fleet, was selected. He was made a lieutenant and given the *Endeavour* bark. In her, he made the first of his three circumnavigations. As a result, and as a compliment to his superior and patron, Cook gave the name Hawke Bay to a notable area of the North Island of New Zealand.

As for Howe, although at that time he was a newly promoted Rear-Admiral, Hawke took the imaginative step of appointing him, at the age of forty-four, Commander-in-Chief in the Mediterranean. When the usual grumbles were heard, Hawke remarked: 'I have tried my Lord Howe on many occasions: he never asked me how he was to execute any service committed to his charge, but always went straight forward and performed it.'

Hawke resigned in January 1771, worn out, as much as ever out of love with politics, and not expecting to enjoy many years of retirement. Fate was kind. He lived for a further decade, and from 1776 was a member of the House of Lords. His peerage, belated reward as it was for manifold services, came as a gratuitous act from the King, since no advantage to any political party could arise from it. That was the meaning of the final sentence on his monument.

Hawke kept up a correspondence with old friends in the Navy. He observed with regret the course of the war with the colonists which opened in 1775, and would have been concerned when, as a result of so few admirals of repute being willing to serve political chiefs who were in the process of losing America, the command of the main fleet fell to men past their best.

One of them was Sir Francis Geary, who had been in his heyday during the Seven Years War, but was in a poor state, mentally and physically. Seeking to brace him, in the summer of 1780, Hawke wrote two letters, which showed with what vigour his mind was working, and how he would have acted had he been in Geary's place.

In June he said he hoped Geary would resume the 'old station off Brest . . . when you are there, watch those fellows as a cat watches a mouse; and if you once have the fortune to get up with them, make much of them, and don't part with them easily'. Two months later he pursued the same theme, passing on to Geary the principles upon which he had always acted. He wrote:

> My good friend, I have always wished you well, and have ever talked freely and openly to you upon every subject relative to the Service. Recollect some of these passages; and for God's sake, if you should be so lucky as to get sight of the enemy, get as close to them as possible. Do not let them shuffle with you by engaging at a distance, but get within musket-shot if you can; that will be the best way to gain great honour, and will be the means to make the action decisive.

At the time of this letter Hawke was seventy-five. In outlook he was as positive as ever, and if Geary was not the man to take up the torch there were younger officers who would do so.

2

Admiral Saunders and the Capture of Quebec

⚓   ⚓   ⚓

Charles Saunders who, like Hawke, became a Knight of the Bath as a reward for services in war, owed the main impetus of his career to Lord Anson. To his patron's steady favour he added qualities of his own, and an enviable measure of luck. Horace Walpole, a fruitful source of naval as well as of most other kinds of thumb-nail character sketch, wrote of him as: 'That brave statue . . . a pattern of the most sturdy bravery. No man said less or did more.' Praise in respect of a member of a Service allegedly silent could scarcely have been carried further.

Saunders has never had a biographer, and such details as are known of his earlier life are few. He was born about 1713 and must have been reported on favourably when still young, for he was a lieutenant at the age of twenty-one, with considerable service in the Mediterranean and in ships of the line. Merit could have been the only reason why Anson, who had many friends to please and obligations to fulfil, should have picked him as first lieutenant of the *Centurion*. This was the ship in which, as a commodore, Anson completed his world voyage in the years 1740–4. Among the smaller ships of the squadron with which he set sail (from which only the *Centurion* herself survived) was the *Tryal* sloop. When Saunders was sent from the flagship to take charge of this vessel, owing to the promotion of her captain, she was already in a critical state from damage, and was nearing Cape Horn. Saunders achieved the feat of rounding the Horn in the face of appalling weather. Previously, another of Anson's lieutenants, Philip Saumarez, had had temporary charge of the ship.

When the *Tryal* rejoined the *Centurion* at the island of Juan Fernandez, only Saunders himself, one other officer and three seamen were in any state to work her. Thirty-four members of the crew had died. A Spanish captain whose vessel Saunders later captured expressed astonishment almost amounting to disbelief that the *Tryal* could have achieved the passage from the Atlantic.

During the course of his voyage Anson made Saunders an acting Master and Commander, and later on an acting post-captain, with seniority dating from 1741. The promotions were confirmed by the Admiralty on his return home. He did not take part in the fight with the Manila galleon *Nuestra Señora de Covadonga* which yielded such an amount of treasure as to require thirty-two wagons to convey it to London. This was the crown of the expedition, but before the time of the encounter Anson had sent Saunders home from Macao with dispatches. Although he lost a certain amount of prize money through the commodore's decision, it was not many years before he made up for it.

Charles Saunders was fairly launched, and he never looked back.

Between the time of his return from the Far East and being in action under Hawke against L'Etanduère, Saunders had much good fortune in the way of prizes. Among them was a Spanish ship valued at around £300,000, of which his own share amounted to more than a tenth.

At the battle of Finisterre he was in command of the *Yarmouth* of 60 guns. Late in the day, in spite of heavy casualties and considerable damage, Saunders proposed to Philip Saumarez of the *Nottingham*, his friend and comrade of Anson's voyage, and to Rodney of the *Eagle*, that with Hawke's permission they should pursue L'Etanduère and the *Intrépide*, which was with the French flagship. The initiative, and the sortie, ended sadly. The British ships were too shattered to be fully effective and Saumarez, to the loss of the Navy, was killed by almost the last shot fired in the action.

Saunders himself continued to prosper. Three years after the battle he became Member of Parliament for Plymouth, and in 1751 he married the only daughter of James Buck, a banker. Then Anson steered him into the lucrative post of Treasurer of Greenwich Hospital, a position which he continued to hold, in plurality, after he had become Comptroller of the Navy, responsible among other matters for ship construction. Promotion to flag rank came in 1756, and as Anson's partiality never wavered he could look for great opportunities to show his gifts in a war which, under guidance of Pitt, was beginning to go well.

It had been hoped by the more optimistic strategists that the capture of the French fortress of Louisbourg on Cape Breton Island by Boscawen and General Amherst in 1758 would come about swiftly. Had the stronghold fallen easily, Boscawen would have taken his fleet up the St Lawrence in an attempt upon Quebec. As it was, when the work was done, only the tail-end of the campaigning season was left. The difficult ascent of the St Lawrence was therefore deferred until the following year.

By the time detailed preparations had been made Boscawen was no longer available. He had been given the Mediterranean command, and the naval force destined for Quebec was put in charge of Saunders, who had recently been promoted Vice-Admiral. This left an aggrieved flag officer in the person of Sir Charles Hardy, who had done well at Louisbourg as Boscawen's second, but Hardy was no particular favourite of Anson and he had to be content with a squadron under Hawke, which at least led to a share in the glory of Quiberon. As Amherst was to have charge of an army which was to advance on Montreal, it fell to Wolfe, who like Hardy had done well at Louisbourg, to lead the land forces in what had every prospect of being an expedition full both of hazard and promise.

Wolfe embarked in no cheerful spirit. His health was poor, and he preferred campaigning on the Continent to adventures on the far side of the Atlantic: but his was, in effect, an independent command, and at the age of thirty-two, a commission as major-general and a mission of importance gave him a golden chance to prove what one of his staff described as 'a very peculiar turn for war'. He wrote to a friend: 'I am in a very bad condition, both gravel and Rheumatism, but I would much rather die than decline any kind of service that offers.'

Anson saw that nothing was left undone to make Saunders well equipped. His fleet was large, and it included the famous *Centurion*. He had two rear-admirals under him. One was Philip Durell, who was wintering at Halifax, Nova Scotia, which was then being busily extended as a counter-weight to Louisbourg farther north: the other was Charles Holmes, who knew the North American station well, as did many of the captains, such as Edward Hughes of the *Somerset*, later to make a name and fortune in India. Durell had actually served in action alongside Saunders under Hawke in the Finisterre battle and, all in all, Saunders could look for better support from his subordinates than could Wolfe from his three brigadiers. These men, Monckton, Townshend and Murray, were all aristocrats, and all were older than their chief. The same unidentified member of Wolfe's staff who wrote of his capacity for war left a series of notes on the expedition in which he castigated their behaviour. He spoke of Murray, the worst disaffected, as being 'the very Bellows of sedition . . . the very mention of another's merit canker'd him'.

Saunders was to be free from that particular sort of trouble. Even so, he had his difficulties. To start with, the voyage to Halifax in the flagship *Neptune*, which began on 14 February 1759, proved exceptionally long and tedious. Wolfe, who at the best of times did not enjoy being at sea, chafed at the delays, which no one could prevent, and when, at the end of April, the *Neptune* reached her destination, admiral and general discovered to their amazement that Durell was still at anchor. His excuse was that ice conditions were unusually severe, but there was more to it than that. Durell's wife had died during his sojourn in Nova Scotia and this, together with a harsh climate, left him depressed and lethargic. About the whole episode, Wolfe's note-taker let himself go.

Admiral Durell and his captains, who had wintered at Halifax with the sole view of blocking the St. Lawrence, began to see themselves in a devilish scrape, and that they should be call'd to a severe account for not being in the chops of the River early enough to prevent supplies going to Quebec. . . .

All mankind join'd in an opinion that nothing could be more scandalous than their proceedings, and all the Bellowing of the Troops at Halifax could not persuade them to leave that harbour for fear of the ice. Canada would certainly have been an easy conquest had the Squadron gone early enough into the River.

There was something in this, for Colonel Bougainville, who had been sent to France the previous year to request reinforcements and supplies for General Montcalm and Quebec, had not only got both, though on a modest scale, but had eluded the British blockade. With three frigates and seventeen supply ships, he was well on his way up the river before Durell, spurred into activity, left port. Once Saunders was in control Durell was efficient enough, but it was left to the senior admiral to redeem in full the honour of the Navy.

There was at least one seaman who did not spend the winter unprofitably. This was James Cook, sailing master of the *Pembroke* who, with the stimulus of a sympathetic captain, set about improving his knowledge of hydrography and surveying. At that time, the soldiers led the way in such expertise, and it happened that there were two technical masters who could teach Cook much. They were both of foreign origin—Samuel Jan Holland who, as his name implies, had been born in the Low Countries, and Joseph Frederick Wallet Des Barres, who came of a Huguenot family. Des Barres in due course made one of the best plans of Quebec, its approaches and the whole scene of action, which has survived. Both Holland and Des Barres had commissions in the army, and it was Holland, whose acquaintance he had first made at the siege of Louisbourg, to whom Cook owed most.

A glimpse of Cook, then aged thirty, occurs in an account by Holland, and provides an explanation of much that was to follow.

> During our stay in Halifax, whenever I could get a moment of time from my duty, I was on board the *Pembroke* where the Great Cabin, dedicated to scientific purposes and mostly taken up with a drawing table, furnished no room for idlers. Under Capt. Simcoe's eye, Mr. Cook and myself compiled materials for a Chart of the Gulf and River St. Lawrence, which plan at Capt. Simcoe's decease was dedicated to Sir Charles Saunders; with no other alterations than what Mr. Cook and I made coming up the River.

Eighteen years later, when Holland had become Surveyor-General of Canada and Cook was at the height of his fame as an explorer, the two met in London. Cook, said Holland, 'confessed most candidly that the several improvements and instructions he had received on board the

Pembroke had been the sole foundation of the services he had been enabled to perform'.

It is uncertain what Wolfe expected of Saunders, once he had reviewed his troops at Louisbourg, found them satisfactory and reported them ready to embark. Both general and admiral had specific orders to co-operate to the fullest extent—there were to be no more Rocheforts. The soldiers were to man the ships 'when there shall be occasion for them, and when they can be spared from the land service'. The sailors and marines were to assist the land forces 'and to man the batteries when there shall be occasion for them, and when they can be spared from the sea service'. There was also to be 'the strictest union' between the two commanders, who were instructed to communicate to each other all orders received from their respective superiors. How far could co-operation actually go?

Wolfe knew at least something of the difficulties of the long passage up the river, and had Saunders told him that he intended to transport the army as far as the Ile de Bic, some 150 miles below the city, supporting it thenceforward with his smaller vessels, the idea might have seemed reasonable. Even the French never attempted to take big ships up to Quebec itself, and indeed Montcalm, the French commander-in-chief, complained more than once that there were no up-to-date charts. Quebec's safety lay in her position. Two previous expeditions had failed. The first, led by Sir William Phips in the time of William of Orange, had at least reached the lines of defence. The other had occurred in 1711, just within the memory of the older inhabitants. That venture got no farther than the estuary of the river when storms dispersed it, and many ships were sunk.

'The admiral is a zealous brave man,' wrote Wolfe. 'I don't know exactly the disposition he intends to make . . . but I conclude he will send four or five of his smallest ships of the line to assist us at Quebec, and remain with the rest at anchor below the Isle of Coudres, ready to fight whatever Fleet the enemy may send to disturb us.'

This was not Saunders's idea at all. After his experiences under Anson, no one on earth could have imbued him with fear of navigational difficulties, even in a river with a huge tide-rise, with swift currents, with winds mainly adverse and with hazards of every kind, most of them to be discovered. His intention was that his whole fleet should proceed, by stages, right up to the basin of Quebec. He would support the army at every point—above all, at the climax.

So constant was the exchange of intelligence, by means of Red Indians and spies, between the rival forces, that the French high command soon knew that the first stage of the operation had been achieved.

The fleet, accompanied by the transports, had negotiated the passage to the Ile de Coudres by early June. They had got to within sixty miles of Quebec without mishap.

From Montcalm's point of view this was grave news. Yet between the Ile de Coudres and the Ile d'Orléans, from which Quebec was in sight, lay the notorious Traverse Passage, which was supposed to be impassable by any ship larger than a frigate. There was reason to hope that Saunders would find the channel too tricky for any but his smaller ships, and that he would suffer loss and discouragement even with them.

Durell, who was now exceeding expectation, lured a number of local pilots on board his ship with a show of false colours, a well-recognized ruse in war. They proved useless, not because that might have seemed to be their duty to their country in the circumstances, but through ignorance, timidity and incompetence. The British sailing masters took over the job themselves. One of them, known to the fleet as Old Killick, gave an exhibition of skill in navigating unknown waters, based on experience under every sort of condition, which was noted by Captain John Knox of the 43rd Foot in a passage sometimes lifted for the anthologies. He wrote:

> I went forward with this experienced mariner, who pointed out the Channel to me as we passed, showing me, by the ripple and colour of the water, where there were ledges of rock (to me invisible) from banks of sand, mud or gravel. He gave his orders with great unconcern, joked with the sounding-boats who lay off on each side, with different coloured flags for our guidance; and when any of them called to him, and pointed to the deepest water, he answered, 'Ay, ay, my dear, chalk it down a d----d dangerous navigation, eh? If you don't make a sputter about it, you'll get no credit for it in England,' etc.
>
> After we had cleared this remarkable place, where the Channel forms a complete zig-zag, the Master called to his Mate to give the helm to somebody else, saying, 'D--- me if there are not a thousand places in the Thames fifty times more hazardous than this; I am ashamed that Englishmen should make such a rout about it.'

Saunders left his heaviest ships at the Ile de Coudres under Durell, with orders to follow him later if there was no sign of a French attack from the seaward. He himself, with four of the smaller ships of the line and all the frigates, made the Traverse Passage and anchored just below the Basin. He had achieved a feat of seamanship hitherto unparalleled.

The army had not had to march a step before being enabled to prepare to invest the city.

Wolfe began to establish a camp, and his own headquarters, on the Ile d'Orléans, on 27 June. The island, its western shore commanding the exit of the Montmorency River with its splendid Falls, higher than Niagara, was a few miles north-east of Quebec. Saunders, with his ships of war and transports, then anchored in the Basin—not without opposition. The French naval forces, light as they were, at first proved enterprising, and Wolfe noted his concern at their activity. The French captains had the great advantage of local knowledge, and it was their hope that an attack by fire-ships, for which they had prepared, would scatter the British.

The fire-ship attempt was made at midnight on 28 June. It was a spectacular failure. The crews abandoned their vessels too soon and the British sailors, using small boats, managed to beach them at points where they burnt themselves out harmlessly, though with a prodigious amount of noise and flame. They provided the onlookers with a thrilling display, but brought no comfort to Montcalm.

Much more serious was a storm which blew up soon after the troops had landed. This led Saunders to write in his dispatch that 'many Anchors and small Boats were lost, and much Damage was received among the Transports by their driving on board each other. The Ships that lost most Anchors I supplied from the Men of War, as far as I was able, and in all other Respects, gave them the best Assistance in my Power'. Some of the transports were American, not subject to fleet discipline, and in a few cases they were sent back down the river. They had done their work.

The next moves, in a campaign with problems novel to him, were up to Wolfe. He lost no time in establishing positions nearer the city, but at first he was both puzzled and fretful. He could, however, complain of no lack of help from Saunders, who landed all the Marines he could spare, mounted batteries and supplied men to work them. Quebec city itself soon came under fire.

The main defences of Quebec were sited to the east of the city, between the river Charles, which flowed close to the walls, and the Montmorency. The position was known as the Beauport Lines, after a hamlet which had been incorporated into the camps. Here Phips had come to grief, and until Wolfe had assaulted the position successfully, or turned it, it seemed to him, as indeed to Montcalm, to be the chief obstacle to the fall of Quebec.

Wolfe lost no time in sending Monckton, his senior brigadier, to occupy Point Lévis, on the south side of the St Lawrence, opposite

Beauport. From near that place, at Point des Pères, Quebec could be bombarded, a destructive activity which became a continuing feature of the campaign. On 8 July, Saunders arranged for a small landing by troops on the north shore of the river, below and near the Montmorency Falls. The sortie took place by night, but came to nothing.

The most impressive move by the Navy was one which Wolfe, even in his rare moments of optimism, might have thought beyond expectation. This was for ships to ascend the river, with a favouring wind and tide, running the gauntlet of fire from the French batteries. The feat was achieved on the night of 18 July by the *Sutherland*, a small ship of the line, by the frigate *Squirrel*, two sloops and two of what Saunders called 'catts', which were bluff-bowed vessels mainly used for carrying provisions. The frigate *Diana* also formed part of the original squadron, but she ran ashore on some rocks near Point Lévis and received so much damage that she had to be sent to Boston for repairs. Cook and some of the *Pembroke*'s men helped to get her away. The effect of the sortie was to inhibit any chance that the British, anchored in the Basin, would be surprised by the sudden advent of the French frigates higher up the river. Saunders did not anticipate trouble from this quarter, and there was now at least a prospect that, after being reinforced, the British ships might find and destroy the enemy.

Wolfe himself took the opportunity of the naval movement to view the situation from above the river, in case he could see possibilities of attack. He found that the French had mounted a battery in the most accessible landing-place, and returned to his headquarters on the Ile d'Orléans. It seemed clear to him that he must try an assault on Montcalm's main position, but before any such operation could be arranged, the French made a second attempt at a fire-ship attack. This occurred on the night of 28 July, use being made this time of what Saunders called 'radeaux'. These were rafts on which explosives and incendiary material were placed. He reported that they 'succeeded no better than the Fire-ships'.

Three days later (belatedly, as some thought), Wolfe made his attempt on the Beauport Lines. Saunders placed the *Centurion* at the general's disposal, also two catts, which were specially armed for use against one of Montcalm's redoubts, which it was believed might be taken by storm, after covering fire from the fleet.

Although Wolfe praised the *Centurion*'s gunnery, he was disappointed that Cook, who seems to have hoped that the catts could be brought very close inshore, for once proved too sanguine in his expectations. Wolfe did indeed land a force of grenadiers from boats, but they tried to rush the French position precipitously, and came under a murderous fire at close quarters. There would have been a complete massacre had not a thunderstorm, blowing up with torrents of rain, soaked the gunpowder on both sides. Wolfe called the operation off, leaving many wounded ashore to the mercy of the Indians. He had no choice. British loss was heavy. It included nearly 60 officers killed or wounded, and well over 700 rank and file.

Saunders referred to the disaster delicately in his messages home, but when Wolfe, in the first draft of his dispatch, attempted to place a portion of the blame on the Navy, the admiral protested in such terms that the remarks were withdrawn.

Seamen burnt the two catts, which were stranded, to prevent them falling into enemy hands. By now Saunders had made up his mind that little was likely to be done against Beauport, where Montcalm was so strong, and he began to concentrate his efforts on getting more ships up the river. The wind was often adverse, but on 5 August he sent twenty flat-bottomed boats above the town. They were to be used for the transport of over a thousand troops under Brigadier Murray. In co-operation with Admiral Holmes, Murray then made a foray up the St Lawrence as far as Deschambault, where stores were destroyed and a fracas occurred with French troops under Bougainville. Holmes did not, as Saunders had hoped, discover the French frigates.

By the time of the return of the expedition, Saunders had succeeded in getting the frigate *Lowestoffe*, three sloops and two catts with provisions to join the *Sutherland*, which was serving as Holmes's headquarters and flagship. Other ships followed. At this stage, Wolfe, who reported himself ill with fever, decided to consult his brigadiers about future plans. Time was running short, and there was no good news to tell the people at home.

The brigadiers were unanimous in their view that any attack, if it were to have a reasonable chance of success, should be made from above the city. By this time only Monckton, the senior of the three, was on tolerable terms with Wolfe, and even he had differences with his superior. Murray never liked Wolfe, though they had served together before, and Townshend had actually produced a series of coarse and insolent cartoons about the general which were causing amusement in the camp. This was not the first time Townshend had done such a thing. On his very first campaign he had got into trouble by using his wit and his skill as a draughtsman in satirizing the Duke of Cumberland.

Knowing Wolfe, his state of health and nerves and his uncertain temper, the brigadiers were careful to enlist Saunders's support before making their recommendation. They held a long conference on board the fleet flagship, and were able to present Wolfe with an idea which had the approval of the sailors. Their report was dated from Point Lévis on 29 August and, if Wolfe should agree that they were right, they were glad to leave the time and place to his judgement.

Wolfe made a personal reconnaissance and decided that the landing-place should be the Anse du Foulon, a small cove about two miles above the city. The party of observation was seen by the French, but the one and only benefit of the reverse of 30 July was to have convinced Montcalm that Beauport remained Wolfe's real objective, and he was not convinced that any new plan was preparing. It now became Saunders's task to confirm him in the view that he was right. This was done by a series of feints and bombardments which kept the defenders on the alert at the wrong place. In so doing, Saunders enabled Wolfe to strike his camp on the Ile d'Orléans, and to transfer the bulk of the troops to Point Lévis across the river without the loss of a man, and—astonishingly—without Montcalm realizing his purpose.

It was becoming clearer every day how wise Saunders had been to entrust Holmes rather than Durell with the work up river, which now called for energy and skill in no ordinary measure. Holmes, although disquieted at the thought of having to land troops by night in the circumstances which would be necessary, prepared to do his best to meet every demand. All the same, he considered it 'the most hazardous and difficult Task' he had ever been engaged in—'for the distance of the landing Place; the impetuosity of the tide; the darkness of the Night; and the great chance of exactly hitting the very spot intended, without discovery or alarm, made the whole extremely difficult . . .'

Saunders picked James Chads as the officer to conduct the flat-bottomed boats to the Anse du Foulon, which would be a supreme test of skill. Chads in the ordinary way commanded the fire-ship *Vesuvius*, but he was attached to Holmes's staff to work out detailed arrangements. Saunders knew he had served earlier in the *Magnanime* under Howe, and that he was well known to Howe's brother William, who was to lead the light infantry in the assault. Saunders might well have chosen another officer of rising merit, John Jervis, who had been first lieutenant in the flagship and had formed a close friendship with Wolfe, but the admiral had by now given Jervis his own ship, and when Saunders recalled that Chads was one of the few who had done well at Rochefort, it seemed likely that he had the right man. All the same, Chads himself was as uneasy as Holmes about what was before him.

Wolfe's note-taker left the only surviving account of an interview on board the *Sutherland* between Chads and the general when the operation was discussed. Chads put up objections. The account runs:

The General told him he should have made his objections earlier, though should the disembarkation miscarry he would shelter him from any Blame, that all that could be done was to do his utmost: that if Captain Chads would write anything to testify that the miscarriage was G. Wolfe's and not Capt. Chads's that he would sign it. Chads still persisting in his absurdity the General told him he could do no more than lay his head on the block to save Chads—then left the cabin.

The British now had a stroke of luck. Quebec was acutely short of provisions, and the quickest though by far the riskiest way of getting them to the city was by boat and at night, the roads being atrocious. It so happened that the French had arranged for a convoy to run down from the Montreal direction on the night of 12 September, the very date chosen for the embarkation of Wolfe's army.

Bougainville, with his infantry and mounted patrols, alert for hostile movements above the city by land or water, was duly informed, so that the shoreline sentries on the watch near the city could be hopeful of seeing French ships slip by on the river—if they had been able to escape Holmes's vigilance. In fact, the convoy was cancelled at the last moment, but Bougainville omitted to tell his subordinates. So when Chads and his flotilla of flat-bottomed boats, racing down with the tide on the fifteen-mile journey from the *Sutherland* to the Anse du Foulon, were hailed in French from the banks, as they expected to be, they had their answer ready, and were believed.

Townshend, in his rough but graphic fashion, wrote in his Journal:

> . . . when ye first corps for disembarkation was passing down ye N. Side of ye River & ye french Centries on ye banks challeng'd our boats, Captn Frazer who had been in ye Dutch Service & spoke french—answered—la france & vive le Roy, on which ye French Centinels ran along ye Shore in ye dark crying laisser les passes ils sont nos Gens avec les provisions . . .

Despite misgivings which were natural enough, and despite a narrow escape from being fired on by the sloop *Hunter* which Holmes had stationed at the end of the first leg of the journey as a mark-boat, Chads won admiration from everyone by landing all but a handful of the first lift of 1,800 troops in the right place during the darkest part of the night. Even the handful, which included Wolfe, who were set ashore a little too far down, were able to scramble back to the Foulon and up the steep path to the Heights of Abraham, facing Quebec, where Wolfe intended to draw up his line of battle.

Chads deserved promotion and in time he got it, though it took seven years. He then became a post-captain, and Saunders was later able to steer him into a Captaincy of Greenwich Hospital, which was a plum well worth waiting for. Cook, who was given a similar post after his second circumnavigation, called it 'a fine retreat, and a pretty income'. Both men had earned it, one by a short and hazardous journey, the other by two long ones.

Saunders is very unlikely to have been preoccupied with the sentiments of Grey's *Elegy*, as Wolfe is reputed to have been on his way to battle. He was busy superintending an elaborate mock attack on the Beauport Lines. Cook and other masters were out all night in small boats, pretending to lay lines of buoys preliminary to a landing. Cook's log, as artless as Townshend's, states that:

> . . . at midnight all the Row Boats in the fleet made a feint to land at Beauport in order to Draw the Enemys Attention that way to favor the Landing of the Troops above the Town on the north Shoar, which was done with little opposition. Our Batteries Kept a Continuell fire . . . all night.

Boats of all kinds were indeed busy, and Chads's work did not end with landing the first wave. Half an hour after his little convoy had set off, Holmes himself weighed anchor with the second contingent of troops, this time carried in catts and in the frigate *Lowestoffe*, to which he temporarily transferred his flag. Chads took the empty boats to meet the admiral, embarking and landing a further 1,900 men. His final duty was to cross to the far shore, where he took on board further men from Point Lévis. By the early hours of 13 September about 4,800 soldiers had been drawn up in line of battle facing Montcalm and the city he was defending. The French were completely surprised.

The work of the sailors did not end with landing the troops. Parties were organized to haul guns up the steep cliff path, and they served them when in position. It is probable that a shot from one of them gave Montcalm his mortal wound when the armies met and the French had been routed by the steady discipline and devastating fire of the British and American infantry.

Whatever may have been his shortcomings as a strategist, however little Wolfe had done to win the affection of his principal subordinates, before his own death on the battlefield he had shown outstanding skill as a tactician and as a trainer of infantry. The contrast between his conduct on the Heights of Abraham and that of Townshend, who succeeded to the command, since Monckton had been wounded, was between a dedicated professional and a limited amateur.

It is true that Townshend took over command in the confusion of battle, but even in his dying moments Wolfe was urging the exploitation of victory. Townshend had complained of neglect by superiors in this respect during his campaigning under Cumberland on the Continent, but he failed no less markedly himself. His fear of an attack from the rear by Bougainville, his obsession with siege tactics against a city dependent on a field army now demoralized, and his lack of grip, do not mark him as a capable soldier even though, long years afterwards, seniority brought him to the elevated rank of Field-Marshal.

By contrast, Saunders continued his aid on a massive, indeed decisive, scale. He moved his biggest ships to positions from which they could cannonade the lower town by direct fire. His sailors continued to haul artillery from the Anse du Foulon; and he ordered Captain Hugh Palliser to prepare landing-parties ready to invade from the river. No man could have done more, and as the threat from Bougainville came to nothing, the garrison commander hoisted a white flag on 17 September, on which day terms of surrender were agreed.

By far the strangest of Townshend's omissions was any reference in his dispatch to Wolfe's leadership and qualities. This was never forgiven nor forgotten by the troops, and although it was no business of Saunders's to repair the ungenerosity in his own report to Pitt, he showed respect in practical ways. Wolfe was embalmed. It was badly done, for facilities were limited but, in the proper conviction that the General would be accorded a State funeral, Saunders had the body placed on board the *Royal William*, one of the largest ships in the fleet, well able to defend herself from any threat during the crossing of the Atlantic.

In one way at least, Townshend did his duty. His tribute to the Navy could not have been better, and it obviously came from the heart.

I should not do Justice to the Admirals, and the Naval Service, if I neglected this Occasion of acknowledging how much we are indebted for our Success to the constant Assistance and support received from them, and the perfect Harmony and Correspondence, which has prevailed throughout all our Operations, in the uncommon Difficulties, which the Nature of this Country, in particular, presents to military Operations of a great Extent, and which no Army can itself solely supply; the immense labour in Artillery, Stores and Provisions; the long Watchings and Attendance in Boats; the drawing up of our Artillery by the Seamen, even in the Heat of Action; it is my Duty, short as my Command has been, to acknowledge, for that Time, how great a Share the Navy has had in this successful Campaign.

In his will, Wolfe left Saunders his plate. This was carried home in the flagship, in which Townshend took passage. He had disliked the whole campaign and was only too glad to leave affairs in Canada to Monckton, who soon recovered, and to Murray, who wintered at Quebec but who was in considerable danger until the reappearance of the Navy, once ice conditions allowed a passage up the river, in the spring of 1760.

When the fleet was nearing the home islands Saunders had word that Conflans might be at sea, and he prepared to alter course to reinforce Hawke's squadron. Before the two admirals could make contact, news of Quiberon came through. Saunders thereupon put in at Dublin, where he was received with rapturous enthusiasm.

The rest of the admiral's career was continued honour and glory. Although he received all the acclaim for his part at Quebec he could have wished he did not get his red ribbon as a Knight of the Bath until 1761. He was, however, given the Mediterranean command, and during the time in which he held it, he had another astonishing piece of luck. The Spanish ship, *Hermione*, bound for Barcelona with a cargo of treasure and nearing home, was captured by the frigate *Active* and the sloop *Favourite*, which were under Saunders's orders. This was one of the best hauls on record, for the *Hermione* was condemned in the Prize Court at £544,648. 1s. 6d. Saunders's share as Commander-in-Chief amounted to £64,963. 3s. 9d. The captains of the frigate and the sloop got £65,053. 13s. 9d. apiece. In this instance, even the subordinate ranks did well. The lieutenants received £13,000. 14s. 1d. and every seaman and marine £485. 5s. 4¾d.

For Saunders there followed service on the Board of Admiralty and a few years of affluent ease. His life was in fact remarkable as a process of uninterrupted success and good fortune. He was painted by notables; he was a close friend of Burke, who eulogized him in the House of Commons; and he was buried in Westminster Abbey near the monument to Wolfe. In his marriage he seems to have been happy, though he and his wife had no children, and he died at the early age of fifty-three.

With a large fortune to bequeath, Saunders was able to benefit a niece who had married an army surgeon, and to leave legacies to naval friends who included Admiral Keppel, a companion on Anson's circumnavigation, to Hugh Palliser, one of Cook's steadiest patrons, and to Edward Hughes, once of the *Somerset*. These sailors were all rich in their own right, but they were comrades, and Saunders felt it right that they should be remembered.

3

Louis-Antoine de Bougainville

⚓   ⚓   ⚓

Bougainville was unlucky at Quebec, but it was not always so. For instance, through the general popularity of the tropical plant *Bougainvillea Spectabilis*, to which his name became attached soon after the earliest descriptions and classification by European botanists had been made known, he is remembered by gardeners when other admirals and venturers are forgotten. He had other reasons for celebrity.

He was born in Paris in 1729; restless vitality, allied with intellectual brilliance, was the predominant feature of his life. He was trained in the law but, discovering a talent for mathematics, became the pupil and lifelong friend of Jean D'Alembert. D'Alembert was later to be a prominent member of Diderot's Encyclopaedists and Secretary of the French Academy. Bougainville's gifts were recognized in England, where he was well known, and where, at the age of twenty-six, he was elected a Fellow of the Royal Society.

There exists a letter from Lord Macclesfield, an astronomer who was then President of the Society, dated 12 January 1756, shortly before the outbreak of the Seven Years War, stating that a volume of Bougainville's 'Calculus of Integers' 'will be very acceptable to me, as well as to the Society . . . who hope that you will contribute to their carrying on the design for which the Society was founded, by communicating . . . such new improvements as yourself shall make in Science'.

Bougainville had social pull as well as natural gifts. A relative of his had been a friend of Madame de Pompadour long before her rise to eminence at the French Court. It was through the recommendation of this powerful woman that he went to Canada, or New France, as it was then called, as a member of Montcalm's staff. He did well, when the tide was flowing in French favour, and it was the Pompadour's advocacy which ensured that supplies were granted, out of a revenue much strained by war, to sustain Montcalm's efforts in the campaign of 1759, during which Bougainville was a comfort to his chief in what proved a disastrous time. Bougainville rose to be a colonel, and the command of the roving force which patrolled the St Lawrence was a measure of Montcalm's confidence.

After the fall of Quebec to Wolfe, and later of Montreal to Amherst, Bougainville had hopes that there might be an extensive repatriation of French citizens to Louisiana. When this proved impracticable, he had ideas for traversing the North American continent, and also of exploring the Pacific, then known as the South Seas. A soldier with a decided nautical bent, he seemed to thrive when afloat. His mathematical genius made navigation easier for him than for many sea officers.

35

Once back in Paris, at the centre of affairs, Bougainville formed an alliance with the Duc de Choiseul, who was then responsible for foreign policy. Choiseul saw in him a born Colonial administrator, and the two men planned that the French should found a colony in the Falkland Islands, that lonely, wind-swept group in the South Atlantic.

The Falklands, which had been visited by Richard Hawkins at the end of the previous century (though they had been sighted earlier by John Davys), belonged, technically, to Spain, but they had never been settled. If such a venture were to prove a success the islands could, thought Bougainville, form a base for further adventures, notably in the Pacific. He had learnt that Anson, after his world voyage, had recommended that the British Government should try to occupy the islands. As nothing had been done, here might be a chance to recoup something of the loss which France had suffered in Canada.

The difficulty was money. The war had exhausted France, and Choiseul could promise nothing from the Treasury for a scheme so full of uncertainties. However, Louis XV authorized the expedition to proceed, provided that Bougainville financed it from his own resources. He also allowed him to exchange into the Navy. At a stroke he was transformed from a Colonel of Infantry into a *Capitaine de Vaisseau*, equivalent to a post-captain in the Royal Navy.

Bougainville raised a large proportion of the necessary funds from a cousin, M. de Nerville, and a wealthy uncle, M. d'Arboulin, who held the office of *Administrateur Général des Postes de France*. Furthermore, a St Malo shipowner, M. Duclos-Guyot, who shared Bougainville's enthusiasm for the project, built him two ships, a frigate and a corvette, and volunteered to sail as second-in-command.

The ships embarked, besides their crews, three families of Acadians, refugees from Canada after Acadia, renamed Nova Scotia, had passed into English hands. These people, who had been living at St Malo on a meagre dole from Louis XV, were glad to accept Bougainville's offer to transport them to a part of the world where they would be given land, and might aspire to a condition of prosperity which would not have come their way in France. It was these families, together with the local character of the whole expedition, which caused the Falklands to be known to the French as 'Les Malouines'.

Bougainville reached the Falklands in January 1764. Having reconnoitred the coast and hinterland, and built a residence and fort commanding Berkeley Sound in East Falkland, he claimed the group for France in a picturesque ceremony which included the unveiling of an obelisk decorated with a medallion bust of the French king. Then he sailed home.

Admiral Hawke in middle life: print by J. McArdell after a lost portrait by George Knapton (1698–1778)

Admiral Saunders in later life, by Richard Brompton (1734–83)

Louis-Antoine de Bougainville after his circumnavigation. Marble bust by F. J. Bosio (1769–1845)

Suffren in later life. Bust by Jean-Antoine Houdon (1741–1828)

Lord Howe: wax profile by John Flaxman (1755–1826)

Left
Admiral Lord Gardner,
by Karl Anton Hickel (1745–98)

Alan, 2nd Lord Gardner:
print by H. R. Cook after a
drawing by Henry Edridge
(1769–1821)

Admiral Sir Joshua Rowley, the most celebrated of the
Rowley admirals, by George Romney (1734–1802)

Sir Charles Rowley as a young officer: a portrait,
hitherto unpublished, by Daniel Gardner (1750–1805)

Opposite
Admiral Lord Collingwood wearing the King's gold medals for the battles of
St Vincent and the Nile, and the Star of the Order of the Bath. A posthumous
portrait by Henry Howard (1769–1847)

Admiral Saumarez, by Samuel Lane (1780–1859)

Danish privateer, the frigate *Cort Adeler* of Copenhagen, unsuccessfully attacked by British forces off Kronborg Castle, 20 August 1808. This night action was typical of many of the time. By C. W. Eckersberg (1763–1853)

Admiral Farragut in 1865, at the end of the American Civil War

USS *Hartford* running past the forts at New Orleans during Farragut's attack, 1862

Farragut's flagship, the *Hartford*, still afloat and flying the Stars and Stripes, 1901

Admiral Beatty, by Sir Arthur Cope (1857–1940): a sketch for a large group of sea officers of the First World War, now in the National Portrait Gallery

The battle cruiser *Lion* flying Beatty's flag during the First World War

Admiral Nimitz in 1939, shortly before his appointment as commander of the United States Pacific Fleet

Admiral Nimitz signing the Japanese surrender, 1945. *Left to right in the foreground:* General MacArthur; Admiral Halsey; Rear-Admiral Sherman, Nimitz's Chief of Staff

By October 1764 his trip to France was over and he returned to the settlement, arriving in January 1765. Learning that the settlers were short of wood, he decided to explore the Straits of Magellan in search of suitable trees to plant. There he sighted, and was himself seen by, the British frigate *Dolphin* and the store-ship *Florida*. The British Government had lost no time in sending out a fast ship, experimentally sheathed with copper to keep her free from barnacles. She was under the command of Commodore Byron, known as 'Foul Weather Jack'. He had been one of Anson's pupils and was grandfather of the poet. He had been ordered to survey the Falklands as part of a voyage of circumnavigation which, though it achieved nothing, was one of the quickest on record.

Byron's intervention was the start of a tragi-comedy which might have led to a European war. At first, all seemed fair for Bougainville. His colonists were in good heart having enjoyed a mild season with plenty of game and fish. Everyone seemed contented, and the population was shortly to increase through a series of marriages. *Le pays*, wrote Bougainville gaily, *est bon pour la propagation*.

Byron was equally enthusiastic, and sent home a report by the *Florida*. Lord Egmont, then at the Admiralty, made haste to dispatch an expedition which made a settlement at a port to which he gave his name. Fortunately, the British landed on West Falkland, and it is some indication of the isolation of that distant area that British and French remained in total ignorance of each other for the better part of a year.

Diplomats then took a hand. The publication in 1756 of his *Histoire des Navigations aux Terres Australes*, by Charles de Brosses, President of the Parlement of Dijon, had a continuing influence not only on explorers but on statesmen. Thoughtful people were beginning to understand the immense possibilities of the Pacific, which was believed to include a vast and as yet undiscovered continent, 'Terra Australis', its land mass 'balancing' that in the northerly part of the world.

Naturally enough, Bougainville had been influenced by de Brosses, whose information and ideas were pirated by a Scotsman, John Callender, and thus became known in Britain. Moreover, the fact that in 1762 an operation mounted from Madras by the British had resulted in the capture and occupation of Manila in the Philippines, one of the byproducts of Spanish entry into the Seven Years War, had made Spain acutely uneasy about the safety of her remoter possessions.

France was then building up strength for another encounter with Britain and could not afford to alienate Spain, particularly over what seemed a trifle. So when the Spanish ambassador pointed out to Choiseul that Bougainville's settlement would encourage the British to do likewise—had, indeed, already done so—Choiseul gave way. Bougainville went to Madrid in April 1766, and there surrendered his claim on the Falklands in exchange for an indemnity of 603,000 *livres*.

Sad as he was at the extinction of his hopes for the future of the 'Malouines', Bougainville, who was as full of energy as ever, conceived his most ambitious project. He would become the first French commander to lead an expedition round the world, and would start on the enterprise after winding up affairs in the Falklands. He was given two ships, the frigate *Boudeuse* of 26 guns, and the supply ship *L'Etoile*, which was to act as a tender.

Bougainville in person handed over the islands to the Spanish in April 1767. He was authorized to continue his voyage across the Pacific to the East Indies, and had broad instructions from Paris to examine in as much detail as possible the ocean and the lands therein which lay between the west coast of South America and the Indies. With him went not only the loyal M. Duclos-Guyot, but Philibert Commerson, the botanist, Verron, the astronomer and, most curious of all, a certain Jeanne Baré or Baret. This person, who acted as valet to Commerson, was a woman in disguise, engaged by her master at Brest in all innocence. She was the first of her sex to sail round the world.

Unknown to Bougainville, the *Dolphin* was once more in southern and Pacific waters. This time she was in the charge of a Cornishman, Captain Samuel Wallis, who, although not to be reckoned among the more distinguished explorers, was a competent navigator with an enlightened attitude towards the wellbeing of his men. Wallis and the *Dolphin* had set out in company with the sloop *Swallow*, Captain Philip Carteret. The *Swallow* was in a shocking state and should never have been sent out in her leaky condition. Wallis, left her, rather unfeelingly as it must seem, soon after the two ships had entered the Pacific, with no firm arrangements for a rendezvous. His lapse could be put down to sickness.

Bougainville, after sailing past the Tuamotas, bird-haunted green islets which he called *l'archipel dangereux* because he could find no holding ground for his anchors, sighted Tahiti on 2 April 1768, the year in which Cook and Banks sailed for the Pacific in the *Endeavour*. Bougainville anchored in what he thought to be a safe bay. It was nothing of the sort. The French lost six anchors in nine days through cables chafing against the coral bottom. Otherwise, apart from the kleptomania among the Tahitians which had also worried Wallis and would shortly worry Cook, all was wonderful. Bougainville, steeped as he was in the classics, thought of Tahiti as *la nouvelle Cythère*, a Pacific version of the Island of Aphrodite. Wallis, who did not have the advantage of learning, regarded the island in a much more matter of fact way, and boldly claimed it for King George III. The islanders seem to have accepted this, in so far as they recognized and hailed the Union flag, whereas the French flag, and the Spanish, when the Spaniards later came on the scene, meant little to them.

From Tahiti, Bougainville sailed west, passing through the Samoan group. This he called *l'archipel des Navigateurs*, from the skill with which the Samoans handled their canoes. He next caught sight of the Melanesian Islands, their people very different from the idyllic Tahitians. Still classical, he called them the Great Cyclades. It was here that Bougainville found earlier maps and charts most misleading, even those published by the Sieur de Vaugondy, Geographer to the King of France. He held on towards the outliers of the Great Barrier Reef on the north-eastern coast of Australia, which gave him warning of what lay ahead. Altering course north-east by north, he prudently avoided dangers which, two years later, nearly put an end to Cook's *Endeavour*.

By this time, Bougainville was desperately in need of a port for refreshment. Through storm and rain, he beat painfully past the eastern point of New Guinea, through the Solomon Islands to New Britain and New Ireland, making for the Moluccas, with his crew by now almost starving. At last he found help at the Dutch island of Boero. By 28 September he was at Batavia, arriving twelve days after Philip Carteret had left that haven in the *Swallow*, the shipwrights declaring that he never would reach England.

The rest of the voyage back to France was plain sailing. Bougainville overtook the *Swallow* in the Atlantic. He sent over a boarding-party, who were not as helpful as they might have been, and who surprised Carteret by knowing so much more about him than he did about them. The incident took place on 26 February 1769. Bougainville was home again at St Malo less than three weeks later.

The crippled *Swallow* did not anchor at Spithead until 20 May, exactly a year after the return of the *Dolphin*. Dr Beaglehole, biographer of Cook, describes Carteret's voyage as 'one of the greatest achievements of the human spirit in the history of the Pacific'. It is good to reflect that Carteret had nearly thirty years more to live and that he died a rear-admiral.

Wallis had taken a Tahitian man to England with him in the *Dolphin*, and Bougainville found much curiosity among the islanders to discover how white people lived. He was urged to take on board Ahutoru, whose brother was a chief. On the long passage back to France, Bougainville took every opportunity to learn from his guest more of the way of life of the Tahitians than he had been able to gather during his brief stay, which had been no longer than thirteen days. When his turn came, Cook was equally glad to make the experiment of bringing a Tahitian back to England. The choice fell on a man called Omai, who was a considerable success in London society.

For some time after the conclusion of his voyage Bougainville gave his energies to assessing the material he had brought back; to reporting to his Government on French prospects in the Pacific; and to preparing a thorough account of his journey. This was published in Paris in two volumes in 1771 as *Voyage Autour du Monde*. It is one of the standard books of travel, and reflects the author's observation, range of learning and charm. Bougainville had a great advantage in this respect over Cook, who had to rely on others to present accounts of his discoveries. They did not always do him justice, and it is only of late years that, for the first time, his Journals can be read without interpolation, the result of the scholarship of Dr Beaglehole, historian of the Pacific.

Bougainville's work became speedily known in Britain, where there was an eager public, as in France, for works of travel and exploration. A translation by Johann Reinhold Forster, who was to serve as naturalist on Cook's second voyage, appeared in 1772.

If Bougainville had deliberately set out to stimulate the philosophers and encyclopaedists, instead of having conducted a highly creditable journey with ulterior objects of a practical kind, he could not have succeeded better than he did. Although Cook, by the incomparable voyages made between 1768 and his death at Hawaii ten years later, filled in the main features of the map of the Pacific, and dispelled for ever the notion of any great Southern Continent larger than Australia, his efforts were backed by his Government in a way which was never attempted by France. But in Paris was to be found the fine flower of civilization. There, *savants* like Rousseau would expound the theory of the Noble Savage. It was true that Ahutoru did not prove a very instructive example, with his leaning towards dissipation, grand opera stars, and the excitement of high society—but, so the wise pointed out, these were temptations to which he would never be exposed at home.

Bougainville, whose acuteness eventually led him to a less romantic view of Tahiti than he had felt at first, when the island had seemed so blissful to a ship's company longing for refreshment and a rest from incessant work at sea, had the matter of interpretation partly taken out of his hands by Diderot, as a useful weapon in his war against the Church. Diderot wrote a *Supplément au Voyage de Bougainville* in which he fulminated against the intrusion of Christians into a community he supposed to be both simple and happy. He warned the Tahitians, in a speech composed in elegant French and put into the mouth of a native chief, that Christians would return with a crucifix in one hand and a sword in the other, forcing them to accept their customs and opinions. Keep away from us, exclaimed the orator, deploring and denouncing any intrusion into the island paradise.

The ultimate fate of both Ahutoru and Omai drew many a moral. Bougainville, who had grown fond of his Tahitian friend, who enjoyed his conversation and learnt much from it, at last persuaded him that he should return to his own people. A ship was chartered for the purpose at Bougainville's expense, but it was too late. Ahutoru's constitution seems to have been undermined by the gaieties of Paris and he succumbed to disease on his way home. Omai had better luck, in that Cook did at least get him back to Tahiti. But civilization had done no good to a character not strong by any standard, and soon the innumerable gifts with which he had been loaded vanished in an orgy of extravagance and eccentricity.

Having enjoyed acclaim as circumnavigator and author Bougainville, whose zeal to serve his country remained as strong as ever, returned to the Navy. He was appointed to squadrons commanded by Admirals de Guichen and du Chauffault. He became as meticulous a student of naval tactics as he had been of mathematics, and the application with which he sought to perfect himself in the art of navigation shows the humility of an exceptional mind, for there was already no better navigator in the French fleet. Although critical both of his admirals and of the service in general, he kept his thoughts to his private Journals, and that he retained the good opinion of the authorities is shown by his appointment to the command of the *Guerrier* in the first expedition sent across the Atlantic in support of the Americans in their War of Independence.

From 1778, for nearly two years, Bougainville was abroad, serving under d'Estaing. He returned to France with his health much shattered and with no very high opinion of the Americans as allies. They were not above insulting the French flag, and at Nantucket, where he was put in charge of the fortifications, he remarked that fifty Americans had not done in twenty-one days what thirty Frenchmen would have done in eight.

During a period of much-needed rest at home he married a twenty-year-old beauty, Flore de Montendre. The difference in age of nearly thirty years had no effect on their happiness or on Bougainville's devotion to Flore for as long as she lived.

When Bougainville next sailed for the theatre of war it was in command of the 80-gun *Auguste*, her original captain, the celebrated La

Motte-Picquet, having fallen ill. He was to serve under the Comte de Grasse, and was given a distinguishing pendant as *Chef d'Escadre*. As such, he took part in two decisive fleet actions of the war, the battle of the Chesapeake in September 1781, so disastrous for the British cause, and the battle of the Saints Passage, Dominica, the following April, where Rodney captured de Grasse together with his towering flagship, the *Ville de Paris*.

At the Chesapeake Bougainville enjoyed his first hour of glory against the British since the days, long before, when as a young ADC to Montcalm he had taken part in French successes at Oswego, at Fort William Henry and at Ticonderoga, during the earlier phases of the Seven Years War. Under de Grasse, his squadron was in the van, and indeed his big *Auguste* was the only French ship of her size to be heavily engaged. Her gunnery matched the fighting spirit of her men, who were as devoted to Bougainville as he was to them. He fought in splendid style before leading away from the British under Graves, who kept to a rigid line of battle. Bougainville's duty to de Grasse was to help keep his fleet together, not to engage in a prolonged *mêlée*. When the ulterior object, to return to the Chesapeake anchorage, was achieved, Bougainville received his full share of credit.

The action against Rodney was a very different matter. It could have been inconclusive but for a sudden shift of wind, which enabled the British to make what one participant described as 'incisions' into de Grasse's line, after which superior training and initiative threw the French into confusion and led to their defeat. Bougainville, whose ship received some damage, left the scene when he saw that there was nothing further he could do to help his chief. Unfortunately, de Grasse grew sour after his capture by the British. His hosts made much of him and flattered him, partly from a sincere feeling of respect, and also because, as they had been able to bring a disappointing war to an end with a feat which did much to restore confidence, they were disposed to be generous.

De Grasse, drinking in the praise of his opponents, began to see himself as the victim of incompetent and disloyal subordinates. He conceived that he had been badly let down; that his humiliation was not his own fault; and he determined, when he returned to France, to find scapegoats. Post-mortems are grisly affairs, and no naval service of any importance has been free of them. It was so now. De Grasse laid particular blame on Bougainville and Coriolis d'Espinouse, another *Chef d'Escadre*, and they were publicly admonished by a court martial for having failed to set a proper example once the line had been broken. Two of his captains were imprisoned, quite unjustly, four more were censured and another was warned to keep his mouth shut for the future. It was all most unfortunate, even for de Grasse himself, for the king refused to receive him and he was 'advised'—virtually ordered—to retire to his estates, where he died in 1788.

In fact, Bougainville's reputation was not much harmed by the episode, and although he swore he would never go to sea again, when the king once more summoned him, as he did shortly before the Revolution, to take charge of the Brest Fleet, he accepted the mission. Subversion was in the air, not to speak of rank insubordination. After struggling for a few months with sailors' committees, Bougainville felt forced to resign. He had always looked after the welfare of his men, but he had insisted on discipline, and this he could not maintain in the circumstances and climate of the time.

In his later years, Bougainville was very close to Louis XVI. When the Paris mob invaded the Tuileries on 20 June 1792, forcing the king to put on the *bonnet rouge*, Bougainville was there to help protect him from further insult. On 10 August, the day on which the Swiss Guard was cut to pieces in the Tuileries Gardens, although Bougainville could not prevent the massacre he did manage to save a few of the wretched survivors by smuggling them out of the city to his home in Normandy.

As the political horizon darkened and the fabric of the *ancien régime* crumbled at a pace which seemed unendurable to ardent royalists, Bougainville prudently retired with his family to La Becquetière, near Coutances on the Normandy coast, but persecution mounted and an order was made for his arrest. He was actually thrown into the Coutances town prison, and only escaped the guillotine through the fall and execution of Robespierre in July 1794.

The rise of Napoleon brought his political troubles to an end. The First Consul of course knew everything about Bougainville, and had read his *Voyage* when a student at Brienne. He sometimes teased the veteran about being a *vieux royaliste*, but he was a good enough judge of men to know that Bougainville would be an ornament to the new aristocracy he would one day try to establish. He consulted Bougainville over his expedition to Egypt in 1798, and even considered making him Minister of Marine, finally deciding that, at sixty-nine, he was too old. However, he created him a Senator, a Count of the Empire and a Grand Officer of the Legion of Honour.

Glad as he was of this recognition, Bougainville's last years were saddened by a series of private bereavements. His second son, Armand, was drowned on the family estate at Suisnes; his beloved wife died in 1806; and his three surviving sons were all far away in the service of their country. In his loneliness Bougainville returned to those scientific studies which had delighted him when young. He was elected a member of the French Institute in February 1796, almost exactly forty years after he had become a Fellow of the Royal Society, and he was President of the Class of Physics and Mathematics.

Bougainville died on 31 August 1811, having long survived the contemporaries who had made the age of his youth and maturity so memorable. At his death, the doors of the Pantheon were opened to receive his body. No interment could have been more fitting.

4

Suffren's Great Adventure

The year 1781, which saw the death of Hawke, the failure of Graves at the Chesapeake, and Bougainville's hour as a naval commander, was also memorable for the fact that Suffren, generally regarded as France's greatest naval tactician, set out on the most important mission of his life. His purpose was to wrest dominance from the British in the Bay of Bengal.

Much had happened to Suffren since the sad day in 1747 when, as a young man, he had been taken prisoner after Hawke's battle with L'Etanduère. By the time of his appointment to the Far East he was a captain of seniority, fifty-two years old and thoroughly seasoned in battle. He was also imbued with ideas which ran counter to those of almost all his French contemporaries.

Pierre André de Suffren was the third son of the Marquis de Saint Tropez, head of a Provençal family. He had entered the service in 1743 as a *garde de la marine*, which was equivalent to midshipman in the British Navy. Within a year he had been in action on board his ship, the *Solide* of 60 guns, at the indecisive battle off Toulon where Hawke first distinguished himself. His wish to emulate this future master of war, enemy though he might be, crystallized when he saw how he handled his command off Finisterre.

Suffren did not return to the French fleet after his captivity in Britain. Instead, he was seconded to that of the Knights of Malta, with whom his family had long-standing connections. The Knights operated a squadron of galleys such as were by then obsolescent elsewhere, except in the Baltic. He served mainly in what was known as the 'caravans', a term which originated from the escort of pilgrims. By Suffren's time the 'caravans' were given over mainly to trading, and to the suppression or combating of the piracy rife in the States of North Africa along what was appropriately known as the Barbary Coast.

Suffren enjoyed his spell at Malta, and was highly regarded there in maritime circles: but in times of crisis or mobilization his duty lay in his own country, to which he returned.

At the opening of the Seven Years War he took part in one of those battles, indecisive in themselves, which lead to results of consequence. This was the action off Minorca where the unfortunate Admiral Byng not only failed to relieve the garrison, but which led to his condemnation under the existing Articles of War. Suffren at the time was a lieutenant in the *Orphée* of 64 guns.

Three years after the action with Byng, Suffren was serving with Admiral de la Clue, and was present when his admiral was defeated by

Boscawen. Suffren was in the flagship which, after suffering heavy damage and casualties, was run aground in order to try to save her from capture. The English sent in boats to see if she could be salvaged, but as the task was hopeless, they burnt her. Suffren was taken prisoner a second time and had another wry opportunity of admiring the devastation caused by a strong offensive spirit.

At the end of the war he returned to the service of the Knights of Malta. He was given command of a xebec, a type of handy vessel, with a low freeboard, commonly employed against the Barbary pirates. He was recalled to French service when his Government decided to support the Americans. He led the French line, as captain of the *Fantasque* of 64 guns, at a battle off Grenada in 1779. His ship, which was heavily engaged, lost 22 men killed and 43 wounded. The English admiral in this case was Jack Byron, whose tracks had crossed those of Bougainville in the years preceding the war. Byron, who was too precipitate, mismanaged the action and suffered heavy loss, but the chance he offered for d'Estaing to inflict a severe defeat on him was missed through over-caution. Suffren's remark was: 'If only M. d'Estaing were as able a naval officer as he is brave as a man!'

When Suffren was sent to the Far East in charge of a small squadron it was with the hope of embarrassing a power already overstretched by the demands of the unsuccessful war in America. Moreover, although the grip of the British on the Indian subcontinent had been immensely strengthened by the successes of Clive and others during the Seven Years War, her position was still vulnerable, and a succession of duels between Admirals d'Ache and Pocock, which had taken place during the earlier conflict, had shown how sea-power might affect the issues on land. Final consideration—the British had a formidable foe in Hyder Ali, ruler of Mysore, and Hyder was a staunch ally of the French.

Suffren's flagship was the *Héros* of 74 guns. With him were three slightly smaller ships of the line, and a convoy. His primary mission was to reinforce the Comte d'Orves, who held overall command in the Indian Ocean, and, in the course of his voyage, to land troops to re-inforce the Dutch at the Cape of Good Hope, Holland having joined the ranks of Britain's enemies.

Being well aware of the importance of the Cape, the London Admiralty had already taken steps. Commodore George Johnstone, with five ships of the line, three large frigates and many smaller vessels to protect a valuable convoy, had been ordered to seize the Dutch settlement. The choice of man was unfortunate. Johnstone was a notorious duellist, a poor tactician and an unpopular leader. The reason for his appointment lay in the fact that the choice of candidates was so limited that the Admiralty was scraping the barrel, and that they were under some obligation to Johnstone for political services in America.

When he was near the Cape Verde Islands which, then as now, belonged to Portugal, Suffren found himself short of water, and he set course for Porto Praia, in the south of San Tiago Island, to replenish. One of his ships, the fast-sailing *Artésien*, ranging ahead, reported ships of war and merchantmen in the roadstead. This, reasoned Suffren, could only be Johnstone. He had, therefore, two courses open to him: he could sail on to the Cape, accepting his deficiencies and thus fulfilling the first part of his mission; or he could attack. If he was successful, Johnstone might be prevented from reaching South Africa at all. Being Suffren, he attacked.

The result was in some ways a foretaste of the future. Johnstone had anchored in an unseamanlike way, suspecting no danger in spite of the fact that the Navy had then been at war for years. However, the wind was light, and he just had time to clear for action when he saw the impetuous Frenchman heading for the harbour.

Suffren sailed boldly in among the British ships of war, dropped anchor and opened with both broadsides. It was an act unique in the annals of the French Navy. The *Annibal* followed the flagship closely, but her captain had not completely cleared for action, thinking that, as the Portuguese harbour was neutral water, Suffren's signals must have been precautionary. He was clearly unfamiliar with a passage in his chief's earlier history, when Suffren had been made prisoner by Boscawen off neutral Lagos. The *Artésien* got into action third, but attacked an East Indiaman which was in Johnstone's convoy, mistaking her for a ship of the line. The Indiaman was taken, but the *Artésien*'s captain was killed at the moment he was about to give the order to anchor, and his ship and her prize drifted to leeward. The other French ships did not attack at all so that the *Héros* and the *Annibal* bore the whole brunt of the return fire, the *Annibal*'s captain being killed. His ship was soon dismasted but for her mizen, which held until she could be headed out of the bay. She was then taken in tow by the undamaged *Sphinx*.

Johnstone, in greatly superior numbers, followed the French as soon as he had recovered some sort of order, and came up with Suffren at dusk. But the Frenchman had his command so well in hand, the towed ship leading, that Johnstone contented himself with retaking the captured East Indiaman. Suffren forestalled Johnstone at the Cape, landed his troops and put his squadron into so strong a defensive position that Johnstone, when he arrived, dared not attack. Suffren's reward was promotion to the rank of *Chef d'Escadre* and to that of Bailli in the Maltese chivalry. It is as the Bailli de Suffren that he is generally known.

Once on station, Suffren's real difficulties began. The Comte d'Orves was an ineffectual officer. He had already missed several opportunities of harassing the British: moreover, the French base at the Ile de France, better known as Mauritius, offered diversions to his officers which they much preferred to active service on the Coromandel Coast, protecting the settlements at Pondicherry and elsewhere, supporting Hyder Ali, and in general showing vigilance. Exile has always seemed hard to a Frenchman, which is not surprising, considering the beauty of his home country, and d'Orves's force did not represent all that was best in the naval service.

Fortunately for Suffren, who might otherwise have been utterly frustrated, d'Orves died soon after his arrival on the East Indies station, and he could consider the situation from the point of view of chief commander. The greatest obstacle to success was the character and capacity of his opponent, Sir Edward Hughes, KB. The Englishman had the advantage of Suffren both in years and in experience of important campaigns. Trained under Saunders, whose close friend he had been, Hughes had not only served with distinction on the Spanish Main and in Canada, but had once before, earlier in the war, been in charge in Indian waters, and was thus familiar with the problems of the command. Over sixty as he was, Hughes was as tough and as stubborn a fighter as he had been when young. Moreover, he was enthusiastically admired by his captains, among whom were men such as Sir Richard King, James Alms, Peter Rainier and others whom Hughes was to turn into a team very differently animated from their opponents.

The first of a series of clashes between Suffren and Hughes took place on 17 February 1782 off Sadras, a place slightly to the south of Madras. A day or so earlier, Hughes had chased and taken six of Suffren's transports, including one full of guns and military stores which were a present from Louis XVI to Hyder Ali. When Suffren sighted Hughes, the French had the advantage of the wind-gauge, which meant that they could choose to attack in their own time and fashion; moreover, they were in superior numbers. Now, at the outset, was the great chance for Suffren to annihilate his opponent, whom he learnt was expecting reinforcements.

Suffren's tactical idea was to approach the British from the rear and to double Hughes's line as his ships came up. He himself would go no farther up the line than Hughes's flagship, the *Superb*, but would also engage the next ahead to prevent her wearing round to the help of the admiral. The plan was frustrated because his own rear ships, some of whose captains Suffren believed to be disaffected, kept to a formal line of battle, much as Graves's captains had done at the Chesapeake. The exception was Saint-Felix of the *Brilliant* who, with de Cuverville of the *Flamand*, gave Commodore King in the *Exeter* a very rough time until Hughes was able to send ships from the van to relieve the pressure.

The losses in the battle were surprisingly even, considering the French advantages. Suffren had 32 killed and 105 wounded, Hughes very slightly less. Suffren was bitterly disappointed at the end of the day. He had had a chance of a clear-cut victory in a fleet action, and it had been missed through no fault of his own. However, there were compensations. By reason of his battle damage Hughes was compelled to sail for Trincomalee in Ceylon. This was a place he had recently taken from the Dutch, with one of the finest natural harbours in the world. Suffren was able to land troops on the Indian coast and to make contact with Hyder Ali. The result was the fall of the British fort at Cuddalore, south of Pondicherry. Suffren could consider that he had scored two successes, and that boldness paid.

Hughes went to Trincomalee after the battle to refit, and then back to Madras. Suffren went to Pondicherry and later to Porto Novo. Then he sailed for Ceylon, with Hughes after him. Suffren's idea was not the immediate capture of the base, but the hope of intercepting the *Sultan* of 74 guns and the *Magnanime*, the 64-gun successor of the ship made famous by Howe at Rochefort and Quiberon, which he had learnt were on their way from England. He was unsuccessful, and when the two admirals next met, Hughes had eleven ships to Suffren's twelve. The newly joined *Sultan* and *Magnanime* were, however, decimated by scurvy and only the *Sultan* was really fit for operations.

The second encounter took place on 12 April 1782 off Providien, an islet on the western side of Ceylon. It was the very day on which, far away in the West Indies, Rodney defeated de Grasse. Providien proved to be a slogging match in which most of the casualties were suffered by the two flagships, the *Héros* and the *Superb*, and by the *Monmouth*, Captain Alms, the latter ship losing her main and mizen masts. Of the 137 killed and 430 wounded on the British side, by far the larger number occurred in their two ships most heavily engaged. The French loss was about the same, and once again, robbed of the outright victory which he had expected, Suffren made plain his displeasure at what he thought was the stupidity and indiscipline of his captains. Hughes's fleet manoeuvred admirably, and his signals were obeyed with intelligence.

The French captains, restless under their leader, whose wish for a *mêlée* differed so markedly from anything they had experienced under other leaders, urged his return to the Ile de France, and indeed Suffren's orders from home enjoined this. But he was the man on the spot. He had given his word to support Hyder Ali and did not intend to go back on it. Every strategic necessity indicated that this was the right course. Lacking any harbour such as Trincomalee, he would refit as best he could on the Coromandel Coast, recruiting lascars and sepoys whenever they were available. Such energy, resilience, resource and determination mark him out as exceptional, particularly in view of the sometimes semi-mutinous attitude of his officers. Their attitude was scarcely surprising considering that Suffren made them fight till they dropped from exhaustion. So much was this so after the action off Providien that the ships of both fleets anchored at first 'higgledy-piggledy, close together,' in Hughes's words, 'like tired worn-out bulldogs after a desperate struggle.' They remained there all night and all next day, at first drenched by tropical rain.

So far, it had been Suffren who had taken the initiative on every occasion, but he had no monopoly in this respect and when the fleets met a few weeks later, it was Hughes who attacked. On 24 June Hughes sailed from Trincomalee and anchored the following day off Negapatam on the Coromandel Coast, the French being farther north at Cuddalore. Suffren appeared with his fleet on 5 July, and Hughes weighed and stood south, to keep the weather-gauge. Next day the French were seen at anchor to leeward, and Hughes bore down upon them, intending to fight a 'line' action in formal style, ship to ship.

The action was very severe and the loss heavy on board the *Brilliant*, which had forty-seven killed and 136 wounded—over a third of her complement—and she lost her mainmast. The captain of the *Sévère*, Cellart, actually struck his colours, but his first lieutenant shut him in his cabin and fought on—to Suffren's enthusiastic satisfaction, as explained later. The *Héros*, as usual in the thick of it, also had many casualties and had by this time lost more men in action than any ship in the whole war except for de Grasse's *Ville de Paris*. The total French loss was 178 killed and 600 wounded, against 77 killed and 233 wounded in Hughes's fleet.

Suffren sent home Cellart of the *Sévère*, also two others whom he thought guilty of misconduct. Then he refitted furiously. Within a fortnight he was ready for sea and sailed for Ceylon, while Hughes was gathering spares at Madras. Suffren's diligence brought him a great triumph for on 21 August, when he had received reinforcements, he decided to attack Trincomalee. The garrison commander surrendered after six days, to the dismay and fury of the British fleet when it arrived after a refit which had certainly been too protracted. They were furious at what they considered to be the shameful loss of their base, owing to an inadequate defence.

Elated by his success, Suffren sailed from Trincomalee on 3 September to give battle to Hughes once again, having a ship superiority of fourteen to twelve. Another slogging match ensued, and again the French loss was the heavier, 82 killed and 255 wounded against 51 killed and 283 wounded in Hughes's ships. Again it was the *Héros* which suffered most, and soon after her mainmast went over the side, Suffren hauled off to the south. Once more his captains did not satisfy him, and on his return to Trincomalee one of his 74-gun ships was lost through sheer mismanagement. He wrote home after the action:

> My heart is wrung by the most general defection. I have just lost the opportunity of destroying the English squadron . . . I can only attribute this horror to the wish to bring the cruise to an end, to ill-will and to ignorance; for I dare not suspect anything worse. The result has been terrible . . .

With the change in the monsoon, which precluded campaigning, Hughes took his ships to Bombay, where he could enjoy dockyard facilities presided over by the great shipwright Jamsetjee Bomanjee. There he was joined by Sir Richard Bickerton with five ships of the line. For his part, Suffren, finding the resources of Trincomalee inadequate, sailed for Achen in Dutch Sumatra, losing the *Bizarre* of 64 guns on the way at Cuddalore through mischance.

It was whilst Suffren was at Trincomalee in January 1783 after his return from Sumatra that he was seen by William Hickey, whose recollections of life in the Far East have given pleasure to so many. Although an Englishman and thus nominally an enemy, Suffren showed the greatest possible kindness to both Hickey and his wife. They had arrived in a Portuguese ship which had suffered dreadfully in a hurricane, and Mrs Hickey seemed to be at death's door. Suffren, in the courtliest manner, did everything possible for her, and so did his officers, providing her with medical attention and, when she had recovered, sending her chocolate, liqueurs, China sweetmeats and Achen fruit. Suffren told Hickey that he had the highest respect for Hughes both as a commander and as a man: 'A braver man does not live,' he said—but it was clear to Hickey that the general view in Ceylon was that Suffren had had much the best of all the encounters, and that the future of the English in India, to which Hickey was proceeding, was likely to be bleak.

It was Suffren's informality, and the nimbleness with which he 'went down the ship's side by a single common rope, and quick and light as any midshipman could have done' which most impressed Hickey, though he was shocked at the state of dirt prevailing in the flagship. Hickey's first impression is worth quoting in full.

Upon my entering the cabin an attendant asked my name, which giving he instantly went in to announce to the Admiral. Five minutes after I was admitted to the after cabin, where Mr. Suffren was sitting at a table having a number of papers upon it which he appeared to be inspecting; his secretary, Mr. Launay, and other persons were writing at the same table. He received me with the most engaging attention and politeness, and, pointing to a chair, desired I should be seated until he finished some matters of business that required despatch. I apologized for my unseasonable intrusion, that as I broke in upon him I would take some other opportunity of paying my respects when he might be less occupied. With the utmost good humour he said he should be at my service in a quarter of an hour, and requested I would sit till then.

Of course, I did so, and this afforded me an opportunity of observing his extraordinary dress and figure. In appearance he looked much more like a little, fat, vulgar English butcher than a Frenchman of consequence; in height he was about five feet five inches, very corpulent, scarce any hair upon the crown of his head, the sides and back tolerably thick. Although quite grey he wore neither powder nor pomatum, nor any curl, having a short cue of three or four inches tied with a piece of old spun-yarn. He was in slippers, or rather, a pair of old shoes, the straps being cut off, blue cloth breeches unbuttoned at the knees, cotton or thread stockings (none of the cleanest) hanging about his legs, no waistcoat or cravat, a coarse linen shirt entirely wet with perspiration, open at the neck, the sleeves being rolled up above his elbows as if just going to wash his hands and arms; indeed I concluded in my own mind that he had been broken in upon and interrupted whilst at his toilette, but afterwards ascertained that he always appeared as above described.

Suffren had started talking English, but broke into French because he hated being at a loss for a word. Although Hickey's French was only tolerable, they continued to converse in Suffren's tongue. Hickey must have appealed to the admiral, for he was invited to dinner, when Hickey remarked:

The table was tolerably supplied, and we had as fine bread as ever I saw on shore, the wines light, but well flavoured, a very coarse table cloth, not over clean, the knives, forks etc. rough in the extreme. The admiral ate voraciously, more than once remarking to me that the heat of the climate did not take any away his appetite, 'though,' he added, 'I have often, with a very keen one, been reduced to a musty biscuit, full of vermin, with a small bit of stinking salt pork, as my only sustenance during the twenty-four hours.'

Through Suffren's kindness, Hickey and his wife were given a passage to Madras and there, in April 1783, they had the chance to pay their respects to Hughes on board the *Superb*. Hughes gave Hickey an account of Suffren in action which is as extraordinary as it is unique. Hickey's Memoir runs:

Sir Edward Hughes received us with the utmost politeness. After asking me a number of questions respecting Admiral Suffren and his fleet, all of which I answered very full, I mentioned the handsome terms in which the French commander always spoke of him, at which he appeared highly gratified, returning the compliment by pronouncing an encomium and panegyric upon Mr. Suffren's qualities and talents as a seaman, saying: 'Mr. Suffren, Sir, is as gallant a man as ever lived, of which I have in many instances been an eye witness.

'In the last action, after fighting his ship in a manner bordering upon desperation and performing wonders, the superior fire of the *Superb* and *Sultan* completely silenced that of the *Héros*. Those two British ships continued pouring broadsides into her without her being able to return a single gun. My ship being within pistol shot, I could distinctly see all that occurred. Her upper deck was more than once completely cleared, scarce a man remaining upon it except Mr. Suffren himself, who ran up and down the quarter-deck like a lunatic, crying out most earnestly for some fortunate shot to take him off.

'I have never thought of the scene but with astonishment, and how the *Héros* sustained such a tremendously galling fire is still incomprehensible to me. A very few minutes must, however, have decided her fate by inevitably sending her to the bottom, when an accidental explosion took place on board the *Superb*, blowing up the entire forecastle, whereby thirty of my brave fellows were destroyed and the rest of my crew thrown into confusion, not only from the lamentable circumstance itself but from the fire's communicating to the middle part of the ship, which was soon in a blaze. The extraordinary exertions of my officers, ably supported and aided by the ship's crew, at last extinguished the flames and saved us from destruction.'

After a long conversation, Hughes summoned one of the lieutenants and ordered him to show Hickey every part of the ship. 'I was equally surprised and pleased,' he commented, 'at the contrast between the main deck of the *Superb* and that of the *Héros*, the former being delightfully neat and clean throughout, the latter disgusting to behold from filth and dirt.'

If Suffren had excoriated some of his captains, Hickey was surprised to hear from Hughes that, although his ships were again all in good order, even he had not been altogether satisfied with the performance of some of them in battle. Sir Richard King had disagreed so strongly about this with his Commander-in-Chief that they had had a quarrel. 'However,' Hughes explained, 'I am glad to say we now understand each other, and this day we are to meet as friends. It is to be a reconciliation dinner.' To his delight, Hickey was invited. The dinner, he noted

. . . was so magnificent, and so capitally dressed, that it would not have discredited the cooks of the London, or any other equally celebrated tavern. Captain Mitchell who sat next to me at table asked me what I thought of Sir Edward's fare, to which I answered I never had seen so splendid an entertainment, and had no idea such a one could have been produced on board a ship. 'Oh,' says my neighbour, 'our gallant admiral likes good living, and always takes care to provide himself with a professed cook. Indeed, he usually has both a French and an English cook. His present chief performer is of the former country, his English cook being killed in the last action.'

Hughes could well afford such prodigality. During his two periods in the East Indies he had been able to amass a fortune reckoned at £40,000 a year. This was 'shaking the pagoda tree', as the phrase was (pagodas being the name of gold and silver coins then current in southern India) to some effect. Fortunate as he was—and as Suffren had been—Hughes's wealth was all dissipated after his death by a feckless stepson.

The capture of Trincomalee had marked the height of Suffren's success. Before his next encounter with Hughes, he had heard first of the death of Hyder Ali, and then of the loss of a convoy of badly needed naval stores. Tippoo Sultan, who became Hyder's successor, would carry on the war with the British, but there was no good alternative source from which Suffren could hope for the stores he wanted.

However, it was always his way to make do with what he had, and when the fleets met near Porto Novo on 20 June 1783 he was as confident as ever.

This time numbers favoured Hughes, who had 18 ships of the line to Suffren's 15. Suffren had the wind-gauge, and came down in his old style, though he was exercising command from the frigate *Cleopatra*. The British were seriously undermanned, having over 600 men in the last stages of scurvy, and the fighting, which lasted some two hours, was more evenly distributed among the French ships than had been the case heretofore. French casualties were 102 killed and 386 wounded, and Hughes lost 99 men killed and 434 wounded in the last of these stubborn affairs. What is remarkable about the five engagements is that no ship on either side was actually sunk, however gravely damaged they may have been, and that the two Commanders-in-Chief, always in the thick of it, remained unscathed.

When the fleets separated Hughes went to Madras, very short of water, and Suffren to Pondicherry, whence he later moved to Porto Novo. It was there that he received word from Hughes, sent by a frigate, that the war was over. This had actually been so for some weeks, but news took time to travel.

Putting in at the Cape of Good Hope on his way home, Suffren was delighted to receive a deputation from the British, led by Sir Richard King, which came to pay their respects to an opponent who had fought so stoutly. The compliment pleased the Frenchman almost as much as plaudits at home, which were on a fitting scale. The King created an extra post of Vice-Admiral in his honour, which was to end with his life. Suffren lived until 1788, and the story, originating from a servant, that he was killed in a duel by a nobleman whose relations he had refused to promote, is now discredited.

Appropriately, seeing that he saw so much, it was Hickey who recorded what French sailors, as opposed to some of their officers, thought of their leader. One day at Trincomalee, as the Englishman was being rowed out to the *Héros*, he asked the boat's crew's opinion of the admiral. The men were bursting with pride in him, and were full of praise. The most eloquent among them, said Hickey, 'concluded the account by declaring the General was the greatest hero upon earth, and ended with—"*Oui, ma foi, c'est un bougre déterminé*." '

Suffren would surely have been content with that rough phrase.

5

Lord Howe and the Relief of Gibraltar

At the time when Suffren and Hughes were at the height of their duelling, Gibraltar was in its fourth year of siege. The Spaniards had never become reconciled to the cession of the rock fortress to Britain by the Treaty of Utrecht seventy years earlier. They were in process of making their most vigorous and sustained attempt to recapture it, backed by their French allies. The defence, conducted by Lieutenant-General George Augustus Eliott, afterwards Lord Heathfield, showed no signs of weakening as time went on, rather the reverse, but the needs of the garrison required the arrival of at least one large convoy annually, with attendant risk of a fleet action.

In the late summer of 1782, when Lord Howe was given charge of the relief (which he considered both at the time and later to have been the most difficult task of his life), he could at least reflect that similar operations during the two previous years provided a good augury. In 1780 Rodney had been responsible. He had defeated a Spanish force in a moonlit battle off Cape St Vincent, capturing four ships of the line and much of a coastal convoy. The following year Admiral George Darby had been equally successful in his mission, and had met with no attempt by the Franco-Spanish fleet to intercept him.

As Howe's convoy, with its attendant ships of war, assembled at Spithead awaiting a fair wind for down-Channel, a tragic episode occurred which was felt as such throughout the entire country. The *Royal George*, Hawke's flagship at Quiberon, which was by then over a quarter of a century old, sank at anchor whilst undergoing a trivial repair, carrying with her Rear-Admiral Richard Kempenfelt and hundreds of her men. Her structure was decayed, and as there was a timber famine in the dockyards she had not been properly repaired before being sent on active service. Kempenfelt was a serious loss to the Navy. One of the most experienced and thoughtful officers of his time, he and Howe between them were in the process of improving the signalling system beyond recognition. As for the ship, the *Royal George* became the subject of speculation, song and folk-lore. William Cowper wrote a poem, 'Toll for the Brave', which, set to a tune by Handel, is still heard. It was well for Howe that his own blue flag flew from the main topmast of the *Victory*.

The *Victory*, as Fleet flagship, had endured some strange roles during the course of the current war, and in some of them Kempenfelt had assisted. Most shaming had been the stage when, with most of the abler admirals refusing to serve afloat—including Howe himself—because they distrusted the Government, or its policy, or both, the protection of the country had had to be placed in the hands of veterans such as Sir Francis Geary or Sir Charles Hardy, once good men, but decayed, and a Franco-Spanish fleet ranged Channel waters at will.

Kempenfelt, as Captain of the Fleet or Chief Staff Officer, had been a steadying influence on these rather palsied men. Moreover, during the December previous to Howe's convoy he had himself gained a neat personal success by capturing a convoy almost under the nose of Admiral de Guichen, who had allowed himself to get to leeward of a convoy he was supposed to protect, and had seen Kempenfelt snap up the merchantmen without being able to get to their help.

Although he had a Captain of the Fleet in the person of John Leveson-Gower, who was Admiral Boscawen's son-in-law, Howe had no need for the advice of such an officer, for he was master of his profession. He was sometimes compared with Anson, on whose circumnavigation he would have served as a midshipman had not his captain turned for home, after reaching the South Atlantic, owing to storm damage. For nearly the whole of his mature life, as a member of the Whig ascendancy, Howe was always at or near the centre of affairs. His taciturnity was proverbial, but he was popular in the fleet where he was known as 'Black Dick' from his swarthy complexion. He smiled rarely, but when he did so the sailors reckoned they were in for a fight. On the mission of 1782, it would be the test of a skilled commander-in-chief to avoid any such thing, at least on an extended scale, since it could serve no good purpose.

The chief difficulty before Howe was that he had to conduct a huge assembly of ships, the larger number of captains not subject to naval discipline, and many destined for places other than Gibraltar, since it was economical to send as many different convoys as possible under the protection of the same covering fleet. All this would be over what the strategists call an 'uncommanded sea'. That is to say, once Channel soundings were left behind, the course lay off hostile coasts, in the harbours of which the enemy was known to have superior numerical strength, though it was uncertain if and where concentrations would be met with.

Early in the morning of 11 September 1782, Howe sailed from the St Helens anchorage off the Isle of Wight. He had 34 ships of the line, five frigates and three fire-ships, useful as scouts or dispatch vessels. The convoys included one for India, one for the West Indies and a third for Oporto, the merchantmen totalling nearly a hundred and fifty. The captains of some of the ships of war sent a stream of complaints to Howe about the state of their commands. The disaster to the *Royal George* had obviously shaken them, and other ships were nearly as rotten. But if the officers concerned expected Howe to release them to return to dockyard hands, they mistook their man.

During the whole summer that year the weather was atrocious. There was no improvement as autumn approached. On 29 September one of the largest transports, the *Duchess of Richmond*, lost her topmasts in a storm. She parted company, and others ran back for shelter to home ports. Three days later all the convoys had dispersed except that for Gibraltar, of which twelve or thirteen ships were by that time missing. The frigate *Latona* was sent ahead to reconnoitre, and on 9 October her captain brought word that 48 French and Spanish ships of the line were anchored off Algeciras, only four miles from Gibraltar. They were the covering force for the 'grand attack' on the fortress which, although Howe did not know it, was already past its climax, and had failed. Two days after the *Latona*'s report Howe sighted the Straits. He then formed his fleet into three divisions, with the transports ahead and to leeward, where he could best watch over them and could run down to their help if they were attacked.

Howe gave the merchant captains his usual meticulous instructions, but these were apt to be involved and sometimes made no allowances for those unversed in the finer points of navigation. He intended the supply ships to sail straight into Gibraltar Bay. His men-of-war would remain outside, cleared for action and under way, ready to meet the Combined Fleet if it emerged from Algeciras. Thus, with the wind astern, the fleet stood into the Straits in the wake of the convoy. The Rock of Gibraltar loomed clearly ahead, and four of the merchantmen went in precisely as ordered, mooring off Gibraltar Mole. The rest were swept on by the tide round Europa Point into the Mediterranean. Howe was compelled to follow them, much against his will, with the Combined Fleet at his rear.

Next day, after a beat to windward under very unfavourable conditions, three or four more storeships reached Gibraltar, but the rest, together with the fleet, were by this time some way to the eastward of the Rock, the Combined Fleet not far distant. It was not until 18 October that all the store-ships had been shepherded back to Gibraltar and safely unloaded. The garrison was now provisioned against all emergencies.

Howe had next to cover the withdrawal of the empty store vessels, and was particularly anxious not to bring on a battle in the confined waters of the Straits. Favoured by an easterly wind, he ran to the west, followed at a respectful distance by the enemy. The sight of Howe and the transports running through the Straits apparently pursued by the enemy was not one which appealed to the Gibraltar garrison, or indeed to Howe, but there was no point in challenging an enemy with a numerical superiority of 48 to 34 until circumstances were more to his advantage.

When the store-ships were clear of danger Howe reduced to easy sail, hoping that as the enemy ran through the Straits to the Atlantic that they would be driven to leeward. De Cordoba, the Combined Fleet's Commander-in-Chief, did not allow this to happen and, seeing that Howe seemed prepared at this stage to offer battle, he accepted the challenge. But he dressed his line with such care, and took so long about it, that it was evening before action became general, and even so it was at long range. There was no attempt by de Cordoba to close with his opponent with the purpose of annihilation, as his numbers might have justified. In fact, Howe soon concluded that he was not facing a serious threat. On board the *Victory*, he ordered the men to lie down and not to fire a shot until they could 'see the buttons on the enemy's uniform'. This never came about. Henry Duncan, the second captain, recorded that 'various were the conjectures of the enemy's intentions on our fleet: I fancy they had no plan, and only thought it incumbent on them to make some show of an action when it was put in their power with so great odds'. A Frenchman might have described the whole affair as a *gasconade*. The total British loss was 68 killed and 208 wounded, and the enemy had 60 killed and 320 wounded. By the fearsome standards of Suffren and Hughes, it was a skirmish rather than a battle.

No eulogy occurred when Howe returned to England, and none was expected. Nevertheless, the admiral was thankful to have accomplished his important task without loss, and the enemy were in no doubt as to the skill he had shown. Captain L. E. Chevalier, historian of the French Navy, described the operation as one of the finest of the war. It was of a kind with which French admirals were particularly familiar. They were never impressed at the thought of a battle without an important ulterior object.

Howe anchored at Spithead on his return home on 14 November. He struck his flag the same day, and went ashore. He had, he said, been 'rendered an invalid' by his recent services in the Channel and Atlantic, 'in a greater degree these five or six months past than I had supposed myself to be for some preceding years'.

The preliminaries of peace with the United States were signed on 30 November, and with the French, Spanish and Dutch two months later. The siege of Gibraltar was formally declared to be at an end on 2 February 1783. It had lasted three years, seven months and twelve days.

Although Howe was able to return to family life—he had a devoted wife and three daughters—he also resumed a political career which had been interrupted by his differences with those at the helm in their treatment of the Americans. He served as First Lord of the Admiralty in the Ministry of the younger Pitt from 1783 to 1788 and in so doing reached the highest post in a service to which he had given unremitting attention since boyhood.

There was a scare of war with France in 1790. George III, who looked upon Howe as his favourite admiral and had made him an earl, insisted that he should fly his flag at sea as Commander-in-Chief, as Anson had done in the time of the sovereign's grandfather. The immediate crisis died down, but not for long. In 1793 there began that immense and costly struggle with Revolutionary and Napoleonic France which, with only one short break, was to spread itself over more than two decades. Howe, again at the King's insistence, was given command of the Home Fleet, in spite of the fact that he was approaching seventy, had taken a prominent part in two earlier wars, and had repeatedly declared his belief that a man was too old for active service at sea by the time he reached the age of sixty.

Howe flew his flag in the *Queen Charlotte*, a splendid three-decker completed three years earlier, with the privilege of having the Union flag at the fore topmast to indicate that he was subject to no authority except that of the King in Council.

It was Howe who, in 1794, won the first tactical victory of the war, far out into the Atlantic, on what was known as 'The Glorious First of June'. He did not prevent a grain convoy from America reaching starving France, but he demonstrated what Mahan called that 'combat supremacy' which was never to be lost at sea by the British until France was defeated. Six prizes looked well at Spithead, and the victory caused general jubilation.

Howe, who had the melancholy satisfaction three years later of settling a mutiny at Spithead which might never have occurred had he not been absent on sick leave, and thus taken no action when petitions were sent to him, lived until the final year of the eighteenth century, to which he essentially belonged. Nelson, in a letter written after his own victory at the Nile, called him: 'our great Master in Naval tactics and bravery'. His words would have been endorsed by every responsible person of his time. Howe had been given the Order of the Garter in 1797, and he was the only officer in history to have received this honour for services purely naval in character.

6

Children of the Service: the Gardners

Howe was reserved in his friendships, but he felt a special affection, undisturbed by the fact that he was capable of smiling at some of his foibles, for one of the heroes of the Glorious First of June. This was Rear-Admiral Alan Gardner.

In the Navy of Howe's time, which was partly his creation, and still more that of Anson and Hawke, there was a phrase in common use in cabins and wardrooms which referred to 'Children of the Service'. By this was meant officers who had risen in the Navy by favour or merit or a blend of both, and their sons. They were looked upon by their fellows as dedicated spirits, who were unlikely to wilt from neglect.

One of the best-known examples is seen in the family of Hood, which produced two Samuels and two Alexanders, all four of whom went far or did well, and who are still remembered, if at times confusedly. There were a number of others, among whom the Gardners, father and son, were outstanding.

Although the elder Gardner won a peerage, both he and his heir (who became a Rear-Admiral at thirty-six, one of the earliest promotions ever recorded) are totally forgotten, for the peerage has long been dormant and biographers have seldom been drawn to sea officers of less than the highest eminence except for reasons not always connected with the Navy. Even those whose business it is to choose ships' names, whose memory sometimes extends to very obscure characters, have never thought of the Gardners.

Alan Gardner was born in 1742, son of a lieutenant-colonel of Dragoons. His home was the Staffordshire market town of Uttoxeter, a place far from the sea, and without a river larger than the Dove. Nevertheless, the fact was not without significance for Anson was from the same county (the family home at Shugborough is still furnished with fine memorials), and a youth who could hitch his wagon to that star could travel fast and well. Anson's favour indeed came about, not directly, but through the medium of Captain Peter Denis, who had been a lieutenant on board the *Centurion* during the famous world voyage, and who rose to be a Vice-Admiral of the Red.

It was with Denis that Alan Gardner went to sea. Denis had command of the *Medway* of 60 guns, and one of his first duties was to escort George II to the Continent on his way to his Electorate at Hanover, Anson being in charge of the fleet. In 1757, the *Medway*, together with the *Eagle*, Captain Hugh Palliser, took the French *Duc d'Aquitaine* after a fight in the Atlantic. On board the *Eagle* was the future Captain James Cook. He and Gardner had a first taste of action together.

The following year, Denis was given the larger *Dorsetshire* of 70 guns, in which he captured the French *Raisonnable*. Then, in November 1759, the ship took part in the victory at Quiberon Bay, after which Hawke is said to have told Denis and Captain Speke of the *Resolution* that they had 'behaved like angels'. Well-blooded as a youth, Gardner was made a lieutenant in March 1760 at the age of eighteen. During the following year, still under Denis but now in the *Bellona*, he was present at the capture of the *Courageux* of 74 guns. This led to hastened promotion. Gardner was appointed Master and Commander of the *Raven* fire-ship, giving him his first taste of independence.

With the coming of peace, the essential further step, to post rank, had necessarily to be waited for, but it was not unduly long in arriving. In May 1766, when still only twenty-four, Gardner was given his captaincy and sent to the *Preston* of 50 guns. This was the flagship of Rear-Admiral Parry, Commander-in-Chief on the Jamaica and Windward Islands station. It was usual for junior post-captains to serve in flagships where they could be under the immediate eye of a still more seasoned officer. To appoint senior men, as was sometimes done, occasionally led to difficulties.

Gardner's next move was to the frigate *Levant*, in which he continued in the West Indies. There, at Jamaica, he married Susanna Hyde, a widow and the heiress of Francis Gale, a man of wealth. The pair had a large family, the boys inclining to the armed services, and the eldest, Alan Hyde, showing brilliance during his short life, as will be related.

Another frigate command followed that of the *Levant*. This was the *Maidstone*, in which Gardner again served at Jamaica, probably at his own request because of his many connections in the island. The opening of the War of American Independence found him still in the West Indies, and when ordered to the American coast to intercept supplies from France, he had yet another of those single-ship encounters of which his career had been full. In November 1778 he chased and challenged a large vessel in the latitude of Cape Henry. She proved to be the *Leon*, a heavily armed French merchantman with a bigger crew than that of the *Maidstone*. After a severe fight the *Leon* hauled down her colours, and was found to have a cargo of upwards of 1,500 hogsheads of tobacco.

The *Maidstone* had been sufficiently damaged to warrant Gardner sailing for home with his prize, since the wind was fair for England. He did nothing of the sort. He shaped course for the West Indies, and after a tedious passage, frigate and prize reached Antigua nearly seven weeks after the engagement. There, the *Leon*'s cargo realized far less than it would have done in the London market. Strict adherence to his duty had cost Gardner several thousands of pounds: even so, he did reasonably well in prize money.

Whilst at Antigua, Gardner was transferred to the *Sultan* of 74 guns, and in her he took part in Admiral Byron's action with d'Estaing in July 1779. The *Sultan*, with 16 killed and 39 wounded, had the highest casualties in the British fleet. There followed another spell at Jamaica, after which Gardner returned home with a convoy, his ship being paid off soon after her arrival.

He had a great piece of luck in his next appointment. Towards the end of the year 1781, he was given command of the *Duke*, whose ship's company had been admirably trained in gunnery by her former captain, Sir Charles Douglas, who had become Rodney's Captain of the Fleet. The *Duke*, a three-decked ship of 98 guns, was only four years old, and was known in the Navy as the 'Tremendous Duke'. This was owing to a bellicose-looking figurehead of the Duke of Cumberland, victor of Culloden, dressed in his red coat. The ship looked fit for war, and she soon showed her worth in action.

The luck lay in the fact that the *Duke* was ordered to the West Indies. She sailed, in company with the *Valiant* and the *Warrior*, to join Rodney's fleet in the one part of the world where, at that time, there might be honour to be gained. She arrived on the station in time to take part in the victory of 12 April 1782, the most satisfying hour, for the Navy, of the entire war. Gardner was one of the few to have been present both at Quiberon Bay and the Saints, twenty-three years apart. He also had the happiness to have his eldest son with him. The lad, who was only ten years old, acted as his father's messenger, and actually received a slight wound during the course of the action.

The *Duke* was just ahead of the *Formidable*, Rodney's flagship, and her captain was one of the first, after a sudden shift of wind, to find himself on the far side of the French line. He confessed later that he had momentary thoughts of the fate of those who had suffered in the past from failure to keep strictly to the Order of Sailing, but his worries ended abruptly when the *Formidable* herself was seen to be following an exactly similar course. The *Duke* had her main topmast shot away, lost 13 killed and had 61 wounded.

The ship was paid off at the peace, but Gardner was not long unemployed for in September 1785 he was appointed Commander-in-Chief at Jamaica, in which was once more seen the hand of partiality. He had the rank of commodore and his pendant flew in the 50-gun *Europa*. He was there three years, and when he returned home, it was to the Board of Admiralty. He also became MP for Plymouth, and when, in 1790, trouble arose with Spain over rights in Nootka Sound, on the north-west coast of America, which resulted in what was known as the 'Spanish Armament', Gardner volunteered to serve as a private captain in the *Courageux*, the very ship he had helped to capture as a youth. She had been taken into the Navy and had had thirty years' useful service.

Three years later, at the start of the war with Revolutionary France, there was a general promotion. Gardner, twenty-seven years after becoming a post-captain, at last received his flag. It had been an exceptionally long wait, and meant that many admirals, who had been posted at an age later than his, were no longer fit for active service.

Gardner was only just over fifty, but his career had been arduous. It had included three fleet actions and many smaller ones, and he had become of a nervous disposition. Sir John Jervis, later Earl of St Vincent, who was only seven years older, once said of him: 'He is a zealous and brave man, with the worst nerves possible, and full of doubts as to the precision of other men.' Gardner's flag captains must have given qualified views of their superior.

Although Jervis's terse description might not indicate an attractive man, there is evidence in plenty that Gardner was trusted by his superiors, respected by his equals and loved by his men. His appointment to the *Queen*, in which he flew his blue flag, would show his qualities at their very best, and in John Hutt he found a flag-captain equal to his most exacting demands.

Three weeks after getting his flag, Gardner was presented to George III on being appointed to a squadron destined for the West Indies, an area in which the Admiralty must by now have considered he had a vested interest. The ships, seven in all, included three seventy-fours and two frigates, of which the *Heroine*, 32 guns, was commanded by the Admiral's son. No service of importance resulted, the French being considered too strong to be attacked at Martinique, their most important island, without sufficient land forces to follow up any initial advantage. In the autumn of 1793 Gardner returned home, when he was immediately attached to the Channel Fleet, under the orders of Lord Howe.

Early the following year Howe had a series of duties to perform which approached in complexity those which he had surmounted in relieving Gibraltar twelve years earlier. He had to safeguard outward-bound convoys, to prevent grain ships from America reaching France, and to seek out and defeat the enemy fleet. Two of these objects he fulfilled, after a series of movements and manoeuvres extending through much of May.

Having seen the convoys safely on their way Howe then sought for the French, having heard from his frigate captains that they were no longer in the security of Brest. He searched far out into the Atlantic, and was rewarded on 28 May when the enemy were sighted, though with the advantage of the windward position. The French Commander-in-Chief was Villaret-Joyeuse, who had learnt his business as a young officer under Suffren during the East Indies campaign against Hughes. It was significant of the changes which had taken place in the French Navy since the Revolution that he had a political commissar on board to make sure that he acted 'correctly'. The man—Jean Bon St André—was one of the most zealous of his breed. He knew little about the sea, but a more indoctrinated Revolutionary could not have been found.

Howe's intention was to gain the weather-gauge: Villaret-Joyeuse's determination was to keep it. At first, all the British could do was to beat up towards the French with their fastest sailing ships leading. In this they had some success. A large French ship was actually captured, but got away during the night.

It was clear to Howe that Villaret-Joyeuse was prepared to stand and fight—on his own terms. There was, in fact, a general action on 29 May, during the course of which Howe managed to isolate two French ships, which would have been captured had not Villaret-Joyeuse borne down to their rescue in strength. In so doing he forfeited the weather-gauge, and was now at Howe's mercy as far as the timing of any attack was concerned, assuming that the fleets kept in contact.

The *Queen* took a distinguished part in the first action, and suffered heavily. Captain Hutt was so badly wounded that he never recovered, dying a few weeks later. The management of the ship therefore devolved directly on Gardner, and on a very able first lieutenant, William Bedford. The damage might not have been so great had better support come from Howe's leading ship, the *Caesar*. Her captain, Anthony Molloy, was one of those men, unlike Gardner or Howe, whose nerve in battle, once good, seems to have failed him. Howe had to signal repeatedly to the *Caesar* to carry more sail or to engage the enemy more closely.

Being neither hasty nor impatient, Howe waited, with the enemy under constant surveillance, until the misty weather, which had been pervasive, began to clear. Then he signified to his captains that he would attack during the early morning on the first of June. His intention was to pass through the French line and to complete the business from the leeward position so that the enemy could not escape.

This was asking a great deal of the intelligence, courage and luck of individual captains, but Howe prophesied that for every ship that

73

fulfilled his orders he would take a prize. This estimate proved true. Six ships were handled in exactly the way he had hoped, and six prizes were the result, plus a seventh French ship, the *Vengeur*, which was sunk by the fire of the *Brunswick*. This was a rare event in sail warfare, so readily could battle damage to wooden ships be repaired sufficiently to get them back to harbour. No British ship was lost, though the casualties were heavy.

The *Queen*'s order of sailing was in the second division of the centre squadron, and Gardner again fought her admirably. One of the lieutenants, Samuel Ballard, entered the following in his log, descriptive of the scene when, battered, partly dismasted and temporarily isolated, the *Queen* would have seemed a likely prize to an aggressive foe.

> Observed eleven sail of the enemy's line and their frigates starting for us. Our fleet so much to windward no hopes of relief from them. Beat to arms. Swayed a fore studding-sail up for a crossjack to keep the ship from falling down on the enemy. At $\frac{1}{2}$ past 1, they began a heavy fire on us, which was so faithfully returned, occasioned them to pass on, not wishing to have any more fire from a disabled British ship.

'*Beat to arms* . . . '—it was a splendid moment in the history of warfare, and the *Queen*'s efforts at self-help were an example to all.

Howe, weary as he was after his exertions, and with much else on his mind, noted the *Queen*'s danger. According to Edward Codrington, one of the lieutenants on board the *Queen Charlotte*, the following incident took place:

> Lord Howe . . . was looking anxiously over the taffrail waiting for the smoke to clear away and to decide what was next to be done. He had made the signal for all ships able to close round the Admiral, and seeing that the *Queen*, Gardner's ship, which had lost her mizen-mast, was a considerable way down to leeward, and in danger of being cut off by the enemy . . . Lord Howe came to the fore part of the poop under great anxiety, and called eagerly to Sir R. Curtis, 'Go down to the *Queen*, Sir, go down to the *Queen*.' 'My Lord, we can't,' said Curtis, 'we're a mere wreck, the ship won't steer.' 'Then send everything else, Sir, directly!' 'My Lord, we're a mere wreck, and there are three sail of fresh ships coming down upon us. What can we do, when the ship herself won't steer?'

Bowen* then burst out with, 'She *will* steer, my Lord.' 'Try her,

---

* James Bowen, the Master of the Fleet, or chief navigator, was a favourite with Howe and indeed with all who knew him. He became a post-captain after the battle, and died as a flag officer.

Sir,' said Howe. And Bowen, with a seaman's eye, watching the movement of her falling off, and getting the spritsail well filled to assist her, got her before the wind with her head towards the enemy.

It was the frigate *Pegasus* which reached the *Queen* first, and before long she had the great three-decker under tow. But what astounded many in the fleet, including Captain Gambier of the *Defence*, himself a hero, was that the *Queen*'s efforts did not end with defending or saving the ship. Gambier wrote:

> She astonished us by her extraordinary exertions. She had lost her main-mast. This was replaced in a most able manner before the evening . . . All her sides were scrubbed, her paint-work looking as clean as if nothing had happened—a good proof of what can be done with good discipline and management.

Gardner had indeed set a shining example, and the mention of the despondent attitude of Sir Roger Curtis, noted by Codrington, bore out the general view that he was a bit of an old woman, and most unpopular. This was all the stranger because, years before, Curtis had been at the heart of the defence of Gibraltar, gallantly supporting General Eliott. He had been taken into the *Victory* when Howe sent her second captain home with dispatches after the relief of 1782. Curtis had been one of Howe's adherents ever since, and it is possible that the Commander-in-Chief was too partial to him. Certainly, the second captain of the *Queen Charlotte*, Sir Andrew Douglas, was much more highly thought of in the fleet.

Douglas, who was badly wounded in the head during the course of the action, had no illusions about the atmosphere of the higher command. Eight weeks earlier he had written to the Comptroller of the Navy, one of whose sons he had promised to befriend: 'No man in his senses, well out of the active service, and at a certain time of life, would wish to come into it again: for it is made up of envy, hatred, malice and all uncharitableness.'

This was perhaps a little harsh, but certainly Howe, probably prompted by Curtis, made a very invidious selection of names for special mention in a supplementary dispatch which he wrote after the fleet had returned home. He omitted completely one flag officer, Benjamin Caldwell, which was bad enough, and he compounded the offence by not mentioning Captain Collingwood, who had fought the three-decked *Barfleur* most ably after his admiral, George Bowyer, who himself received due praise, had his leg shattered by a cannon-ball and was carried below. Collingwood never forgot the slight, nor did Caldwell.

Gardner had every just reward for his part in the battle—a baronetcy, a gold chain from the King, the official thanks of Parliament, together with the other flag officers, a major-generalcy of the Marines; but he was never quite the same man again. Howe, who had often seen him in the stern gallery of his ship, rising several times a night to make sure that the lantern on the poop above his cabin was brightly lit so that the next astern should not overrun the *Queen* in the darkness, thought that for his own good he should retire. Gardner did not agree, but his exertions, both in an action fought by Lord Bridport off L'Orient in June 1795, which resulted in a success, though not a distinguished one, and two years later at the time of the Spithead Mutiny, lessened his resilience still further.

With the new century, Gardner was made a peer, taking his title from his birthplace at Uttoxeter. He held various commands in home waters, but never at critical times or places. Collingwood, one of the most eagle-eyed men in the Navy, would have liked to see Gardner as Commander-in-Chief, had not Cornwallis been available for that responsible post. In April 1805, a few months before Trafalgar, he wrote from his flagship:

> Lord Gardner joined us a week ago, to command the Fleet in the absence of Admiral Cornwallis. I saw him yesterday for an hour or two, and was sorry to find him altered for the worse—old and out of spirits; yet I think, if he were established he would recover again, and be as active as ever, for there is no officer a more perfect master of the discipline of the Fleet than he is.

There were, indeed, brief returns to former activity. For instance, in 1807 he again held chief command for a short time, with his son acting as his Captain of the Fleet, but this was only an interlude. The seasoned warrior, active in so many fights, lasted until 1809. He died worn out, and it was no wonder.

Young Alan Hyde Gardner succeeded to his father's peerage at the age of thirty-seven, by which time he had already become a Rear-Admiral of the Blue. His promotion had been startling, for he was made a lieutenant in 1787 at the age of fifteen, which was against regulations (often more applied in the breach than the observance when concerned with 'Children of the Service'). Two years later he became a commander, and in the general promotion of 1790 which brought his father a flag he rose to be a post-captain, and was appointed to the *Daphne*, later to the *Circe* and then to the *Heroine*, in which he sailed with the squadron to the West Indies.

He did not serve in Howe's fleet. Instead, he was sent to India under the orders of Commodore Peter Rainier, who was soon to get his flag. This officer, one of the many who made a fortune in the Far East, could claim to have had more service in that area than any other living man. As a youngster he had taken part in the duels between Pocock and d'Ache during the Seven Years War. Later, as captain of the *Burford*, he was in all Hughes's battles with Suffren. Now, his efforts, though principally directed 'to protecting the Trade against the Enemy's cruisers', as his Orders put it, would also be made against those Dutch possessions which had been so much in dispute during the War of American Independence. One of the first warlike actions of Revolutionary France had been against Holland, and in consequence this country was once again, this time most unwillingly, numbered among Britain's enemies.

Gardner's first assignment was to a small squadron, commanded by Rainier himself, whose purpose was to recapture Trincomalee. The expedition sailed from Madras on 21 July 1796 and a landing within striking distance of the Trincomalee fortifications was made on 18 August. After a short siege, with not much more than formal resistance, the place surrendered. This time, the most valuable base and harbour remained in British hands throughout the war.

Rainier then took his larger ships on an expedition against the Moluccas, leaving Gardner in charge off the Coromandel Coast and in Ceylon. The young man's most important success occurred in February 1797. This was the reduction of Colombo, in co-operation with troops under Colonel Stuart, which was achieved without loss of life.

Gardner returned home the following year and was appointed to the *Ruby* of 64 guns, which was attached to the fleet commanded by Lord Bridport. Afterwards he removed into the larger *Resolution*.

There was an uneasy interlude of peace in 1802 and for part of the following year. When war was resumed, Gardner was given charge of the *Hero*, 74 guns. Once more he served under Lord Bridport, but had no further action until 1805. In the summer of that year the *Hero* was one of the ships detached from the main fleet to intercept Admiral Villeneuve and the Combined Franco-Spanish Fleet on their way back from a foray in the West Indies, the preliminary to Napoleon's grand plan for the invasion of Britain. Calder's dispositions were such that a battle took place off Finisterre, during which two Spanish ships were captured. In this engagement Gardner led the van, his conduct being singled out for praise in Calder's dispatch.

Calder's satisfaction at having beaten a fleet superior in numbers to his own was not echoed in Whitehall. St Vincent and Nelson had by this time set new standards for the Navy, and Barham, the First Lord, did not think Calder had been sufficiently zealous in following up his success. Greatly chagrined, Calder demanded a court martial, and this was agreed to. The outcome was that he received an official reprimand, a verdict which many thought to be unjust. However, he forfeited any sympathy by his action in claiming a share of the Trafalgar prize money: this in spite of the fact that Nelson had allowed him to go home in his flagship, the *Prince of Wales*, instead of transferring him to a frigate, as the Admiralty intended. Calder was duly slapped down by Collingwood and, as he was already rich, he should have blushed at his own greed. He was later restored to official favour and ended his career as Commander-in-Chief at Plymouth.

Gardner had one further slice of luck, before a series of dull appointments on blockading duties, as captain and junior admiral, stretched before him until the end of hostilities. His ship was one of a squadron detached from the Channel Fleet under the orders of Sir Richard Strachan, which won a small-scale victory, a few weeks after Trafalgar, by capturing four French ships of the line which had escaped the holocaust a few weeks earlier.

In this action, as in Calder's, Gardner's ship was in the van. The losses were not heavy among the British, but the *Hero* suffered nearly half the total—10 men killed and 51 wounded. Strachan, who was ever afterwards known as 'the delighted Sir Dicky', from the exuberant tone of his dispatch, received the King's gold medal for this action, as did all his captains.

Gardner had no further service of note, but he could look back upon a career which had begun under Rodney when he was a child and had ended in the aftermath of Nelson's annihilating victory.

⚓   ⚓   ⚓

The present writer possesses a run of the *Naval Chronicle* which once belonged to Admiral Benjamin Page, who earlier in his life had served in the Suffren–Hughes duels, and was later ashore and afloat in the East alongside the younger Gardner. In the volume of the *Chronicle* in which occurs a notice of Page's old comrade-in-arms there is a print of a drawing of Gardner by Henry Edridge. On the top of this print Page has written: 'This is a formal and stiff likeness of the Merry and Lively, Original and most Gallant Officer.' Sad to say, the subject of the picture scarcely survived the end of the war which had brought him so much credit. He died three days before Christmas in the year of Waterloo.

7
Children of the Service: the Rowleys

⚓   ⚓   ⚓

When, during the Second World War, a frigate was christened *Rowley* (which afterwards saw active service in the Atlantic and off the coast of Normandy), she commemorated Sir Joshua Rowley, the second of various notable admirals of the same family. It was another instance of 'Children of the Service' distinguishing themselves in the fleet. There were Rowleys in the Navy long before the elder Gardner was born: they continued long after the younger Gardner had died.

Out of a considerable number of possibilities, the Rowley grandees best worth considering are four in number: Sir William, who was born when William and Mary occupied the throne of Britain, and who lived to become senior admiral; Sir Joshua, who was Sir William's eldest son; Sir Josias, who was Sir William's grandson, and finally Sir Charles, another grandson who, like his cousin, Josias, survived into the reign of Queen Victoria.

Sir William Rowley, who rose higher in the Navy than any of his descendants, though he was not the most distinguished, became a post-captain before he was thirty. He was first heard of commanding the *Bideford* of 20 guns when for some years he was active against the pirates of Sallee, who were among the hazards of the Barbary Coast throughout the eighteenth and early nineteenth centuries. He next had charge of the *Lively*, and for nearly nine years was stationed in Ireland, pirate-hunting once more, and helping the Customs officers against smugglers.

In 1741, at the time of the War of the Austrian Succession, he was sent to the Mediterranean in the *Barfleur*. It was in this ship that, as a Rear-Admiral, he commanded the van in Mathews's action off Toulon, which led to a crop of courts martial and to the rise of Hawke, whose ship, the *Berwick*, was in Rowley's division. Rowley proved a good friend to Hawke, both at the time and after he had replaced Mathews as Commander-in-Chief.

One of the captains at Toulon was Richard Norris of the *Essex*, who showed himself so craven in the face of the enemy that the authorities had no option but to 'inquire into his conduct', as the phrase was. His first lieutenant, Hugh Palliser, later eminent as captain, admiral and patron of James Cook, reported the appalling example he had shown to his crew. At one critical stage he had exclaimed that the *Essex* 'must not go down' to the help of ships under attack, for 'if we do, we shall be sunk and tore to pieces'.

Rowley handled the affair in a manner extremely partial to Norris, for whom there was really no excuse. His attitude was almost certainly due to his respect for the captain's father, Admiral Sir John Norris, who was very senior, much admired, and still living. Richard Norris was allowed to leave the fleet and he disappeared by going abroad via Gibraltar. The King and the Board of Admiralty were so disgusted that Anson persuaded his fellow members to recall Rowley from his command. It was six years before he was forgiven, but in 1751 amends were made. He became a member of the Board, and shortly afterwards received a Knighthood of the Bath.

In 1762 Rowley found himself at the head of the list of flag officers, and thus became Admiral of the Fleet, of which there was then only one. He enjoyed this eminence until his death in 1768, when Hawke succeeded him.

With plums falling ripely, those familiar with the ways of the Navy could have predicted that Joshua, the admiral's eldest son, would attain captain's rank at an early age if he chose to follow the sea profession. It is often true that sons of well-known men, impelled faster along the road than their natural pace or their merits warrant, sometimes disappoint the hopes of their sponsors. In Joshua's case this was not so. Although he was indeed 'posted' before he was twenty, as the younger Gardner had been, he saw a great deal of hard service, some of it under Howe and still more under his father's beneficiary, Hawke.

He was born in 1734, and the start of the Seven Years War saw him in the *Montagu* of 60 guns in the Mediterranean. He had his first taste of battle as one of a small squadron under Admiral Henry Osborne. The ships concerned were employed in blockading a French force under de la Clue which had taken shelter in the Spanish harbour of Carthagena. The British had news that de la Clue was expecting a reinforcement of three ships of the line and a frigate from Toulon, and Osborne planned to intercept it. His object was achieved on 28 February 1758, when two of the larger French ships, the *Foudroyant* and the *Orphée*, were captured, and the third, the *Oriflamme*, driven ashore, only the frigate escaping. It was with the *Oriflamme* that Rowley was concerned, but as the British were in greatly superior numbers, it was not an affair which made much stir.

Joshua was later detached from the fleet to take part in a number of combined operations. These consisted of landings on the French coast, a favourite idea with Pitt to dissipate the enemy's strength. They involved work with specially designed flat-bottomed boats which were used as landing craft. During an operation at St Cas, with Howe in charge, Rowley had the misfortune to be wounded and captured together with three other post-captains.

He was soon exchanged. He celebrated his release by marrying Sarah Burton, the only surviving child of Bartholomew Burton, Deputy

Governor of the Bank of England, and an heiress. He then returned to the command of the *Montagu* and was engaged in Hawke's wearying blockade of Brest. Rowley was, however, present at Quiberon Bay, thus sharing the glory as well as the ardours of his chief.

Quiberon was his great day, as it was for most of those present. Another came three years later when Rowley, by then in the 74-gun *Superb* in company with Captain Jervis of the *Gosport* of only 44 guns, and Henry Martin in the still smaller *Danae*, were faced by a French force which far outnumbered them. Their duty was to defend a West Indian convoy of immense value. The French admiral happened to be on his way to attack St John, New Brunswick. True to the tradition of his Service, the Frenchman held that the 'objective' came first, and made no serious attempt to defeat Rowley and capture the merchantmen. Seeing that the *Gosport*'s captain was the future Earl of St Vincent and already a renowned fighter, discretion was probably wise.

Rowley saw no further service of importance until the War of American Independence, when he took part in the indecisive Atlantic cannonade between Keppel and d'Orvilliers, which led to two courts martial, one on Keppel, the other on Palliser, which split the Navy and had political overtones. Rowley's ship, by then the *Monarch*, was not heavily engaged, having two men killed and nine wounded.

After transferring to the *Suffolk* of 74 guns and receiving an honorary appointment as Colonel of Marines, Rowley was sent to the West Indies in charge of a squadron of ten ships, with the rank of Commodore, in order to reinforce Admiral Byron. He was present at the battle with d'Estaing in July 1779, but his own ship once more escaped lightly, with seven killed and 25 wounded.

When he was in the *Conqueror*, another 74, and senior officer of four ships of the line, Rowley had a success off Guadeloupe in December 1779 when he came upon three French frigates which were chased and captured. Rowley next came under Rodney's orders; he found him a hard Commander-in-Chief to serve in that he did not always make his intentions clear to his captains, whom he kept at a distance, and of whom he expected too much. Rowley was in action against de Grasse in April 1780, when his casualties were heavy in an inconclusive engagement, and again a month later. He did not escape Rodney's criticism for misunderstanding tactical instructions, but at least the Commander-in-Chief did not put his inadequacies down to disaffection, as he was at times inclined to do with many of his subordinates. Rowley got his flag when with Rodney's fleet, but he missed the triumphant battle of the Saints Passage in 1782 and had no further opportunity to distinguish himself.

In 1786, when the war was over, he was made a baronet, an honour he lived four years to enjoy. His eldest daughter, Philadelphia, married Admiral Sir Charles Cotton, a man of the highest character and attainments who never had opportunities equal to his merit. The union provided yet another of the countless links between Service families, and it was later and to some degree to influence the career of Charles Rowley, a promising young kinsman.

Sir Josias, nephew of Sir Joshua and grandson of Sir William, was born in 1765 and joined the Navy under his uncle's aegis. He received early promotion to lieutenant, but had to wait until he was thirty before he reached post rank. By that time, war with France had reopened, and he could hope for a chance to shine on active service. He was sent to the East Indies Station for three years, but Admiral Rainier had things so well in hand there that no fleet action took place although, as was usual in time of war, prizes were fairly plentiful and captains seldom returned home without substantial additions to their means.

In the action between Sir Robert Calder and the Franco-Spanish Combined Fleet under Villeneuve, which was fought in July 1805, Rowley, who was by then with the Channel Fleet, commanded the *Raisonnable*, now quite an old ship. He saw further service at the Cape of Good Hope, which was occupied and retained, and at Buenos Aires, under the orders of Sir Home Popham, who in one respect was a principal successor of Howe and Kempenfelt in that he devised a Vocabulary Signal Book which was in use at Trafalgar. Popham, co-operating with General Sir David Baird, famed for his exploits in India against Tippoo of Mysore, although successful at the Cape, met misfortune when he traversed the South Atlantic to cross swords with the Spaniards at Buenos Aires. This time, Popham was acting with William Carr Beresford, later the commander of the Portuguese in the Peninsular War. Beresford's troops were defeated, he himself being taken prisoner. On the return of the Fleet to England, Home had to face a court martial. He received a reprimand, though this had little effect on the upward trend of his career.

Rowley, who had by then been so long in the *Raisonnable* that he must have felt the ship belonged to him, was later sent as senior officer of a squadron serving in the area of Mauritius, which since 1789 had replaced Pondicherry as the official headquarters of the Far Eastern outposts of France. Naturally in the circumstances, the island was strongly held, but this did not apply so well to neighbouring Réunion, then known as Bourbon. Rowley had much success against both merchantmen and ships of war using this island as their base. He crowned his work in March 1810 when, having at last transferred his pendant to the *Boadicea*, he made a landing at Réunion, which capitulated.

Failure resulted from an attack on Mauritius organized by Captain Samuel Pym, who was repulsed and captured. He had not waited to be reinforced by Rowley who, when he arrived off the main island, found he could achieve nothing. He had no choice but to return to Réunion, from which he organized a blockade of Mauritius which was highly effective.

The end of the war found Rowley a baronet, a Rear-Admiral, and just under fifty years old. He was in fact of an age and seniority which gave him the prospect of important peace-time commands. In due course, one came his way. Josias was given the Mediterranean in 1833, a post of which Lord St Vincent once said that it 'required an officer of splendour'. Rowley received the highest grade of the Order of St Michael and St George to join the insignia of the Bath, of which he was already a Knight. He died in 1842, one of the last of those who had taken a considerable part in what our ancestors called the 'Great War', and his title died with him, for he never married.

Sir Josias's cousin Charles, who was five years younger, began his sea career at the age of sixteen under the eye of Prince William Henry, third son of George III and one day to succeed to the throne as William IV. As a young man the Prince was a martinet, a heavy drinker, and excessively conscious of his elevated birth. His ships could not be described as happy, for he was apt to take violent and unreasonable dislikes to the officers.

Probably because of his age, Charles Rowley survived two commissions with the Prince, one in the frigate *Pegasus* and the other in the *Andromeda*. He became sufficiently in favour to become the recipient of a vast correspondence from his august patron, chiefly on naval subjects. The *Pegasus*, when in the West Indies, brought Charles into at least distant contact with Nelson, who for a time was senior officer on that Station, where he found the Prince a handful.

Charles Rowley became a lieutenant at the age of nineteen, and during the earlier part of the Great War served in the *Resolution* on the North American Station, the ship flying the flag of Rear-Admiral George Murray. He reached post rank in 1795, the same year as Josias. Five years later he served as flag captain to Sir Charles Cotton in the *Prince George*, Cotton of course being connected to him by marriage. During the later stages of the struggle, Charles commanded the *Eagle* in the Mediterranean and the Adriatic. In the Mediterranean he was for a time under the immediate orders of Rear-Admiral Sir Sidney Smith, who in 1806 was operating off the coast of Calabria and elsewhere,

Collingwood being Commander-in-Chief. On 11 May, acting with two Neapolitan gun-boats and a party of Royal Marines, Rowley expelled a hostile force from the island of Capri.

After Collingwood's death at sea in 1810, Rowley had the pleasure of serving with Sir Charles Cotton once more, Cotton succeeding Collingwood for some sixteen months before leaving for England. Cotton appointed Rowley senior naval officer in the Adriatic, where in 1811 Sir William Hoste, with a detached force, gained a splendid small-scale victory off Lissa, flying the signal 'Remember Nelson' as a reminder that he had been one of the great admiral's pupils.

Cotton was replaced as Commander-in-Chief by Sir Edward Pellew, and under his superintendence, and that of Rear-Admiral Thomas Fremantle, Rowley, Hoste and others conducted a spirited, almost self-contained warfare whose object was to expel the French from Austrian possessions. Rowley and Hoste played the most active part in the capture of Fiume in July 1813. Rowley was made Governor, with Hoste as Lieutenant-Governor under him. The pair, both full of dash, got on excellently, Hoste writing of Rowley as 'a very fine fellow, and my good friend'. Both later received the Order of Maria Theresa of Austria, as did Fremantle, the flag officer most directly concerned here and at the capture of Trieste, where Rowley and Hoste were again prominent.

Josias and Charles had both become Rear-Admirals and Knights of the Bath by the end of hostilities, after which Charles held chief commands at the Nore and in Jamaica. In 1834, after his early patron had succeeded to the throne, the King, as William IV, made his old shipmate a Knight of the Guelphic Order of Hanover. He also joined the Board of Admiralty, and received a baronetcy in 1836. William certainly favoured old friends.

Charles Rowley married a daughter of Sir Richard King, who had been Hughes's stalwart second in the days when Suffren was in India. She was a dark-haired beauty and a woman of great force of character, well fitted to be hostess in the high appointments of her husband's later life. The admiral died, full of years and honour, in 1845, having fulfilled the promise shown in a charming portrait painted of him in youth by Daniel Gardner, and having enjoyed the Navy's principal shore command at Portsmouth.

During the course of nearly a century and a half, Rowleys were always to be found on the list of flag officers, the family producing a succession of men who proved themselves in command. There was Sir William, first of this naval dynasty and at one time a member of the controlling body of the sea service; there followed Sir Joshua, present at some of the greater fights of his era, during which there were so many; then

Sir Josias, who exercised his talents in the Far East; and Sir Charles, who took part in the Marryat-like campaigning of the Adriatic at a time when initiative was at a premium and when the nineteenth century was young with, in Conrad's phrase, 'an air of fable about it'.

An Admiral of the Fleet, three baronets, and three Knights of the the Bath was no mean harvest for a single family, if it is also remembered that lesser favours were extended to various other members not quite so illustrious. The Navy did well by the Rowleys, but they, in turn, had done well by the Navy.

8

Nelson's Collingwood

⚓   ⚓   ⚓

Cuthbert Collingwood, who ranks not far below Nelson in the hierarchy of leaders of the classic days of sail, is always associated with his friend, since their lives touched at so many points. The two men, each in his way so remarkable, were in fact about as different in character as it is possible to be, and it is Nelson's more sparkling qualities that have attracted more attention. For much of the earlier part of their careers, the pair were so close that to study the one is to know the other.

Collingwood and Nelson, who, like the Gardners and the Rowleys, made their names against the navies of France and Spain, owed their first dramatic rise in life to the War of American Independence.

For their country, this sad struggle was a story of ineptitude and misfortune; yet it provided for the pair their great chance of future fame. During its course both became post-captains, thus ensuring that in the next conflict in which their country engaged, the war with Revolutionary and Napoleonic France, they were in positions of such seniority as to ensure that their influence within their profession would be of consequence.

Until recently, it was not known precisely when Collingwood made the acquaintance of the man under whom he was one day to serve, as second-in-command, at Trafalgar. But in 1965, a bequest to the British Museum of a bundle of letters from Collingwood describing some of the greater events of his career, disclosed one illuminating fact: when Collingwood and Nelson first met, Nelson was a lad of fifteen and Collingwood a man of twenty-five. Neither had yet reached commissioned rank, but Nelson had a good deal of sea experience. Collingwood—having gone to sea at twelve in the frigate *Shannon*—had still more.

The letter referring to the beginning of the friendship was written soon after death had ended it. It was sent from sea by Collingwood to a kinsman, Walter Spencer-Stanhope, within five months of Trafalgar, where Nelson had died in the hour of victory. It was dated 6 March 1806, and runs as follows:

I have indeed had a severe loss in the death of my excellent friend Lord Nelson. Since the year '73 we have been on terms of the greatest intimacy: chance has thrown us very much together in service, and on many occasions we have acted in concert. There is scarce a naval subject that has not been the subject of our discussion, so that his opinions were familiar to me, and so firmly founded on principles of honour, of justice, of attachment to his country, at the same time so entirely divested of every thing interested to himself, that it was impossible to consider him but with admiration. He liked fame, and was open to flattery, so that people sometimes got about him who were unworthy of him. He is a loss to his country that cannot easily be replaced.

In 1773, the key date referred to in the letter, Great Britain was at peace, and Nelson, having already visited the West Indies, served in North Sea, Channel and Atlantic waters, and been on an expedition in the Arctic, was preparing for a long voyage to the East Indies. Collingwood had an extensive acquaintance with home, Atlantic and northern waters, and had visited the Mediterranean more than once, as midshipman and master's mate.

The actual difference in age between Collingwood and Nelson is valuable to remember, for many works of reference lessen it by two years, asserting that Collingwood was born in 1750, which is not so. The error stems from a memoir written by G. L. Newnham Collingwood, first published in 1828 and for long the principal biography. As the author had the benefit of the information at the disposal of his wife Sarah, the elder of the admiral's two daughters, his mistake is all the more surprising. The register of what is now the Cathedral Church of St Nicholas, Newcastle upon Tyne, states that Cuthbert Collingwood was baptized on 24 October 1748. Family records state that he was born on the 26th of the previous month. The matter is important as emphasizing that there were ten full years between them, since Nelson was born on 29 September 1758. A decade is a long stage in youth, and the slow rise of Collingwood towards rank that would give him command of a ship could well have soured him. He had many virtues, but few people would ever have thought of him as being lucky.

When, after Trafalgar, Collingwood became famous, Joyce Gold, publisher of the *Naval Chronicle*, wrote to the admiral to ask him to supply a sketch of his life. Collingwood sent a letter home in which he said he intended to produce something sensational. This was by way of a joke. What he actually composed was brief and dignified in the extreme: so much so that the journal employed a hack to concoct an elaborate article which could have pleased few, and certainly not Collingwood. Much later, Gold printed the admiral's plain text, in which that austere man described his first promotion in fewer than fifty words. He wrote: 'In 1774 I went to Boston with Admiral Graves, and in 1775 was made lieutenant by him on the day the battle was fought at Bunker's Hill, where I was with a party of seamen, supplying the army with what was necessary to them.' As an example of compression, the sentence has everything to commend it. It told a contemporary naval officer exactly what he wanted to know.

The action in which Collingwood had taken part, a Pyrrhic victory if ever there was one, was fought out between soldiers and taught him nothing except coolness under fire and how to support a force ashore. His conduct had been exceptional, his promotion merited, but his fate, for the next few years, was sad. He was sent home so that he could be appointed to a new ship. The Admiralty ordered him to the sloop-of-war *Hornet*, in which he crossed to the West Indies. The ship's co-mander, Robert Haswell, proved impossible to admire and almost impossible to serve. He had been eighteen years on the lieutenants' list and was to remain as long on that of the commanders before he was at last relieved because of advanced age. Haswell missed chance after chance of prizes, bullied his officers and men, and at one stage had Collingwood court martialled on charges so trivial that his judges must have wondered why they had been called upon to waste their time.

Although Collingwood was duly acquitted, he had still many months to endure before Admiral Sir Peter Parker, soon after his arrival in the capacity of Commander-in-Chief, Jamaica, had him transferred to a crack frigate, the *Lowestoffe*. Her captain, Locker, had made a name as a young man under Hawke, and the ship had brought Nelson out from England. Nelson had only recently been made a lieutenant, but his uncle, Captain Maurice Suckling, was Comptroller of the Navy, and with Sir Peter Parker also his friend, he was likely to get a good start. This was exactly what happened. In December 1778, Nelson was given command of the brig *Badger*. Six months later, while still short of the age of twenty-one, Parker transferred him to the frigate *Hinchinbrook*, which gave the rank of post-captain. Collingwood followed his young friend step by step, first to the *Badger* and then, when Nelson was given charge of a still larger ship, to the *Hinchinbrook*. So, within a few months from being a despondent lieutenant serving a man he despised, Colling-wood had reached a rank, promotion from which, to that of admiral, could only come by seniority. In the process, Nelson, with influence behind him, had got ahead. He was nine months senior to Collingwood as a post-captain. When the time came, many years in the future, for them both to gain flag rank, Nelson would do so at the age of thirty-eight. Collingwood had to wait until he was fifty.

Collingwood and Nelson remained grateful to Sir Peter Parker for the chance he had given them, and repaid it whenever they could by favouring his relatives and those he recommended. In the entire correspondence which survives from his hand, Collingwood never suggested by a single innuendo that he considered Nelson's lightning elevation unjustified; neither did he ever show a sign of jealousy at Nelson's later meteoric rise to fame as a result of the battles of St Vincent and the Nile. He and Parker were of exactly the same opinion about this extraordinary little man. They recognized his brilliance, natural leadership and imagination.

⚓   ⚓   ⚓

When Spain joined France in support of the Americans, the situation offered to Great Britain an obvious chance to strike at enemy possessions overseas. Nicaragua was supposedly one of the more vulnerable Spanish territories, and an expedition, in which both Collingwood and Nelson were involved, was mounted from Jamaica. The planners had learned nothing from a succession of past failures in the area of Central America. The season was ill-chosen; the possible advantages of success had not been weighed against the effort entailed, and in any case the force was inadequate. Nelson did well ashore, but went down with fever and was compelled to go home. When Collingwood arrived at the scene of operations, the port of San Juan, he found nothing but desolation. Sickness reigned supreme. 'My constitution survived many attacks,' he wrote in the sketch which he sent to the *Naval Chronicle*, 'and I survived most of my ship's company, having buried in four months 180 of the 200 which composed it. Mine was not a singular case, all the ships that were as long there suffered in the same degree: the transports' men all died . . . but transport ships were not wanted, for the troops they brought were no more; they had fallen, not by the hand of the enemy, but sunk under the contagion of the climate.'

One misfortune followed that of Nicaragua which Collingwood was never again to experience: he was shipwrecked. After taking the *Hinchinbrook* back to Jamaica, he transferred soon afterwards to the *Pelican*. He had not been many months in command of this frigate when in August 1781, in the course of what he called 'a most tremendous night', the ship was driven on to the rocks of Morant Keys, thirty-five miles south-east of Jamaica, by the force of a hurricane. After great difficulty, the ship's company were got ashore on rafts made of broken yards, and there, with little food and water, they were stranded for ten days. Collingwood contrived to get a boat away to Jamaica and another frigate came to take them off.

After the American war had ended Collingwood found himself back in the West Indies and involved in one of the complications arising out of the separation of the United States from the former Mother Country. As a result of the independence they had achieved Americans found themselves debarred from their old trade with the British Caribbean islands, which had been a source of profit to both parties. Henceforward, since they were foreigners, American traders must be treated as such. This suited no one in the area, and the way around had been to wink the eye and to continue the old traffic. But Collingwood, Nelson (who had taken the frigate *Boreas* to serve on the station), and Collingwood's younger brother Wilfred, who had charge of the sloop *Rattler*, were men of zeal who intended to see that the law was enforced, and this despite any lack of firm support from their admiral, Sir Richard Hughes.

That Collingwood was as active as even Nelson, who was always to the fore in trying to suppress the forbidden trade, is shown by a letter dated 16 December 1784 addressed to Governor Shirley of Antigua. In the course of this missive he reported that his frigate, the *Mediator*, had detained an American ship and repaired her in so short a time as five hours—thus preventing her master from taking her cargo into port as had been his intention.

This letter stirred up the wasps' nest of which Collingwood was fully aware. Soon, governors, local law officers, traders, and even the spineless admiral were ranged against the officious captains. Then, and for the rest of their service among the Leeward Islands, the two Collingwoods and Nelson found life extremely difficult. Although Nelson took the precaution of writing to the authorities in London to ensure that he and his friends would be backed up in what they did, he and Collingwood were not best pleased when they discovered that the admiral had been officially congratulated on his stand! Hughes, who in Nelson's words 'bows and scrapes too much', would gladly have winked both eyes in order to prevent trouble.

Collingwood departed for home in the late summer of 1786, leaving his brother Wilfred in the *Rattler* under Nelson's orders, for Hughes had also left for England. The little squadron was reinforced in November by the frigate *Pegasus*, in charge of Prince William Henry. The prince was already a seaman of experience—he had served in battle as a midshipman under Rodney, and he was ready enough to fall in with Nelson's policy against the interloping trade, while Wilfred Collingwood wore himself out in the service, dying at sea on 21 April 1787.

Only once was Collingwood to cross the Atlantic again, though his naval career had over twenty years yet to run. In 1790, at the time of what was known as 'the Spanish Armament', he was given command of the frigate *Mermaid* and proceeded to the West Indies with a squadron under Admiral Cornish. This 'Armament', or war scare, arose from the fact that the officer commanding two Spanish ships of war seized some British vessels lying at Nootka Sound, off what is now Vancouver

Island, which was held to be within waters controlled by Spain. The crews were sent as prisoners-of-war to a Spanish port, and since, as a result of the voyages of James Cook, particularly his third circum-navigation (1776-9) British interest in the area had much increased, and since, moreover, Spanish sea power was held in some contempt, a high tone was taken by the government of George III and preparations made accordingly. In the upshot, Spain climbed down since she found no support from France, and Collingwood's cruise was uneventful.

He was wont to complain of his lack of influence, and his good fortune in being given the *Mermaid* derived from his known zeal and efficiency. Many others were less fortunate, Nelson among them, and he was five years on the beach. He made no bones about his envy of those who, through influence or otherwise, found themselves at sea. After he had returned home Collingwood enjoyed his only really long spell ashore, at home in his beloved Northumberland. In June 1791 he married Sarah, daughter of John Erasmus Blackett, who was then mayor of Newcastle upon Tyne, and a prosperous man of business. Sarah's maternal grandfather was Admiral Roddam, under whom Collingwood had served as a young man. The marriage was happy, in spite of the very long separations caused by the exigencies of a service life. There were two children, both girls; Sarah, born in 1792, and Mary Patience, born the following year. Collingwood was destined to see very little of his daughters, but his distant care over their education and upbringing was unceasing, and his directions to that end occupy many pages in his future son-in-law's *Memoir*.

Early in 1793, Great Britain found herself once again at war with France, as she had done so often during the course of the century. At first, Collingwood was in his usual state of worry about whether he would get an appointment, but he had made friends with George Bowyer, at that time a rear-admiral, and Bowyer invited him to become his flag captain. Collingwood wrote to his eldest sister on 17 February 1793:

> I am well content with my situation for many reasons. In the first place it is an appoint't of great trust and respectability; in the second, it gives me a claim in future to a line of battle ship in preference to a frigate, into which I will never go again if I can help it . . . I will never command a two-decked ship when I can get one with three; in the third place, it was proposed to me in so handsome a way that I should have been wrong to have refused it.

Collingwood's decision was justified. Although rather senior on the post-captain's list for such a position, he knew and liked Bowyer both as an officer and an individual, and it soon became clear that the ship, the *Prince*, would be ordered to serve under Lord Howe in the Home Fleet, the situation which Collingwood would have chosen at that stage of the war. Howe was the most accomplished admiral then flying his flag at sea, and was the elder brother of General Sir William Howe, the British commander at Bunker Hill, where Collingwood had been present.

It was not in the *Prince* but the *Barfleur*, a faster ship, to which Bowyer and Collingwood transferred, in which they took part in the first fleet action of the war, the Atlantic battle of 1 June 1794.

Collingwood fought the *Barfleur* splendidly and as, during the course of the fight, Rear-Admiral Bowyer was badly wounded, Collingwood was disappointed in the extreme not to be included among captains who were cited for honours by Howe. Bowyer got a medal and a baronetcy; Collingwood got nothing; the fact was anguish to him, and so remained. Many fellow captains in the fleet were surprised at the omission, which had the effect on Collingwood of making him wish for the opportunity of showing Lord Howe the full measure of his injustice.

The chance came nearly three years later, after a gruelling and dull spell of blockade. It was eagerly taken, and was followed by the most flattering recognition. Collingwood had been sent in the *Excellent* to the Mediterranean, where he once again became the close companion of Nelson, who was serving in that area. On 14 February 1797, they took a leading part in Sir John Jervis's victory over the Spaniards— who had by that time joined the French—off Cape St Vincent. There, fifteen British ships defeated twenty-seven of the enemy, capturing four ships of the line in the process. Collingwood wrote an account of the action to his cousin, Edward Collingwood of Chirton, which is included among the new letters bequeathed to the British Museum. It bears out Nelson's well-known description in every respect. The friends were near one another in action and could see exactly how well they were doing. Collingwood wrote:

On Valentine's day in the morning we discovered them, and immediately made an impetuous assault upon them, which divided them into two parts; then, turning our whole force on the larger division . . . stuck close to them 'till near close of day, when we collected the fruits of our victory, two first rates . . . of 112 guns each, an 80 and a 74 gun ship. I had the good fortune to get the *Excellent* early into action and was warmly and well engaged all day . . . We fought our way through their line until we got up to the

Santissima Trinidada of 130 guns . . . I had an envious longing for the *Santissima Trinidada* which is the largest ship in the world, a four decker, and at one time had no doubt of her . . . Three ships that *Excellent* engaged was not more distant than the breadth of your dining room, so we literally burnt their whiskers. Two of them that ran on board of each other Commodore Nelson boarded and took sword in hand and (what may never happen again) received the submission and swords of the officers on the quarter deck of the first rate *San Josef*, while one of his seamen made a bundle of them, with as much composure as if he had been tying faggots. I lost eleven men and have a few wounded; the protection of Providence was great, considering what a scene we were engaged in.

The *Barfleur* had also been in the battle, and it was particularly sweet for Collingwood to receive the warmest notes from her captain, Dacres, and her admiral, Waldegrave, both of whom remembered Collingwood's sadness after Howe's victory. As for the Admiralty, they seemed determined to right an old wrong as well as to recognize fresh service, for Lord Spencer, who was then reigning over the Board, sent Collingwood gold medals for both actions, suitably inscribed. At long last, honour was satisfied.

While Nelson was gathering acclaim and a peerage for his victory at the Nile, the friends were separated. One brief meeting they did have, in 1801, when Nelson was on a flying visit to Lord St Vincent at Tor Abbey near Plymouth, his victory having brought Jervis an earldom.

Collingwood was waiting for his wife and elder daughter to arrive by coach from Northumberland and they were announced when the admirals were dining together. Collingwood wrote to his father-in-law:

I flew to the inn where I had desired my wife to come, and I found her and little Sarah as well after their journey as if it had lasted only for the day. No greater happiness is human nature capable of than was mine that evening . . .

Nelson joined the family later, Collingwood writing to a mutual friend from the old days in the West Indies: 'How surprised you would have been to have popped in to the Fountain Inn and seen Lord Nelson, my wife and myself sitting by the fireside cosing, and little Sarah teaching Phillis, her dog, to dance.'

Over eight hard and weary years spent at sea in watching the enemy's Atlantic ports, with but a few months at home during the brief Peace of Amiens, lay between the glories and consolations of St Vincent and the autumn of 1805, the climax of Collingwood's career. Then, in the waters off Spain which they both knew so well, Collingwood and Nelson faced the combined fleets of France and Spain under Admiral Villeneuve.

The pattern of the Trafalgar campaign is well known. What is seldom realized is that it was Collingwood who, with a minute force, shepherded Villeneuve into Cadiz and watched over him night and day until at last he emerged to face annihilation, and that it was Collingwood who, unrelieved until his death, bore the full weight of his friend's burden of command after death had struck Nelson down.

During the course of the next four and a half years, that burden, the Mediterranean Command-in-Chief, was to wear Collingwood out, and there are two remarkable facts about it. The first was that, even before the news of Trafalgar had been properly assimilated, it was taken for granted that Collingwood, who was then a vice-admiral of only eighteen months' seniority in that rank, and with no experience whatsoever except in subordinate sea commands, would be Nelson's only possible successor. The second was the strange way in which Collingwood, although he himself had proved an admirable flag captain in his time, was totally unable to delegate, even in the smallest particulars. The result was that a position which would in any case have proved taxing, became one of whose difficulties he never ceased to complain. Collingwood, who never appointed a Captain of the Fleet to ease his way administratively, was without Nelson's gift of trust in his subordinates. In this respect he resembled Howe, who liked to see everything himself, in his case because experience had taught him not to rely on his captains.

The matter of succession to the command was decided by George III in person. The moment he had had detailed news of Trafalgar, that sovereign, who knew a man when he saw one, caused his secretary to write as follows to the Admiralty:

> ... every tribute of praise appears to His Majesty due to Lord Nelson, whose loss he can never sufficiently regret ... His Majesty considers it very fortunate that the command, under circumstances so critical, should have devolved upon an officer of such consummate valour, judgement and skill as Admiral Collingwood has proved himself to be, every part of whose conduct he considers deserving his entire approbation and admiration. The feeling manner in which he has described the events of that great day and those subsequent, and the modesty with which he speaks of himself, whilst he does justice, in terms so elegant and so ample, to the meritorious exertions of the gallant officers and men under his command, have also proved extremely satisfactory to the King.

This letter became Collingwood's proudest possession. 'It is there,' he wrote to his wife, 'I feel the object of my life attained.' Next to the letter, in his regard, was the praise of every officer in the fleet. 'Many of the captains here,' he wrote, 'have expressed a desire that I would give them a general notice whenever I go to Court; and if they are within 500 miles they will come up to attend me.' But the letter also sealed his fate. Wherever the King commanded, there his place would be, however protracted his exile from the home he loved, and though it wore him out.

⚓   ⚓   ⚓

All the time that Collingwood was in charge in the Mediterranean, Britain's affairs were never less than complicated, and her policy sometimes uncertain. Moreover, the slowness and the unreliability of communications required that commanders on the spot should take decisions without, in many cases, the chance to consult their superiors. Collingwood's habit was to anticipate orders, and never once was his judgement questioned or were his dispositions deemed less than adequate.

The result of Trafalgar, so far as France was concerned, confirmed Napoleon in his pursuit of a continental strategy: he realized, once and for all, that any project for the invasion of Britain was doomed to failure. His fleet, such of it as remained operational, would be used first to contain his enemy and then, when the chance offered, to further his designs in Italy. In 1806, Britain had only two bases which she could use in the Mediterranean. One was Sicily, where a small army supported the Bourbon dynasty, exiled by force of arms from Naples, and the other was Malta, which flourished under the protection of Collingwood's fleet. They proved to be enough. Schemes for the conquest of Sicily failed. Malta was never in danger.

In 1807, relations with Turkey grew difficult, owing to aggressive action by the Tsar of Russia, who was at that time the ally of George III. Collingwood sent a force under Admiral Duckworth up the Dardanelles to try to persuade the Sultan's government to return to an earlier benevolence, but Duckworth failed and had to withdraw. Collingwood himself anchored off Imbros a few months later, but could do nothing. Presently the Tsar, defeated at Friedland by Napoleon, began to change his allegiance, a movement which was concluded when he met the French Emperor at Tilsit, and agreed to exclude British trade from his dominions.

An unexpected turn of the tide came in 1808 when, after their royal family had been humiliated and a French monarchy imposed on them, the Spanish people made spontaneous attempts to throw off their foreign yoke. Collingwood was welcomed when he landed in August at Cadiz, and was able to give active and continuing support to the nationalist forces active in Andalusia and Catalonia.

There had been a single chance of a further fleet action during his tenure of command, when the French Admiral Ganteaume eluded the guard off Toulon and made a sortie to Corfu. Owing to a succession of mischances, the battle to which Collingwood had looked forward with the utmost confidence never took place. Ganteaume eventually returned to his base, having accomplished nothing.

In 1810, British land forces successfully invaded and occupied the islands of Zante, Cephalonia, Ithaca and Cerigo, while Collingwood's admirals defeated a French attempt to supply Barcelona, destroying two ships of the line and thirteen transports in the process. He had shown that he remained master at sea in the Mediterranean.

Collingwood wrote to his sister-in-law:

> While I can serve to the satisfaction of my King, and benefit of the country, I feel the reward in my act, and look no further for it. But my fear, my only fear, is that my strength of body, impaired by length of days and weight of years, should unfit me for the arduous duties I have to fulfil. Fourteen or sixteen hours of every day I am employed. I have about eighty ships of war under my orders, and the direction of naval affairs from Cadiz to Constantinople, with an active and powerful enemy, always threatening, and though he seldom moves, keeps us constantly on the alert. I leave nothing undone that I can devise for the public good. Where I fail it will be my misfortune, not my neglect. When there is fault it will be all my own. In the plan, I involve no one, for I never ask for counsel, and this I do from principle, not pride. But I look for success, and I know I shall glad your heart when the world allows I deserve it.

His fear was not unfounded. In March 1810, he became so ill that he was forced to resign, dying—still at sea—in his great flagship, the *Ville de Paris*, on his way home from Majorca. He was buried in St Paul's, beneath one of the plainest tombs in the cathedral, and among the mourners were Sir Peter Parker, the Earl of St Vincent, and a succession of First Lords of the Admiralty whom he had served so ably. Collingwood's life had been a sad one, illuminated by brilliant flashes, and during his last few years he had conducted the entire policy of his country's government in the Mediterranean theatre of war.

When he lay dying, Collingwood found Europe a sad place, and saw little anywhere to comfort him. He could not know that his great adversary, Napoleon, was later to say that what he called 'the Spanish ulcer' was a major cause of the downfall of his empire. Although final victory was still five years in the future, Britain, to all appearances so involved and shaken, would emerge from the conflict more powerful than ever before. It was the skill and endurance of Collingwood and his like, and the land victories of Wellington in Spain and Portugal, which had helped to ensure that result. Collingwood and Nelson had been among the first to realize that they were involved in what was for the time a new kind of war, and that the price of defeat might well be national extinction.

Collingwood was by no means a colourless personality, but he was unknown outside the Navy, and within it had only one close friend, Nelson. He founded no school of tactics, and fellow officers were apt to regard his standards as impossibly high, his detachment inhuman. All admitted that he was peerless in the exercise of his profession, but only his family, whom he never saw during the last seven years of his life, knew what a many-sided and even laughter-loving person he could be, when the times allowed him to be his fullest self.

Famous men of letters wrote tributes to Collingwood, among them the Frenchman, Alfred de Vigny, who saw in his whole career the apotheosis of Roman virtue, and his fellow countryman, Thackeray, who in *The Four Georges* asked when in history there could be found 'a nobler, kinder, more beautiful life of duty, a gentler, truer heart?'

The verdict that Collingwood himself might have valued most, because it was brief and exact, came from a frigate captain to whose vessel he transferred his flag when the *Royal Sovereign* had been critically damaged at Trafalgar. It was in the cabin of the *Euryalus* that Collingwood composed the dispatches which so moved all who read them. Blackwood, the captain in point, described Collingwood, in a letter home to his wife which was sent off immediately after the battle, as 'a reserved, though a very pleasing good man, and as he fought like an angel I take the more to him'.

9

Lord de Saumarez

Both Collingwood and Nelson received peerages while on operational service. Sir James Saumarez, well known to them both, and Nelson's second-in-command at the battle of the Nile, had to wait. Although he saw as much fighting as any other officer of his era, Nelson not excepted, and was the last to survive among Rodney's captains at his victory of 1782, Saumarez somehow missed the high recognition everyone felt to be his due. His peerage was, in fact, even more belated than Hawke's in an earlier generation, but Saumarez retained enough love of reward to be as pleased when it came as he would have been when younger.

'Wonderful is it yet to me,' wrote his wife to her eldest son, on hearing the great news in October 1831, when the Admiral was seventy-three, 'so suddenly, so unexpectedly did it come at last . . . . The accounts of the reception everywhere, from all classes and parties, have no parallel, and it seems to me as if the dignity had been deferred to prepare it for greater glory and additional lustre.'

Allowing for wifely partiality, it was indeed time that Sir James became a lord, such was the variety and importance of his services to the nation from the day he joined the Navy until he gave up his last command at Plymouth in 1827.

Undoubtedly a 'Child of the Service'—his uncle Philip was the captain killed under Hawke's command off Finisterre—James Saumarez belonged to an ancient and well-known Channel Island family, long settled in Guernsey. He had another uncle, Thomas, also distinguished at sea.

James Saumarez was born in March 1757, and at the age of twelve went to the Mediterranean in the frigate *Montreal*. His captain was James Alms, who was later to do well in command of the *Monmouth* during the Suffren–Hughes campaigning in India. Saumarez was away for six years and he visited most parts of the Mediterranean, including Turkey. There, his knowledge of French (for like most Channel Island people he was bilingual), made him acceptable to the many families who spoke that language. Altogether he was lucky in his first appointment, though, not unnaturally, he suffered bouts of acute homesickness.

Alms, who was of humble origin, was an officer of already great experience who encouraged his 'yonkers', as did later captains of the *Montreal*. They might one and all have been surprised at Saumarez's propensities, for he had strong religious inclinations. He once astonished his mother by spouting long passages from *Paradise Lost* which he had learnt by heart.

When the War of American Independence broke out, he was one of the first to benefit from the patronage of Sir Peter Parker, who gave Nelson and Collingwood such help. He served for a time, as did Nelson later, in Parker's flagship, the *Bristol*, in North American waters. It was Parker who ensured Saumarez's promotion to lieutenant, an acting commission as such being dated July 1776 from 'Five Fathom Hole, off Charleston.' It was confirmed in January 1778.

When, after varied service across the Atlantic, Saumarez returned to England, he was appointed to the *Victory*, a ship of which he was to see much later in his career. At the time he joined her she was flying the flag of Sir Charles Hardy, Kempenfelt being his Captain of the Fleet.

In 1781 Saumarez exchanged into the *Fortitude*, which flew Sir Hyde Parker's flag. The admiral, no relation of Sir Peter's, was the father of the flag officer under whom Nelson was to serve at Copenhagen. His nickname was 'Vinegar', which gives an idea of his nature, though not of the explosive qualities he also possessed.

Hyde Parker took to Saumarez, as did all his superiors, and it was while with the admiral that he experienced his first fleet action. This was an old-style slogging match fought with the Dutch near the Dogger Bank on 5 August 1781. Parker was covering a convoy to the Baltic. So was the Dutch admiral, Zoutman, and although the fight itself was a draw, Parker at least had the satisfaction of seeing the Dutch convoy return to port while his own proceeded on its way.

When the squadron returned home George III paid a visit to his sailors. Parker received the monarch with a remark very much in character. 'I wish your Majesty better ships and younger officers,' he said. 'As for myself, I am now too old for the Service.'

Parker presented Saumarez to the King, who inquired if he was related to the Captains Saumarez he remembered, one of whom had served with Anson. 'Please your Majesty,' said Parker, 'he is their nephew, and as brave and good an officer as either of them.'

Old as he deemed himself, Parker accepted command of the East Indies station, that sure source of wealth, with his flag in the brand-new *Cato* of 50 guns. It was lucky for him that James got promotion at this time, for on her way to India the *Cato* foundered in the South Atlantic and was lost with all hands.

Kempenfelt had remarked Saumarez's efficiency when he was serving in the *Victory*, particularly an aptitude for signalling which he cultivated all his life, and he was glad of his promotion to 'Master and Commander', as the rank then was, in August 1781. He was sent to Sheerness, to commission the newly built fire-ship *Tisiphone*, which was armed with carronades. These were large-bore weapons of massive destructive power at close range. At that time they were being sent to the fleet as fast as the foundries at Falkirk could turn them out.

When the *Tisiphone* was ready, Howe ordered Saumarez to place himself at the disposal of Kempenfelt, who had recently got his flag. The admiral was even more religious-minded than Saumarez. Four years earlier he had published a collection of 'Hymns and Poems' under the pseudonym of 'Philotheorus' including an invocation of the Day of Judgement in the most startling manner:

> Horrors invest the skies;
> Graves burst, and myriads rise;
> Nature in agonies
> Yields up her store . . .

Kempenfelt was a disciple of John Fletcher of Madeley, one of the most influential evangelists of the age. The first consignment of Bibles ever sent to a man-of-war—no fewer than 400—went to Kempenfelt's flagship the following year from the Naval and Military Bible Society. It is legitimate to wonder how many of the sailors could read, even if they wanted to.

As for Saumarez, during the December of the same year as his experience with the Dutch, the young commander was able to observe at close quarters the conduct of a master of tactics when Kempenfelt captured twenty-one ships, including troop transports loaded with 11,000 soldiers ordered to America, without loss to himself, in spite of a powerful covering squadron.

Saumarez had his own particular satisfactions. He was first to sight the enemy. Moreover, he engaged a frigate which formed part of the close escort, capturing his opponent after an action lasting twenty minutes. At that time, the French had nothing to equal his carronades. When the engagement was over, Kempenfelt sent Saumarez across the Atlantic to warn Hood, who was commanding in the West Indies during Rodney's absence on leave, that the French squadron was on its way west, and in what strength.

Saumarez now had the luck of a lifetime. On 7 February 1782, Hood signalled him to repair on board the *Barfleur*, his flagship, so that he could be sent home with dispatches. What followed is best described in Saumarez's own words:

> I was in my own boat, with the despatches in my hand, and with a heavy heart had ordered the bow-man to shove off, when Captain Stanhope of the *Russell* came alongside, and seeing me called: 'Hallo, Saumarez, where are you going?' 'To England,' said I, 'I am sorry

to tell you!' 'Sorry,' replied Stanhope, 'I wish I was in your place; I want to go home on account of my health; and if I had known, I would have exchanged with you.' 'Perhaps it is not too late,' said I. 'Hold on then,' said he, 'till I speak to the admiral, since I have your leave.'

By this time the *Russell*'s boat was alongside the admiral's ship, and at the word 'Hold on' the bow-man hooked the quarter of the *Russell*'s barge, where I remained in breathless suspense, after which Captain Stanhope appeared at the gangway and called, 'Come up, Saumerez.' I was on deck in an instant and found that, on the captain of the *Barfleur* being asked to submit the proposal to the admiral, he said: 'Let Captain Saumarez do it himself, he is the fittest person.'

When Sir Samuel Hood heard the application, he was silent, and after reflecting for a few minutes he said: 'Captain Saumarez, you know not how much I wish to serve you; Captain Stanhope shall go home as he desires, and you shall have command of the *Russell*.' Accordingly, before the close of that day, Captain Stanhope was on board the *Tisiphone* on his way to England; while her late commander was in possession of his post-rank, and captain of one of his Majesty's ships of the line of seventy-four guns; and all this effected in less than two hours.'

Even this stupendous piece of good fortune was not the end of it. Within little more than two months, the *Russell* took part in Rodney's victory over de Grasse, and was of material help in forcing the surrender of the *Ville de Paris*. Saumarez had 12 men killed and 27 wounded and his ship suffered damage to her fore and mizen masts. At five and twenty years old, he could have thought himself a veteran with more battle service than many admirals, and every prospect of a splendid future.

Like most officers at the end of a long and exhausting war, he was glad enough when his ship was paid off and he could at last look forward to home comforts. There was also a most important matter to attend to. He had formed an attachment early in life to Martha le Marchant, only daughter and heiress of a longstanding friend of the Saumarez family. The pair were married in October 1788, when the bridegroom was just over thirty. They 'lived happily ever after,' as the saying is. There was no scandal in Saumarez's life, and with his elegant manners, his tall and graceful person, his general good looks, he might have been considered too flawless to be interesting had he not also been proud, touchy and ambitious, characteristics which at certain stages of his life he was unable to conceal.

When, in 1793, war broke out anew with France, Saumarez was one of the first to be given a ship. She was the frigate *Crescent*, nine years old, and her looks and capabilities pleased her captain. In one respect, he was exceptionally and continuously lucky—he seldom had difficulty in finding men. They followed him from the Channel Islands, as being the leading sea officer from those parts. Their quality, as volunteers bred to a seafaring life, was first-class. Frigate service, when a prize or two might be expected, was always more popular than that in big ships, but even four years later, when war-weariness was setting in, an examination of Saumarez's muster-book when he was commanding a ship of the line shows that some seventy-six men out of a complement of 590 were set down as being Channel Islanders, and the actual total was probably higher, since places of origin were not invariably accurately recorded.

The *Crescent* was soon in action. On 20 October 1793, when off Cape Barfleur, Saumarez encountered the French frigate *Réunion*, and he engaged her at once. The enemy captain was confident in his skill, his size and his large crew, added to the fact that he was near Cherbourg, from which help would, he felt, be sure to arrive. He was, however, no match for Saumarez, who ordered his gunners to aim at the *Réunion*'s rudder, which was soon disabled. After an action lasting two hours and ten minutes, the Frenchman struck his colours. 'I am singularly happy in being able to inform their Lordships,' wrote Saumarez to the Secretary of the Admiralty, 'that she has been obtained without the loss of a single man . . . although her own loss has been very considerable.'

This single-ship action, early in the war, had a tonic effect. It set an example such as Howe was to extend to the whole fleet the following June. To signify his pleasure, George III sent for Saumarez and knighted him. Saumarez was overjoyed, for he would have said, with Henry V: 'If it be a sin to covet honour, I am the most offending soul alive.' Every zealous officer of the time felt as he did.

The following summer, soon after Howe's battle, Saumarez gave the Channel Islanders an exciting display of his skill when his own ship and two others were chased close inshore of Guernsey by a much superior French force. Shot flew thick and fast, and all three British ships were saved from capture. Saumarez was by now eager to command a ship of the line, as he had done under Rodney. Being a favourite with the Admiralty, he was given the 74-gun *Marlborough*, and later the *Orion* of the same rating. He was in action near L'Orient on 23 June 1793 under the command of Lord Bridport, brother of Admiral Hood, who took charge of the fleet in Howe's absence through ill-health. The French lost three ships and would have fared much worse had Bridport followed them closer inshore, as Hawke had done long before at Quiberon, where Bridport had himself been present as a junior officer. The *Orion* had eight killed and 18 wounded, and she suffered a good deal in hull, masts and sails.

Having been in battle under the elder Hyde Parker, Rodney, Kempenfelt and Bridport, it was now Saumarez's good fortune to be sent to the fleet commanded by Sir John Jervis, the strictest disciplinarian and one of the finest seamen in the history of the Navy. This was at a stage in the war when everything was going the French way by land—so much so, that Britain had to withdraw for a time from the Mediterranean. Jervis based his ships on Lisbon and the Tagus, with an additional force at Gibraltar.

Saumarez played a distinguished part in the *Orion* on Valentine's Day 1797, when Jervis beat a greatly superior Spanish fleet under Admiral de Cordoba and took four prizes. Among others present were Nelson, who flew the broad pendant of a commodore in the *Captain*, Collingwood of the *Excellent*, noted for an astonishing rate of fire, and Troubridge of the *Culloden*, who was reckoned by Jervis to be the most accomplished officer of his seniority in the fleet. At one stage the *Orion*, along with other ships, engaged the towering *Santissima Trinidada*. Saumarez believed that the Spaniard struck his flag to him, but she escaped in the aftermath of the battle and did not meet her fate until more than eight years later, at Trafalgar.

The earldom which Jervis received in recognition of his victory at St Vincent, and Nelson's knighthood, were equally pleasing to Saumarez, whose own ship escaped lightly. There were no killed and only eight wounded. The *Orion*, being little damaged, was assigned the difficult task of towing one of the prizes into the Tagus. This was the *San Josef*, whose capture had been due to Nelson's initiative. Writing home, Saumarez was generous in praise of the commodore, who was soon to have news that he had received his flag. Saumarez wrote that he 'distinguished himself most eminently, his bravery on this occasion is above all praise'. Nelson himself, as was his way, made sure that his own exploits were fully publicized, a matter not always acceptable to his contemporaries.

After the battle, no invidious exceptions were made, as had been the case with the Glorious First of June. Every admiral and every captain of a ship of the line received the King's gold medal, suitably inscribed. Saumarez, along with the rest, always wore his, suspended from its blue and white ribbon, with particular pride, and Nelson said of the award that it was one that no duke could buy.

Saumarez shared with Nelson and others the ardours of the inshore watch on Cadiz after the battle. Hand-to-hand fighting was not uncommon, and there was no respite when the weather became boisterous. After a year of such routine duties, Saumarez was ordered to the Mediterranean with a small squadron of observation in charge of Nelson. This consisted of the *Vanguard*, flagship, the *Orion*, the *Alexander*, Captain Ball, and some frigates.

The object of the foray was to discover the purpose of a vast French armada then preparing, with Bonaparte at the head of the troops and Admiral Brueys of the ships. The mission was a failure, and a typical Gulf of Lions storm dismasted the *Vanguard*, which was saved only by the exertions of Saumarez and Ball. Much to Nelson's vexation, the frigates returned to Gibraltar.

So important did the Admiralty consider the matter of the French expedition that at the first possible moment St Vincent reinforced Nelson with eleven ships of the line, bringing his force up to fourteen, although he only had the *Mutine* brig suitable for scouting purposes. The squadron had a frustrating time casting between Egypt and Sicily before the French were at last discovered, on 1 August 1798, embayed and at anchor at Aboukir. Of this tense period Saumarez wrote: 'Fortunately I only act here *en second*; but did the chief responsibility rest with me, I fear it would be more than my too irritable nerves would bear. They have already been put to the trial in two or three instances this voyage.'

When battle was joined with Brueys, Saumarez played his part splendidly, taking the *Orion* inshore of the French line, an example being set by Captain Foley in the *Goliath*. An enemy frigate, the *Sérieuse*, foolishly tried to intervene, which was against all custom. She was sunk by a single well-directed broadside from Saumarez, who then gave his full attention to the *Peuple Souverain* of 74 guns. She struck, after a brave defence.

Saumarez, like Nelson, was wounded in the action, being hit in the side by a large splinter when the French flagship *Orient* blew up. Necessary attention to his wound meant that he could not pay his respects next day to Nelson. Instead, he sent him an admiring letter, referring to 'the most complete and glorious victory ever yet obtained'. When he was able to visit the *Vanguard*, he and Nelson had a difference (which Nelson did not allow to develop) on the wisdom of ships doubling their opponents, that is to say, ranging up on the enemy from both sides. Although he had done it himself, Saumarez did not agree with the idea on principle, chiefly because of the danger of damaging each other by crossfire. Nelson later wrote home to his wife telling her that had Saumarez's wound been very little deeper, 'it would have done his business, but as it is he is not the worse'.

It was at this point, when Nelson's and Saumarez's ways were to separate, Nelson going to Naples, there to conduct a misguided series of military operations, Saumarez to Gibraltar with the prizes, that their attitude to one another, in general so generous, came under strain. Despite the close friendship of their wives, Nelson would have been less than human had he not been jealous of Saumarez's brilliant record of service, more varied and extensive than his own. Their temperaments, in some ways alike, did not readily accord; they were both wounded and shaken; and there is no doubt that Saumarez felt hurt when he discovered that Nelson had not mentioned him specifically in his dispatch. The reason was more complex than it may seem. Nelson would not have wished to mention Saumarez without also extolling the services of his particular friend Troubridge, who was also St Vincent's favourite. This he could not do because, in approaching Aboukir Bay, Troubridge's ship had run on to a sandbank. Her captain was driven nearly crazy as he vainly tried to get her off in time to join the fighting not many hundred yards away.

⚓   ⚓   ⚓

On 14 February 1799, the second anniversary of the battle of St Vincent, Saumarez, who was by then high on the list of post-captains, was made a Colonel of Marines, a sure sign that he would receive his flag before long, when the appointment—and its emoluments—automatically ceased. He was also given command of the *Caesar*, one of the best-looking ships afloat and the first two-decker to carry 84 guns. Her captain at the Glorious First of June, Molloy, had done badly, in Howe's opinion, and had been dismissed his ship as the result of a court martial held at his own request. Saumarez was determined that the *Caesar*'s good name should be rebuilt, but at first, since she was sent on blockade duty, it did not seem probable that she would see much action.

In July 1800 St Vincent, who had succeeded Lord Bridport in command of the Home Fleet, picked Saumarez for the most exacting work he had to offer. This was charge of the 'Advanced Squadron off the Black Rocks' upon which fell the close watch on Brest. 'Really and truly,' wrote the Commander-in-Chief with his usual candour, 'after Sir John Warren, who neither knows nor fears dangers of any kind, Thornborough and Saumarez are the only men within reach I dare confide that port to.' Saumarez was now to endure the severest continuous strain of his life, ensuring that no enemy ship escaped from the French anchorage. Collingwood, when allotted the same duty, exclaimed that the Admiralty should invent a patent mechanical admiral as the work was more than flesh and blood could stand. Certainly it reduced Saumarez to looking 'as thin as a shotten herring', in St Vincent's words. All the same, he was well fitted for the duty, and he treasured a letter from his chief which gave him as much pleasure as anything in his Service life. 'I repose such unbounded confidence in your zeal and judgement,' wrote St Vincent, 'that I sleep as soundly as if I had the key of Brest in my possession.'

Saumarez received his flag on New Year's Day, 1801 and continued in his former ship, Jahleel Brenton becoming flag captain and Philip Dumaresq, a Channel Islander, her first lieutenant. Saumarez had already asked St Vincent to submit his name for a baronetcy, a request with which the Earl willingly complied. 'The merit of Sir James cannot be surpassed,' he wrote in appropriate Court language, adding, 'nothing can gratify me more than that officers who have signalized themselves under my auspices should be amply rewarded.' The honour was gazetted in June, and Saumarez also heard that he had been given command of a squadron whose duty was to watch Franco–Spanish forces at Algeciras and Cadiz. It was thus that, having at last received special recognition for his services at the Nile, Saumarez began to embark on a series of duties, increasingly important, where he would for the most part be independent.

The mission began with a reverse. With six ships of the line, Saumarez made a bold attack on the enemy at Algeciras on 6 July—it was only six miles from Gibraltar across the bay. There, it was the French under Linois he was after, for he could see three big ships, and the Venetian-built frigate *Muiron*, on board which Bonaparte had escaped back to France from Egypt. The enemy were moored under the formidable shore batteries, and the plan was rash. Nothing went right, for soon after action had been joined the wind dropped, and one of Saumarez's squadron, the *Hannibal*, ran aground, was fired at from all sides and forced to surrender. Saumarez withdrew to Gibraltar as best he could, having suffered damage and casualties, including the Master of the flagship. He was not only beaten but humiliated, and Linois was quick to announce a victory. He had captured a British ship belonging to a superior force, a fact which nothing could conceal.

That the event should have occurred so near Gibraltar, with memories still vivid of Heathfield's triumphant defence twenty years earlier, was specially unfortunate, but Saumarez refused to be flustered. He sent word to St Vincent of the *Hannibal*, and the Earl reacted as he always did when he believed in those concerned. He sent reinforcements, saying to his staff, 'We may have lost a ship, but I well know the man, and the men who were there, and I'll pledge my life the Nation has lost no honour.'

Three days later, the *Superb* and the *Thames*, which had been off Cadiz, were seen approaching the Mole under a crowd of sail, with the signal flying that the Spaniards were at sea. The enemy were soon in sight, anchoring near Linois at Algeciras. It was the general belief that their their destination was Cartagena.

Every exertion was made to re-equip the squadron, particularly the *Caesar*. Her crew worked watch and watch, night and day, and they replaced her mainmast. By 12 July, a mere six days after the reverse, the squadron was once more ready for sea. The *Caesar*, *Superb*, *Thames*, *Audacious*, *Spencer* and *Venerable*, in varied states of repair, sailed to seek battle with a force consisting of six fresh Spanish ships, including three of very large size, and three Frenchmen, elated with success, under an able admiral. If the original attack on Algeciras may have seemed rash, the sequel seemed more so, yet it reflected the spirit not only of the Gibraltar garrison, but of Saumarez's own men. They were out for revenge, and the admiral never had a greater tribute from the lower deck than the fact that two seamen from the *Caesar*, wounded on 6 July, escaped from hospital and rowed out to the squadron just before their ship got out of reach.

The prognosis of enemy movements proved wide of the mark. Far from trying to force its way into the Mediterranean in the face of opposition, the Combined Squadron was soon observed to be heading for Cadiz. Linois had intended to sail the *Hannibal* with the rest, strongly escorted, but he could not work her out of the Bay of Algeciras.

It was nearly nightfall before the enemy were within striking distance and Saumarez, in the manner of Hawke, ordered a general chase. This suited his captains. One of them, Richard Keats of the *Superb*, an officer whom Prince William Henry, now Duke of Clarence, had served as a youngster, provided the best account of an extraordinary night action.

As his ship sped towards the enemy with every sail set and at a speed which her partial captain estimated at between eleven and twelve knots, Keats summoned a meeting of experts. He reported:

I ordered the first and second captains of the guns to be assembled on the quarter-deck. I then told them that I had had the advantage of having been in action with the enemy by night, and predicted what precisely took place—namely, that the Spaniards would blow up, and that we should have more to apprehend from our own careless-ness of powder, than from any efforts of the enemy.

The *Superb*'s Master, an excellent look-out, reported that the ship with which they would first come up was a three-decker. This proved to be the Spanish *Real Carlos* of 112 guns. When darkness was complete, shortly after eleven, Keats fired a broadside into the vessel. The effect was staggering. The Spaniards had no effective watch on deck, and most of the officers were at a meal in the great cabin, which was brightly lit, helping to make a good target. The first, and in some cases the last, that most of the Spanish party knew of the immediate presence of the enemy was the arrival of shot.

This was not the worst. Much of the *Superb*'s fire flew beyond the *Real Carlos* and hit the *San Hermenegildo*, which was sailing close to her consort on a parallel course. Thinking that the shots came from the *Real Carlos* and that she must therefore be hostile, the *San Hermenegildo*, whose gunnery was better than her recognition, discharged a ragged return broadside so that, within a few minutes of Keats's arrival, the *Real Carlos* had been engaged from two directions. When she herself began to reply—and it was not for some time since the Spaniards were untrained in night actions—her shooting was wild and ineffectual.

It was soon clear to Keats that he need concern himself little more with the two Spaniards. They would destroy one another, as he had forecast. This they proceeded to do with shattering thoroughness, falling behind the rest of their squadron, soon to be lost in smoke.

Having discharged two valedictory broadsides, Keats went on to attack the French *St Antoine*, 74 guns, which was by now nearest to him. Her commander, who proved to be Commodore Julien Le Ray, resisted for over half an hour, until the arrival of Saumarez in the *Caesar*. Saumarez then witnessed the French surrender with the greatest satisfaction, a fitting riposte for the loss of the *Hannibal*. Meanwhile, the *Venerable*, commanded by Samuel Hood, one of the heroes of the Nile and a kinsman of the admiral, which had suffered much from the fire of the forts at Algeciras, was seen to be grappling with another Frenchman, but in difficulties. She was soon supported by the *Thames*, on whose arrival the French ship made off.

As soon as it was light, Saumarez received Keats at the gangway of the *Caesar*, saying that he could not find language to express the sense of the services Keats had rendered to his country. Keats said he hoped he had not made too much of his part in the affair. 'That is impossible,' said the Admiral.

There was much sympathy for the wretched Spaniards, of whom not many survived, so proud, so gallant, and so courteous, yet so inept at naval warfare and much at the mercy of their French allies.

The scene at Gibraltar when Saumarez returned with his ships was almost frenzied. 'The Royal Standard was hoisted,' reported Captain Brenton, 'twenty-one guns were fired at the King's Bastion, and the whole of the noble fortress was brilliantly illuminated in honour of the victory.' Revenge is sweet, all the more so when it comes swiftly.

Unfortunately, the affair went to Saumarez's head. His more admirable side was shown in adversity. Once he had achieved success, which, though of a spectacular kind, owed more to Spanish ineptitude than to any other single factor, he became touchy, looking for higher rewards than he could reasonably expect. St Vincent, in sending him reinforcements, had put them in charge of a senior post-captain so that Saumarez should not be superseded. This was a thoughtful act, in addition to his quick response to what he believed to be Saumarez's difficulties. But in the Mediterranean, where Lord Keith held sway, it was different. Keith announced that he considered Saumarez's force to be within his own command, a double humiliation in Saumarez's eyes, since not only could he no longer deem himself independent, but—Keith being notorious for the acquisition of prize money and prize bounty—Saumarez feared that he would have to share the reward which could be expected from the capture of the French ship and the destruction of the Spaniards. He protested to the Admiralty about this and other matters, and was justly, though very mildly, rebuked for his pains.

When the fuss had died down, there came the question of honours. There is little doubt that Saumarez hoped for a peerage. Had this been granted, it would have been quite out of scale. Nelson had received a barony for the Nile, but the contrast between the two encounters was marked. Nelson's was a tactical masterpiece. Saumarez's was a fortunate act of aggression. The authorities solved the problem by giving him the Star of the Bath, something for the baronet to wear on his coat, in the Nelsonic manner.

Both St Vincent and Nelson eulogized Saumarez in the House of Lords, while the Duke of Clarence, never at a loss for a word or two, spoke up on behalf of his old shipmate, Keats. If the reporters caught his words aright, Nelson said that he:

. . . was not surprised at the matchless intrepidity and zeal of his gallant friend when he considered the professional school in which he had been bred—viz: the late Lord Howe, Lord Hood, Lord Bridport, and his noble friend the noble Earl who sat next him. (The Earl of St. Vincent, feeling the full force of the compliment, made the noble and gallant lord a very low bow.) From such masters he

116

could not but have learned everything that was courageous, spirited and magnanimous.

Saumarez was voted a pension of £1,200 a year, and received the official thanks and a sword from the City of London. What pleased him as much as anything was a Resolution, in elegant French, from the the States of his home island. Although he was kept in the Mediterranean for some time after the action, and indeed until after the preliminaries to the brief Peace of Amiens with France had been signed, he could at last look forward to an interlude at home. He was in fact offered the Mediterranean command before he struck his flag, but did not wish for this in time of peace.

When war was resumed in 1803, Napoleon being ready for the next round, the possibility of invasion was real. Napoleon had his Grand Army encamped in the Pas de Calais and he maintained a threat to the Channel Islands from the Cherbourg Peninsula. There was a useful little harbour at Granville which could serve for troop-carrying barges, and more important facilities at St Malo, a great centre of privateering. It was to the Channel Islands station that Saumarez was next appointed. He was given a miscellaneous force, mainly small ships, which were constantly active and in danger. Jahleel Brenton, for instance, commanding a frigate, was driven ashore in a fog and taken prisoner. He was three years in France before he was exchanged. Saumarez himself led an attack on Granville and was lucky to escape with his life from the burst of a mortar.

In 1806 the Earl of St Vincent resumed command of the Home Fleet and asked for Saumarez as his second. On 7 January 1807 he hoisted his flag on board the *San Josef*, the ship he had towed into the Tagus ten years earlier. Later he transferred to the *Prince of Wales*. He struck his flag in August 1807 and returned to Guernsey, where he flew it on board the frigate *Inconstant*. He then received the offer of chief command in the East Indies, which he declined. This was fortunate for the country, for an opportunity arose for detached service in the Baltic. Saumarez was appointed, and thus began the most important phase of all his years as an admiral.

By the year 1808, when Saumarez first made intimate acquaintance with the Baltic, matters had reached a crisis in the north. Earlier in the war the old idea of an Armed Neutrality had been revived, first mooted at the time of the struggle with the American Colonies. The Powers concerned, namely Denmark, which then included Norway, Sweden,

Russia and Prussia, proclaimed their right to free use of the seas, which meant that they intended to trade with all belligerents. To an island kingdom fighting for its life, as Britain was until the downfall of Napoleon, such a combination represented an intolerable threat and rendered blockade meaningless. It was seen as such by all responsible parties in London.

It was to dissolve the Armed Neutrality that the younger Hyde Parker had been dispatched with a fleet, with Nelson as his second. The resultant fighting at Copenhagen fell to Nelson, and it was so severe and difficult that when Saumarez first got hold of an account of it, he was so overcome that he could not continue reading.

Although the expedition was successful, Nelson had prophesied that such a proud nation as the Danes would not for long submit to having their fleet immobilized. He was right. In 1807, after Napoleon had attempted to close all Continental ports to Britain, there was renewed danger from the north. A second and larger expedition was mounted, under Admiral Gambier and General Cathcart, which bombarded the Danish capital and towed away most of the larger ships. The result was as before. Denmark remained more firmly than ever within the orbit of France, and although she could no longer mobilize a fleet, she built and equipped gunboats which kept up a ceaseless, gallant and sometimes successful guerrilla warfare against the British until the very end of the fighting.

Saumarez's duty was to maintain a presence in the Baltic during the ice-free months, and he was given the *Victory*, with Philip Dumaresq as his flag captain and George Hope Captain of the Fleet. He had served in the famous ship when young, had watched the signals run up from her halyards by Jervis at St Vincent as he took his fleet into battle; Nelson had died in her cockpit at Trafalgar. By now, Saumarez himself held the rank of Vice-Admiral of the Blue, and in choosing him for this appointment the Admiralty showed inspiration. His task was to ensure, by means open or by subterfuge, a flow of trade with the United Kingdom, the most vital commodities being naval stores, which the northern countries produced in such quantities, and which were essential munitions. The island of Heligoland had been seized as an *entrepôt* for trade, serving much the same purpose as Malta in the Mediterranean. The Danish island of Anholt in the Kattegat was also seized under Saumarez's direction, for military as well as trading purposes. It had the additional virtue of a first-rate supply of fresh water.

The mission was as much diplomatic as naval, and was almost as important as Collingwood's duties in the Mediterranean. Saumarez was ideally suited for it, and there were few on the flag list who approached his standard of sophistication, dignity and skill. Besides these qualities, he had sufficient ships to make his presence influential, and often decisive. Samuel Hood, now a Rear-Admiral, and Richard Keats were particularly gratifying appointments to the fleet, since both had been Saumarez's supporters in battle.

Sweden was the key to the situation. When Parker and Nelson had entered the Baltic by way of the Sound, it was noted that whereas the guns mounted on the battlements of Elsinore on the Danish side thundered defiance, those of Hälsingborg opposite in Sweden were silent. That was because the eccentric Swedish king, Gustavus IV Adolphus, while agreeing the notion of an Armed Neutrality, had such a revulsion for Napoleon, whom he believed to be the incarnation of the Beast of the Apocalypse, that he was unwilling to do anything active against any country which was fighting the dictator. The situation did not stay in that happy state, but throughout the four years of Saumarez's command, Sweden, whatever her formal position may have been, was either openly or secretly friendly, welcoming the presence of a fleet in the anchorage off Göteborg known as Vinga Sound, called 'Wingo' by every British sailor.

The chief people in Sweden spoke French, and Saumarez's ease in this language was one of his greatest assets. It proved to be all the more so after a number of senior naval officers, who when young had done their training in the French service in the fleet commanded by de Grasse, discovered that Saumarez, years earlier, had been one of Rodney's captains, and had indeed been present when the French admiral was taken prisoner. Here was a man they could respect.

Nothing was simple at that time in northern affairs. Earlier in the war, Russia had been Britain's ally; then her Tsar, Paul I, made terms with Napoleon. The country's alignment altered once more after Paul's murder, for his son Alexander maintained a different attitude until he came to an agreement with Napoleon at Tilsit to join the Continental system directed against Britain, with the understanding that he should be given a free hand against Sweden, whose Finnish territory he coveted and intended to take by force.

By the time Saumarez had arrived off the Swedish coast the situation in Finland had become critical for the Swedes. Russian successes by land and sea included the capture of the great fortress at Sveaborg, which fell after a negligible resistance. In August 1808 Samuel Hood in the *Centaur*, supporting Captain Byam Martin in the *Implacable*, captured the Russian ship of the line *Sevelod* within sight of the Tsar's main fleet. When Saumarez himself arrived on the scene in the *Victory*, which was accompanied by some Swedish ships, he was in favour of pressing the attack further, but was dissuaded.

During the spring of the following year, when the admiral was at home, events at Stockholm gathered momentum. In March, Gustavus IV Adolphus was declared to be mad and was deposed. The throne was assumed by his ageing and childless uncle, the Duke of Södermanland, who reigned as Charles XIII. One of his first acts was to give Saumarez the Grand Cross of the Order of the Sword, gratifying to one who valued decorations. But the old King had to bear not only the loss of Finland to Russia, but the Åland Islands in the Gulf of Bothnia, strategically valuable to his country.

By the year 1810 Napoleon was in a position to force Sweden to abandon her attitude of non-belligerency. This made little difference to the general attitude of the people or even to the flow of trade, which in view of the hostility of Denmark had to be routed by way of the navigationally difficult Belt rather than the Sound. But when influential Swedes offered the reversion of the throne to the French marshal Bernadotte, it appeared that the policy of the country might alter radically.

Napoleon, after hesitation, allowed the Gascon soldier to accept the offer, and the British, believing that matters might appear very differently within a short time, allowed the marshal to proceed to his new country unhindered, and indeed escorted. He arrived in Sweden in October 1810, much astonished at the spectacle of so many British ships pursuing their business in Swedish waters. He later told an officer serving with Saumarez that this was

> . . . the most beautiful and wonderful sight he ever had beheld, one of which he had never formed an idea. The day was very fine, the Fleet was anchored in a close compact body, with the *Victory* in the centre, bearing the Admiral's flag at the fore, surrounded by six ships of the line, and six frigates and sloops disposed for the complete protection of the convoy.

Saumarez's own view concurred with that of the home Government that henceforward Swedish policy would be guided solely by her own interests, not by those of France. This proved to be so. Although the country made a formal declaration of war against Britain, no hostile acts ensued. Instead, guided by Baron von Platen, Bernadotte, who was styled Crown Prince until the death of Charles XIII eight years later, took summary powers, and soon made himself popular. In due course an alliance with Russia came about, a key condition being that the Tsar would support the acquisition of Norway from Denmark in compensation for the loss of Finland.

The Baltic watch was at no time maintained without loss, even although large-scale battles did not occur. The sick lists were apt to be high, in the Swedish as much as in the British forces. Scurvy was not always treated, even by this time, in the manner which had been suggested by James Lind, a naval surgeon, in a treatise published as early as the time of Hawke, and proved by dietetic experiment. The difficulty of regular supplies of fresh fruit and vegetables was, however, greater in the Baltic than, for instance, the Mediterranean. There were also victims of Danish enterprise, and losses from marine causes.

The route to the Baltic was at most seasons inclined to be stormy, and in order to make good as many passages as possible during a limited season, ships were apt to leave the final journey home late, sometimes rashly late. The worst losses suffered by Saumarez were that of the *Minotaur*, ship of the line and veteran of the Nile, which in 1810 was lost with all hands off the Texel on her way to England, and that of the *St George*, *Defence* and *Hero* the following winter, just before Christmas.

The loss of the *St George* and *Defence* was the fault of Rear-Admiral Reynolds who, against advice, insisted on sailing home, in spite of previous damage and in a season of storms. Some two thousand men perished on a lee shore on the peninsula of Jutland. It was the most shocking and unnecessary tragedy since the *Royal George* foundered at Spithead thirty years before.

The crucial year was the last of Saumarez's command, and it saw every difficulty resolved. Napoleon occupied Swedish Pomerania, the last of those Continental territories which had once made the northern kingdom a major power. Then he marched against Russia, and the Swedish–Russian agreement became operative. At later stages of the European struggle Bernadotte was adroit in the way in which he managed not to involve his troops directly against the French until it was impossible to do otherwise.

Although the Emperor's advance to Moscow was a land matter, the British fleet supported the Russian flank: moreover, it was largely through Saumarez, and the information he collected, that the world was enabled to learn the truth about the large-scale disaster into which Napoleon had plunged his army. From the French-controlled newspapers it might have been gathered that the famous Retreat was almost a picnic.

The *Victory* was paid off in November 1812, and Saumarez could at last enjoy the prospect of ease, since he had no further operational duties. Two years earlier, after the death of Lord Collingwood, he had once more been considered for the Mediterranean command, but his presence in the Baltic was held to be so vital that the post went elsewhere. In retiring, Saumarez could pride himself on the terms in which their Lordships of the Admiralty had expressed their approbation. Equally pleasing must have been the warmth of congratulation sent by Swedish friends. This was best expressed by Baron von Platen, who wrote of Saumarez as

> ... the guardian angel of my country; by your wise, temperate and loyal conduct you have been the first cause of the plans which have been formed against the Demon of the Continent. Once more I must tell you that *you* were the first cause that Russia dared to make war against France: *had you fired one shot when we declared war against England*, all had been ended, and Europe would have been enslaved.

⚓ ⚓ ⚓

At the end of the war, all the naval Commanders-in-Chief were given, or were offered, peerages. Saumarez was not. This was a bitter blow to him, particularly as he had continued in the Baltic at the special request of the Government. A promotion to the highest grade in the Order of the Bath was no consolation to a man who had set his hopes on something else.

The compensations were mostly small beer—the honorific Rear-Admiralty of the United Kingdom, followed by the Vice-Admiralty, which had once been conferred on Hawke, and the last appointment as General of Marines to be given to a naval officer.

More substantially, the Admiralty gave Saumarez the Plymouth Command in 1824, and he held it for three years. During his tenure, Earl Grey was his guest, and in the course of a speech to the Navy Club he said of his host:

> ... I wish I could see him ennobled by his Sovereign, as his services entitle him to be: for who would deny him that honour, who recollects the career which has run from Rodney's glorious day, the battles of Cape St. Vincent and the Nile, down to his own brilliant exploits in the *Crescent* and as Commander-in-Chief at Algeciras, and not to say, if ever a name should or would have graced the peerage, it should have been that of Saumarez.

The chance for Grey to put his sentiments into effect came in 1830, when he became Prime Minister. To his surprise, he found opposition in the last quarter he would have expected—from William IV, the 'Sailor King'. William liked to favour his naval cronies, but such they had to be, and he was a man of extreme, irrational and quite unpredictable prejudices. Saumarez happened to be among them, and it was the better part of a year before he was shamed into doing his duty.

Lord de Saumarez, as he became in 1831, had five years of life in which to enjoy his dignity. He devoted himself to philanthropy and to church-building, and was gratified that his heir was in Holy Orders, since his own inclinations had been so much that way.

Saumarez died in 1836, only a short time before his ungracious sovereign. During both the wars of the present century his name was given to a destroyer. The ship of 1915 was a flotilla leader which served with the Grand Fleet. Her successor of 1940 gained various battle honours and had a gallant part in the destruction of the German battle cruiser *Scharnhorst*, appropriately enough in northern waters. Greater men have not always been so well commemorated.

10

Farragut: the American Paragon

When Saumarez died there was a lieutenant serving in the Navy of the United States, not yet forty years old, whose career was to be one of the strangest on record. David Glasgow Farragut, born at Campbell's Station, near Knoxville in eastern Tennessee, spanned the era between sail and steam. He first saw serious fighting as a boy of twelve when the ship in which he was serving, the *Essex*, fought the British Frigate *Phoebe*. The *Phoebe* was commanded by James Hillyar, who had been well known to Nelson, under whom he had served in the Mediterranean. When Farragut was next engaged in full-scale warfare it was as a leading officer of the Federals in their civil war with the Confederate States, of one of which he was a native. A more remarkable preparation for high command could not easily be imagined, yet it was enough to ensure Farragut a place in the history of his country.

The so-called 'War of 1812', in which the United States and Britain became involved largely because of high-handed behaviour on the part of the British at sea, was unnecessary, and led to no satisfactory results in spite of campaigning extending from Canada to South America. It would never have occurred had communications been better and swifter. During its course the Royal Navy received some salutary shocks in the way of defeats in frigate actions, and the Americans fortified a tradition of gallantry which had been established by Paul Jones and others during the previous century.

At that time many of the same customs (not to speak of the same harsh discipline of the lash) obtained in the Navy of the United States as in that of her opponent. For instance, aspirants to quarter-deck status could receive advantages through a senior officer being their patron. They were taken into his 'family' or retinue. In Farragut's case the benefactor concerned was Commander David Porter, who was in charge of the naval station at New Orleans. He adopted young David, and was ever afterwards his faithful friend; and in one matter at least the United States service was specially helpful. Midshipmen could intersperse formal schooling with periods at sea when the chance offered, as it often did in a Navy with few ships in commission.

Young Farragut had no inherited love for the British. His father, George Farragut, was of unmixed Spanish descent, having been born at Minorca at a time when the island was temporarily in British possession. Although he was entitled to British citizenship, he had never set foot in the United Kingdom and, after he had emigrated to North America, felt himself very much at liberty to serve the Colonists in their struggle for independence. His wife was a native-born American, and together they moved to Louisiana from eastern Tennessee shortly after the State purchase of Louisiana from France. George Farragut served, at least for a time, as a sailing master, but as he died when David was still in his teens he had no influence on his future career. The boy was, in fact, orphaned at an early age and quickly learned to rely on himself. He had a brother, also attracted to the naval service, and a sister, but they were adopted by others and David saw them rarely.

Farragut's first protracted voyage under Porter, who had been promoted post-captain, was the most varied he ever experienced. He joined the frigate *Essex* in August 1811, when he was ten years old and his captain just over thirty. The *Essex* had been built at Salem, Massachusetts, in 1799, and had already been round the Cape of Good Hope on an earlier voyage. She was armed with forty carronades and six long guns. Her primary mission was to attack the British whaling fleet in the Pacific, which at that time included armed vessels used for privateering.

The voyage began with a visit to the scene of Suffren's surprise attack on Commodore George Johnstone twenty years earlier in the Cape Verde Islands, preliminary to the stretch down to Cape Horn. Once in southerly latitudes, the frigate took three weeks to reach the Pacific against adverse westerlies and high seas, the crew being on half-rations.

After putting in at Valparaiso, Porter had some success in taking whaler prizes. Then he moved north, to the Galàpagos Islands, which served as a base for some of the British ships, and whose astonishing natural life made such an impression on Charles Darwin when he visited them in the *Beagle* twenty years later.

Porter equipped and armed a prize, which he christened the *Essex Junior*, into which he put a crew of sixty. On one occasion he gave young Farragut charge of another smaller prize, and was pleased when the lad refused to be intimidated by the former captain. Porter soon had news that the British were sending a frigate and two sloops to protect the whaling fleet, and thereupon he trained his men, who were already smart, in every form of ship-to-ship fighting.

Part of the year 1813 was spent at the Marquesas, which gave Farragut a glowing idea of Pacific island life. Then the captain returned to Valparaiso, where he arrived early in 1814.

Within a few weeks the British frigate *Phoebe* was sighted, in company with the sloop *Cherub*, and as the ships were in territorial waters, icy courtesies were exchanged between Porter and Hillyar, who had met before, on service in the Mediterranean. Porter was well aware that Hillyar, given the chance, would make light of Chilean neutrality. The opportunity came on 28 March, when the *Essex*'s anchor cable broke during a storm and Porter was forced either to let his ship drive ashore, or put to sea. He chose the latter course and, as he fully expected, was soon in action.

Hillyar knew from long experience that the carronade was useless at long range, and when fighting began at about four o'clock, he kept his distance. He was careful not to close until, after a most gallant defence lasting for two and a half hours, Porter was forced to surrender. His ship was badly battered and his casualties were high—58 killed, 65 wounded and 31 'missing' out of a total complement of 253. Porter had done his duty well.

Farragut, who was still just under thirteen years old, had some narrow shaves, but escaped with bruises. He remembered one experience all his life when he observed a quarter gunner, Roach, who had shown himself one of the bravest of the crew earlier in the voyage, desert his post; he would have been shot, on Porter's orders, had he been found. Actually he had escaped ashore, with six others, in the only serviceable boat. Farragut remarked, as many had done before him, that 'personal courage is a very peculiar virtue'. It was not to be relied upon at all times and in all places.

The young midshipman was invited to dinner with the two captains on board the *Phoebe*, Hillyar saying: 'Never mind, my little fellow, it will be your turn next perhaps.' He was sent home, with the other survivors, in the *Essex Junior*, arriving after a three years' absence with a story to tell which would have made the most adventurous-minded envious.

This was as well, for there followed for young Farragut almost a half-century of routine service, during which his upward progress was slow. It was also not without setbacks and sadnesses.

One matter over which Farragut could never justly have complained was that he lacked variety of employment. Sent to a ship of the line, he became a favourite with the captain, but Farragut disliked the methods by which a 'taut hand', or over-strict disciplinarian, cultivated smartness through discomfort. It had not been Porter's way, and Porter had nothing to learn about creating a 'happy ship' atmosphere or training an efficient crew. 'My experience,' wrote Farragut later, 'determined me never to have a "crack ship" if it was only to be attained by such means.'

In a later appointment Farragut had an extended tour of the Mediterranean, during which he attracted the particular notice of the ship's chaplain, Charles Folsom, who acted as schoolmaster. In 1817 Folsom received an appointment as American Consul at Tunis. Taking Farragut with him, he was able to give his pupil the chance to study mathematics,

English literature, French and Italian, during a stay ashore of nearly a year. Farragut had some aptitude for languages, and at this as at every other stage of his life he was an avid learner.

When he returned for duty with his squadron Farragut was made an acting lieutenant, and although it was long before the rank was confirmed, it gave him occasional chances of independence such as he had enjoyed earlier under Porter. He wrote: 'I consider it a great advantage to obtain command young, having observed, as a general rule, that persons who come into authority late in life shrink from responsibility and often break down under its weight.'

Farragut's next service was in the Caribbean with what was known as the Mosquito Fleet, to which the duty was assigned, in collaboration with the British Navy, of extirpating the last of the pirate gangs which infested the area, as they had done for centuries. Farragut's patron, Commodore David Porter, was in charge of the fleet, and he himself was appointed to the *Greyhound*, commanded by John Porter, the Commodore's brother. The work was tough. 'I never owned a bed during my two years and a half in the West Indies,' wrote Farragut, 'but lay down to rest wherever I found the most comfortable berth.' Unfortunately, the expedition led to the resignation of the Commodore. He was held to have exceeded his orders, was court martialled, sentenced to six months' suspension of duties, and was so indignant at the verdict that he resigned from the Navy. He took service with the Mexican Republic, but this led to nothing but frustration. When Andrew Jackson became President in 1829 he offered to reinstate Porter in his old seniority or to give him alternative employment. Porter chose the latter, and became Minister Resident in Turkey.

In September 1823, after his return from the Caribbean but before his confirmation as lieutenant, Farragut married Susan Marchant of Norfolk, Virginia, where he made his home when not employed afloat. His lieutenant's commission at last came through in August 1825, together with orders to join the frigate *Brandywine*, which had been chosen to take Lafayette back to France after a triumphant visit to America. Lafayette, one of the stalwarts of the War of Independence, remained a hero in American eyes, and not least of those on board the frigate. From France, the *Brandywine* crossed to England, and then proceeded to the Mediterranean, returning in May 1826.

Farragut had another opportunity of admiring French genius when, in command of the sloop-of-war *Erie*, he was sent to Mexico and was an observer of the actions taken by Admiral Baudin to obtain reparation for injuries received by French subjects at the hands of the Mexican authorities. Baudin first tried blockade. Then he took by assault the castle of San Juan de Ulloa, an uncommon example of success by sea forces against a shore position of strength.

Not long after his return home, Farragut's wife died. Her health had long been precarious, and Farragut had been a faithful nurse when his duties allowed. One of his wife's friends said he had been such a good husband that, when he himself came to die, 'he should have a monument reaching to the skies, made by every wife in the city contributing a stone'.

Shortly after his bereavement Farragut became a commander, and his first acquaintance with steam, apart from a fleeting episode with a primitive example in the Mosquito Fleet, was when, as a captain, he was given command of the *Brooklyn*, one of a batch of six sloops-of-war just completed. This was in 1858, when he could have thought of himself as being close to retirement. By that time he had married again, he and his second wife, who like his first was a Norfolk woman, being supremely happy.

It was ten years since Farragut had served afloat, for he had been given a succession of important shore jobs, including a long spell in California. Fortunately, he retained his earlier assiduity and eagerness to learn, and was determined to make himself a thorough master of handling what he realized to be the type of vessel which would make up the fleets of the future.

The *Brooklyn* and her class were built for broadside firing, in the traditional way. They were fitted with 9-inch smooth-bored Dahlgren muzzle-loading guns, together with one, or in some cases two, additional 'pivot guns' of a larger bore. These, as their name implied, gave them a useful traverse. They fired shells, not the solid shot of the days of the *Essex*. These ships had a full set of sails in addition to the engines which gave them a maximum speed of about eight knots.

Farragut was in the *Brooklyn* for two years. In October 1860 he returned to Norfolk, having completed the last commission of his life in a 'private' ship. Henceforward, his responsibilities would be greater.

⚓   ⚓   ⚓

No decision of Farragut's life was more difficult to make than when, at the outbreak of the American Civil War, at a time when he was living at Norfolk with his wife and son, he became convinced that his allegiance to the central Government, guided by President Lincoln, outweighed all other considerations. Born a southerner, domiciled in a southern State, married to a Virginian, there was yet no doubt in Farragut's mind what he should do, at a time when the divisions which every civil war entails were causing anguish. As his biographer, Alfred

Mahan, wrote, it is impossible for most people, 'however conscious of right, to bear without suffering the alienation and the contempt visited upon those who, in times of keen political excitement, dare to differ from the general passion which sways the mass around them'.

Farragut's wife was of the same mind as he was, and in April 1861 the pair left Norfolk, together with their only son and Mrs Farragut's sister and her young family, never to return to it as their home. They made their way to New York, partly in a crowded canal boat, only to realize when they arrived that it must be some time before Farragut could be fully accepted into the confidence of his own Service, where suspicion of treachery was sometimes justified.

He was at first employed on a Board whose purpose was to recommend officers for retirement, there being then no regular system. But a more active role was contemplated. There was an official in the Navy Department, Gustavus Vasa Fox, who had extensive sea experience, who knew what ships could and could not do, and who realized the importance of New Orleans to the Secessionists. It was Fox who proposed an expedition against that place, and it was he who urged the appointment of Farragut to undertake the naval side of the task. Fox was impressed both by Farragut's enthusiasm for the project and his confidence that he would succeed if given the chance to carry it out.

Also to be concerned in the assault was Commander David D. Porter, the able son of Farragut's first captain. The auspices were good. 'Keep your lips closed,' Farragut wrote to his wife, who was at Hastings, on the Hudson River. 'Perfect silence is to be observed . . . I am to have a Flag in the Gulf, and the rest depends upon myself.'

The colourful personalities of the leading generals, the drama and vicissitudes of the land campaigns in the American Civil War, have led to some neglect of the bearing of the sea upon its fortunes. For their sinews the Confederates depended upon the use of their ports, and these were blockaded. Ships such as the *Alabama*, which proved that the seaward watch could be evaded, afford a romantic story, and this vessel, together with others of her kind, did much harm to the Federal cause. Nevertheless, the *Alabama* was in the end defeated in battle, and so was the side she represented.

It would have been an even longer war than it proved to be had not the Federals discovered in Farragut, at the age of sixty, a born leader of men. Hitherto he had had no opportunity to apply his gifts in a sphere to match them. Now at last, just before it was too late, he was given the most responsible maritime command within Lincoln's gift.

On 9 January 1862 he was formally appointed to the 'Western Gulf Blockading Squadron'. His duties covered the area from St Andrew's

Bay to the mouth of the Rio Grande. The steam sloop-of-war *Hartford* was chosen as his flagship, and she was similar in design to the *Brooklyn*. Farragut's orders were to reduce the defences of the Mississippi, a task which was to exercise him for much of the war. He took over command on 21 February, and for the next few weeks was engaged in assembling, assessing and training his miscellaneous little fleet.

At this time, steam was still regarded as auxiliary in larger ships, all of which were equipped with sails. In the sea campaigns of the previous decade, when the British and French engaged the Russians in the Baltic and the Black Seas, most of the larger vessels had auxiliary steam power, but naval engineers were a despised race and would remain so for at least a generation. In the navies both of the Federals and the Confederates there was a different attitude. The Americans were forward-looking, and the armoured duel in Hampton Roads between the Federal *Monitor* and the Confederate *Merrimac*, in the year that Farragut took over command in the Gulf, was one of the chief episodes which brought about the transformation from sail and wood to steam and metal.

Farragut had at his disposal four wooden, steam-powered sloops-of-war, including the *Hartford*. These, although of only 2,000 tons, were his capital ships, around which he made his dispositions. There were three other sloops, about half the size of the larger ones, also the *Mississippi*, which was a paddle-wheel steamer of about 1,700 tons, and nine gunboats which had been hurriedly built to meet the exigencies of war. In addition, there were steamers attached to a mortar flotilla by which it was hoped that the defences of New Orleans would be reduced. These defences were Fort Jackson and Fort St Philip, which were sited, one on each bank of the river, some distance downstream from the city.

A secondary but important object of the operation was to join forces with Federal land forces far up the river. Right from the start of planning there were two schools of thought as to the best procedure. One, whose advocates included Commander Porter, believed that the most effective way to set about matters was by steady bombardment of the forts by the ships, in which mortars would play the main part. The other, headed by Farragut, believed that the fleet could force its way past the forts, in the face of enemy fire, without the necessity of reducing them first, which he knew might be a lengthy process. If success were achieved, the forts would be under threat through the severance of their river communications. Their fall would thereupon be a matter of time and not, in Farragut's view, a very long time. Planning went ahead as if the more conventional view prevailed. The forts would be reduced as a preliminary to anything further.

The mortar bombardment proceeded as arranged but, as Farragut had predicted, it was without decisive effect, in spite of creditable marksmanship. After three days he called a Council of War. When the captains were assembled, he listened carefully to their views, Porter's being set down in writing and read out with due attention on the part of all concerned.

Farragut then told the meeting that his mind was made up. He intended to take the ships past the forts with all the attendant risks of such a plan. The Council had been summoned not because he had any doubts, but simply so that he could listen to suggestions. His detailed orders for the attack were dated the same day, 20 April 1862. The document began, in a manner somewhat reminiscent of Nelson at Copenhagen:

> The Flag Officer, having heard all the opinions expressed by the different commanders, is of the opinion that whatever is to be done will have to be done quickly, or we shall again be reduced to a blockading squadron, as we have nearly expended all the shells and fuses and material for making cartridges.

Farragut had already ordered every effort to be made to sever the chains across the river, which, with a timber boom, were considered effective obstacles by the Confederates. Gallant work had been done by picked officers and men, who believed, rightly as it proved, that they had cleared a practicable channel for any fleet proceeding up-river.

On the night of 24 April, Farragut led the *Hartford* in to the attack. It was the first time he had come under close fire from an enemy since boyhood.

Everyone present agreed that the effect was tonic. Farragut had been confident before, basing his belief in success largely on deductions made at the time of Admiral Baudin's manoeuvres against the Mexicans under equally difficult conditions. Action stimulated him to the highest pitch. He exuded resolution, infecting those around him in the manner of a born commander.

All went well, but there were tense moments. At one time fire-rafts were seen to be drifting down on the *Hartford*, and they actually set her alight, the flames roaring through the open ports and driving men from their guns. 'Don't flinch from the fire, boys!' shouted Farragut. 'There's a hotter fire waiting for those who don't do their duty!' When a steam tug was seen to be trying to nose the raft more firmly against the sloop, Farragut said: 'Give that rascally tug a shot'—very much in the manner of Saumarez when attacked at the Nile by a frigate. The tug was disposed of, and by dawn Farragut was through and on his way to the Louisiana capital.

There was panic in the city, followed by riots, looting and partial evacuation of civilians. Moreover, long before they could have been bombarded or starved into submission, the garrisons mutinied, and Farragut's retreat was safe. This was highly important, for although his armed ships could look after themselves, they required an attendance of colliers and supply vessels which were vulnerable to both ship and shore fire.

The central Government, elated at the swift success, wished Farragut to proceed higher up the Mississippi and under far more difficult circumstances than anyone sitting at a Navy Department desk could appreciate. Farragut was as willing to take risks as anyone alive, as he had shown already, but he needed assurance that the objects in view were worth the cost in life. It was soon clear to him that conditions beyond New Orleans, over which the Union's flag now flew, would not warrant protracted operations, since the Federal army had not been able to fulfil its own expectations in the way of an advance.

Despite implied protest, once he had rendered the *Arkansas* ineffectual, the solitary Confederate iron-clad ship known to be up-river, Farragut prudently went back to the Gulf. There he would continue the harassing and all too often disappointing work of blockade. This required patience and endurance, in neither of which qualities had he shown himself lacking.

Just before leaving New Orleans, Farragut received a commission in the rank of Rear-Admiral, which was dated 16 July 1862. Three other officers were admitted to the grade, which had never before existed in the United States. Farragut was the senior promotion. By December he could report that, with the exception of Mobile, the Federals at that time held the entire coast of the Gulf of Mexico.

When Farragut next ascended the Mississippi, it was with the purpose of interrupting the stream of supplies which was reaching the Confederate forces from Texas by way of the Red River. His duty was also to co-operate with General Grant in the reduction of Port Hudson and Vicksburg. This was a wearing campaign, and at an early attempt only the *Hartford* and one other ship managed to pass the river forts. There were, in fact, heavy losses in the squadron, some due to mechanical failures, some to damage to ships' engines by enemy fire, some to errors in pilotage in an area which offered tough problems. By now, the Navy Department had grown more nervous over losses than ever Farragut had been himself. They were urging caution where once they had hoped for miracles.

Despite setbacks, Farragut gave every necessary help to the army, and he blockaded the Red River. Co-operation between the two Services was excellent, as would have been expected when a soldier of the calibre of Grant was involved. Farragut could also place complete reliance on Porter, who in a swift promotion had become an acting Rear-Admiral. At one stage Farragut had with him on board the flagship his son and only child, Loyall. The youth bore himself well under fire, but the responsibility, added to the cares of campaigning, seemed to Farragut incompatible, and he arranged for Loyall to return. 'The anxieties of a father,' he wrote to his wife, 'should not be added to those of the commander.'

Vicksburg and Port Hudson surrendered in July 1863, after which Farragut turned over the command above New Orleans to Porter. He himself then sailed north in the *Hartford*, so that his ship, by now much battered, could receive an extensive refit in a well-equipped yard. On 10 August Farragut anchored at New York, and remained ashore until the start of the following year. 'I am growing old fast, and need rest,' he said. Rest was his due, but the crown of his work must, he felt, be the reduction of Mobile.

⚓   ⚓   ⚓

The next few months, tedious for the most part, represented a critical stage in Farragut's life. The war, against expectation and even probability, had been going badly for the Union, which had lost control, through defeats on land, of part of the Gulf coast. This in turn had led to the inevitable loosening of the blockade and to increased efforts by sympathisers abroad to bring the Confederates what they needed.

In resuming personal charge of the fleet, Farragut became subject to moods of depression, which were unnatural to him. They were due to the events of the war and to pressure of work. Although he allowed himself freedom in his letters to his wife, like every wise commander he permitted no expression of gloom among his officers and men. A different impression might be conveyed to his immediate staff, and in particular his flag captain, Percival Drayton, with whom the Admiral formed the closest friendship, but it would not go beyond the cabin. What Drayton most disliked—and in this he was seconded by his chief —was the incessant paper-work which fell to his lot. These were still the days of minute staffs. Farragut wrote letters on business in his own hand: clerks merely copied them. In the half-century which had elapsed since Collingwood made similar complaints from his Mediterranean flagship no attempt had been made, in any Navy, to systematize appreciably or lighten the administrative burden which fell to commanders-in-chief.

Not that matters were wholly without alleviation. For instance, one day a messenger arrived with a splendid gift for Farragut. This was a sword with a massive scabbard of gold and silver, the hilt set with brilliants. It came from the Union League Club of New York, where Farragut had many friends and admirers. The letter accompanying it spoke of the Admiral's 'brilliant services to the Nation'. It was a fortifying reminder that, whatever the future might hold, his fellow-citizens were not unmindful of the immediate past. Moreover, he was so much liked by all ranks that he never had need to consider that anyone was intriguing to supplant him.

Farragut had reason to pause before his final preparations for the assault on Mobile. There was an iron-clad in the port, against which he could pit only wooden vessels such as he had used with such effect at New Orleans. The enemy ship was the *Tennessee*. She used her guns broadside, having two 6-inch rifled weapons on each quarter. Fore and aft were additional single 7-inch guns. Her armour included a formidable ram, for use in a mêlée, and although her engines could give her a speed of only six knots at best, she was a tough proposition.

The Federals, when Farragut's fleet was complete, would be strengthened by four monitors. These, first devised by the Swedish engineer, John Ericsson, were in essence round forts, heavily plated with iron, resting on a raft almost flush with the water. The forts, or turrets, carried two heavy guns side by side, the turret revolving by machinery in the direction required. Above the turret was a fixed conning-tower, but this was subject to such disadvantages from smoke and from concussion when struck, that many captains preferred to remain outside and exposed, giving orders to the helmsman through sight-holes pierced in the armour.

The monitors were of two kinds: one was sea-going, armed with two 15-inch guns; the other, of lighter draught, mounted four 11-inch guns. The larger vessels were the *Tecumseh* and the *Manhattan*, the smaller being the *Winnebago* and the *Chicasaw*. Their guns, unlike those of the *Tennessee*, were not rifled.

Besides the *Tennessee*, Farragut would have to face the thirty-eight guns of Fort Morgan, and others in Fort Jackson and Fort St Philip. Even this was not all, for the Confederates were using what later came to be known as mines, but which in those days went by the name of 'torpedoes'. This derived from the genus of cartilaginous fish, related to the skates and rays, with apparatus in the head which could give a lethal electric shock. The mine, and later still the locomotive torpedo, had a transforming effect on all naval warfare. When combined with an efficient submarine (an event some distance in the future), they would inhibit the action of surface ships to a marked extent.

The 'torpedo', as Farragut would continue to call it—the original was delightfully described in Dr Johnson's Dictionary as 'a fish which, while alive, if touched even with a long stick, benumbs the hand which so touches it, but when dead is eaten safely'—had already had an effect on operations. It had been exploited by the Germans at Kiel during troubles in the 1850s over Schleswig-Holstein; by the Russians in the Baltic and the Black Sea; by the Austrians against the French; while Farragut himself had experience of its use by the Confederates. He had lost a gunboat in the Mississippi in December 1862 when she struck two 'torpedoes' and sank in twelve minutes.

At Mobile two types were employed, laid in triple lines. Elsewhere, the Confederates sometimes made use of what were known as 'Davids', so called in honour of David Bushnell, who vainly tried to blow up Howe's flagship, the *Eagle*, during the War of Independence. The 'Davids' were not submarines in the strict sense. They were so constructed that they could run awash, by taking in water ballast, their weapon being a torpedo mounted on a spar, fired by chemical fuses when brought into contact with the hull of a ship. Farragut was to be spared this form of attack.

The operations at Mobile differed from those at New Orleans in that Farragut could expect co-operation from the Federal army, who would attack and besiege the forts, although with small prospect of success if the fleet could not ensure their isolation. The sailors had, in the event, excellent relations with General Granger, with whom the admiral arranged for the attack to begin on 3 August.

Delay resulted from the non-arrival of the monitor *Tecumseh* from Pensacola. That it was not serious was due to the initiative of Captain Thornton A. Jenkins of the *Richmond*, who supplied the iron-clad with coal when her bunkers were empty. The energy shown by Jenkins was specially pleasing to Farragut, for this officer had formerly served as his Chief of Staff.

When at last all was ready, Farragut wrote to his wife, on 4 August 1864, and once more there were echoes of Nelson. 'I am going to Mobile in the morning, if God is my leader, as I hope He is, and in Him I place my trust. If He thinks it is the proper place for me to die, I am ready to submit to His will in that as in all other things . . .'

Farragut wanted a flood tide, to sweep him up the river, and a west wind, to blow the funnel and gun-smoke towards the forts and to help conceal his own movements. On the tide he could depend, and when, during the restless early hours of 5 August, his steward told him that the wind was favourable too, preparatory signals were made at once. The fleet weighed anchor about half past six.

To his great regret later, Farragut did not lead in, as he had at first intended. The *Hartford* took second place in the column to the *Brooklyn*. As with all the larger wooden ships, she had a paddle-wheel gunboat secured to her port side. In the case of the flagship the vessel concerned was the *Metacomet*, in charge of Lieutenant-Commander James E. Jouett. Although the days of battle under sail alone ended at Navarino Bay in 1827 with the destruction of a Turkish fleet by an Allied squadron composed of British, French and Russian ships, close-quarter fighting was still very much the rule, as it was to be for some years to come.

In order to have a clear view of his fleet and its task Farragut, during the approach, stood in the rigging of the *Hartford*. Although this was a peculiar position for a flag officer in battle, it was dictated by common sense. His size—just over five foot six—his nimbleness and constant physical exercise made such activity natural to him. It was only the particular circumstances which would have called for any remark.

Not far from the Admiral was Jouett of the *Metacomet*, standing on top of his wheelhouse, as much exposed to fire as the captains of the monitors, who spurned the protection of their iron conning-towers. The pilot was in the *Hartford*'s main-top, again in an odd post, but with the advantage of complete freedom from smoke. As this increased and rose higher, Farragut himself changed his position until he was almost beside him.

Captain Drayton became alarmed for the Admiral's safety and sent a seaman, Watson, aloft with a lashing. Watson remarked that if the Commander-in-Chief insisted on standing where he did, he might as well make himself fast. 'I thanked that dear boy for his consideration,' said Farragut later, 'and took a turn around and over the shrouds and around my body for fear of being wounded, as shots were flying rather thickly.'

The two-column approach which had been decided on, monitors nearest to Fort Morgan, wooden ships with their attendant ships parallel, soon neared the known minefield and the narrowing of the navigable channel which was thought to be clear. The *Tecumseh* seemed to be reserving her fire for the *Tennessee* which, with the other Confederate ships, was in position beyond the Fort. Then came disaster. Both the *Tecumseh*'s and the *Brooklyn*'s captains seemed to be in doubt as to the true line of the channel. The columns were bunching and were in immediate danger of confusion, right under the guns of the Fort. The *Tecumseh* then steered directly for the Confederate iron-clad, and, whether by accident or calculated risk, crossed the line where torpedoes were known to have been placed. Almost at once there was an underwater explosion. The monitor lurched to starboard and sank bows foremost, her screws revolving as she disappeared.

Farragut stood on. As the *Hartford* passed the *Brooklyn*, her captain still in perplexity, with his engines at slow and his bows now headed towards the Fort, he shouted across to the Admiral that there were torpedoes directly ahead of him. Farragut's answer came swiftly. 'Damn the torpedoes!' he shouted. 'Captain Drayton, go ahead! Jouett, full speed!'

The decision was justified. There were indeed torpedoes where they had not been expected. Some were actually heard knocking against the *Hartford*'s plates; primers snapped, or so it was believed, but no explosions followed, and the *Tecumseh* was the only loss from this sinister form of defence.

When he had negotiated the minefield, Farragut ordered the paddle-wheel steamers to detach themselves from the wooden ships of war and chase the smaller Confederates, an order which was obeyed with zest. Then, at 8.30, an hour after firing began, the flagship anchored about four miles from Fort Morgan, and the men were sent to break-fast.

The *Tennessee* meanwhile had moved under the batteries of Fort Morgan which, though unsubdued, could do Farragut no harm since he was now beyond the traverse of their guns. The right tactics for the captain of the *Tennessee*, Franklin Buchanan, who had been in charge of the *Merrimac* in her duel with the prototype monitor at Hampton Roads, would have been to stay where he was. If he moved, he should have tried to keep his opponents at as great a distance as possible, since his guns had the range of anything the Federals pos-sessed.

Now that Farragut was past the Fort, Buchanan knew that the Confederate gunboats would get short shrift from the superior Federals. He therefore felt it his duty, as well as a point of honour, to attack, making the *Hartford* his principal target. Even before Farragut's men had finished their meal the *Tennessee* had shifted position and was heading towards them. Farragut sent an order to the monitors to intercept, using the Fleet Surgeon, Dr Palmer, as messenger. 'Happy as my friend Perkins of the *Chickasaw* habitually is,' recorded Palmer later, 'I thought he would turn a somersault overboard with joy when I told him: "The Admiral wants you to go at once and fight that *Tennessee*!"' Lieutenant-Commander George H. Perkins, the officer concerned, had served enthusiastically in all Farragut's previous operations.

Three hours after the Confederates first opened fire, Buchanan surrendered. He was wounded, and his ship had been so rammed and blasted that he had no choice. Mobile Port had been entered at a cost to the Union of 335 men, of whom 113 lay coffined in the iron hull of the *Tecumseh*. The *Hartford* had 25 killed and 28 wounded out of a ship's company of some 300, and the *Brooklyn*'s list was much the same. The work of the fleet was soon completed by the army, and when all the local forts had surrendered, General Granger wrote a tribute to the Navy very much like that of Townshend after the capture of Quebec.

> I am pleased to record the perfect harmony existing between the two branches of the Service. For my own part, I cannot sufficiently acknowledge the assistance rendered by the Fleet and the Admiral in command in transporting and disembarking the troops, guns and materials employed by me in the operations. In brief, during all our operations, the officers of the Fleet, with their distinguished Commander, displayed in a high degree those qualities which mark their gallant service.

Farragut stayed in the area of Mobile Bay for some months after the engagement—indeed, up to the limit of his endurance. 'This is the last of my work,' he wrote home, 'and I expect a little respite.'

Those who knew him best, men like Captain Drayton, grew anxious. 'I was talking to the Admiral today,' wrote Perkins of the *Chickasaw* shortly after Fort Morgan had surrendered, 'when all at once he fainted away . . . It gave me quite a shock, and shows how exhausted he is, and his health is not very good, any way. He is a mighty fine old fellow.'

Word at last reached the Navy Department about the Admiral's condition, and he was released. He sailed from Pensacola on 30 November 1864 and reached New York twelve days later. There, he received a frenzied welcome, and an address which must have been drafted by someone of particular sympathy. It read:

> The citizens of New York can offer no tribute equal to your claim on their gratitude and affection. Their earnest desire is to receive you as one of their number, and to be permitted, as fellow-citizens, to share in the renown you will bring to the metropolitan city. This desire is felt in common by the whole community.

The words were accompanied by the gift of $50,000, which in those far-off days was enough to ensure that Farragut could acquire a residence in the city. The United States Government, not to be outdone in courtesy, created the rank of Vice-Admiral, to which the veteran was at once appointed.

When the Confederate city of Richmond was occupied by Union troops in April 1865, Farragut was among the first to visit the fallen capital, whence he returned briefly to his old home in Norfolk. This was perhaps unwise, for feelings remained bitter long after the fighting was over, and the Admiral was happier on some of his later visits, for instance, to New England, and later in Europe.

In July 1866, Congress passed a law creating the rank of Admiral. This was at once given to Farragut, and he was duly succeeded in the rank by David D. Porter, his companion-in-arms and friend. The following year Farragut was posted to the European Squadron, with his flag in the steam frigate *Franklin*. Without any request on his part, the Navy Department allowed Mrs Farragut and a kinswoman to accompany him.

The cruise was triumphant. It had been many decades since Farragut had had the chance to visit the Mediterranean, and he did not neglect Minorca, the home of his ancestors. He left the Mediterranean in April 1868 and England was included in a tour of ports in Northern Europe. He was presented to Queen Victoria, against whose grandfather's Navy he had fought as a boy.

In the summer of 1870 the Navy Department placed the steamer *Tallapoosa* at the disposal of the admiral and his family. He took her to Portsmouth, New Hampshire, where he was the guest of the Commandant of the Navy Yard. It was his last sea voyage. Farragut died at the Commandant's house on 14 August 1870, aged sixty-nine. His funeral was attended by General Grant, who by then was President of the United States.

The *Hartford* long survived the man whose flag she had flown in battle. A photograph dating from early in the present century shows her at sea, and even under sail, square-rigged on fore- and mainmasts, fore- and aft-rigged on the mizen, the Stars and Stripes flying from the peak. The ship succumbed at last to old age and sank at the very Yard where Farragut died. Many of her fittings were salvaged as reminders of her glory.

It is not enough to say that Farragut never wronged anyone and never made an ememy. The affection he inspired was as simple, as firmly rooted and as genuine as he was himself. He was denied the supreme test of an admiral's stature in his own profession, a fleet action against a powerful enemy, but in every other respect he proved himself the complete sea commander, with attributes, in his later years, generally found only in younger men.

11

Beatty of the 'Lion'

From America's David Farragut to Britain's David Beatty might appear to involve a long step, though it was not in fact so far as all that. Beatty was born in 1871, less than a year after Farragut's death. Some of his early training was done, like all of Farragut's, in sail. But Beatty epitomizes naval warfare under steam and, to those whose memory extends back to the earlier years of this century, he is pre-eminently associated with the battle-cruiser *Lion*. She was his flagship for three crowded years. In her he fought three of the major surface engagements of the First World War.

Beatty was an Irishman who shared his compatriots' love of horses and the chase. His great-great-grandfather had fought at Waterloo, and his father at one time held a commission in the 4th Hussars, the regiment in which Winston Churchill later served. His mother came from County Meath, but settled with her husband first near Nantwich and then at Rugby, in the heart of hunting districts. There were five children, four boys and a girl, all of whom became fine riders. The boys proved themselves good officers when the country needed leaders in time of war. The daughter, Kathleen, who shared her brothers' interests, married an army officer. The whole family thought in terms of hunting or steeplechasing, and of them David, the second son, proved to be the most thoughtful. He decided at an early age that he wanted to be a sailor. He had a good share of brains, otherwise he could not have passed tenth out of 99 competitors into the training ship *Britannia*. Thirty-two candidates were successful, and of these, seven reached flag rank.

Beatty's first appointment was to have been to the China Squadron. When she heard the news, his mother thought she could do better for him. She took the train to London on the plea of shopping, saw her hunting friend Lord Charles Beresford, who knew those in high places, and suggested that her David should be sent to 'the best ship in the Navy'. Beresford was susceptible to charm, and enjoyed wire-pulling. The result of the London trip was that Beatty went to the *Alexandra*. She was the flagship of the Commander-in-Chief, Mediterranean, and the fastest battleship in the Navy. The admiral was H.R.H. the Duke of Edinburgh, second son of Queen Victoria, an officer of high attainments, like so many earlier and later members of his family. Prince George of Wales, afterwards King George V, was serving in the ship as a lieutenant.

When Beatty joined in January 1886, shortly after he had reached the age of fifteen, it was at a time when the Navy was in transition.

The *Alexandra*, which had been completed in 1877 and served as a flagship throughout her active career, was fully rigged, and she had side armour of malleable iron. She had been given 11-inch and 10-inch muzzle-loading guns arranged in broadsides on two decks within a central citadel. If such ordnance appeared to be old-fashioned, the *Alexandra* was one of the last ships to be thus armed, and one of the first to be equipped with a device which had been developed by Robert Whitehead, working at Fiume. This was the first practicable locomotive torpedo. From Whitehead's day onwards, mines were known as such. The word torpedo came to denote a much more flexible weapon, fired by air impulse.

The *Alexandra* was a good start to a career, and Beatty made the most of it. Besides the illustrious in cabin and wardroom, there were those in the gunroom, the midshipmen's mess, who were to rise to distinction. They included Walter Cowan and Reginald Tyrwhitt, friends and fellow-admirals in Beatty's later years.

Beatty's next ship was a contrast. She was the *Ruby*, described as a 'masted corvette'. She had been built in 1876, and he joined her for 'intensive seamanship training'. While serving in her, he got a step in rank to sub-lieutenant. The captain, W. A. Piggott, was a seaman of the old breed. 'I really think he loved the *Ruby* most when she was half-submerged like a good swimmer doing the crawl,' wrote one of her officers. Piggott disliked using his engines and once made a passage under sail of nineteen days from St Vincent to Trinidad.

After the *Ruby* it was back to battleships, first to the *Camperdown*, which had been involved in a tragic collision on manoeuvres with the *Victoria*, and then to the *Trafalgar*, by which time Beatty was a lieutenant, a rank he attained during a few weeks' service on board the royal yacht *Victoria and Albert*. Like most young officers he preferred the life of a smaller ship to the spit-and-polish inevitable in a larger one. He was in luck, for Stanley Colville, who was the *Trafalgar*'s commander, was given charge of a flotilla of river gunboats which were to work in support of an army engaged in the Sudan against the Khalifa, leader of the people who, eleven years earlier, had been responsible for the death of General Gordon at Khartoum.

This was adventure, and a chance to show initiative. It also made Beatty acquainted with a young man, three years his junior, who had attached himself to the field army as a war correspondent, against the express wishes of Kitchener, the Commander-in-Chief. Winston Churchill, in his book on the Sudan campaign, *The River War*, stressed the vital importance of Colville's gunboats, among which the *Abu Klea* was commanded by Lieutenant Beatty. They were shallow-draught steamers with stern paddles, lightly protected, and armed with quick-firing Nordenfelt guns.

During his first serious engagement, at Hafir, near the Third Cataract, the *Abu Klea* was hit by a shell which lodged in the magazine but did not explode. Beatty, realizing the danger to the ship, picked it up and threw it overboard. He did not report the incident, but it was of a kind which more than once in the past had earned the Victoria Cross. Colville, who was badly wounded, had to turn over the command to his subordinate. The gunboats were the first to occupy Dongola, in September 1896, and Beatty, on Colville's recommendation, which was strongly supported by Kitchener, was awarded the Distinguished Service Order, and his name was noted at the Admiralty for early promotion.

Beatty was given leave of absence during the campaign, but he returned home to the very sad news of his mother's death. When he was once more on active service, it was for the final stages of the advance against the Khalifa. Beatty narrowly survived the capsize of his gunboat *El Teb* in the Fourth Cataract, and was then given the newer *Fateh*. He was present at the culminating battle of Omdurman, at one stage helping the 21st Lancers with his fire. It was with this regiment that Winston Churchill took part in the last of those cavalry charges which played such a spectacular part in nineteenth-century warfare.

On flotilla service with Beatty were two special friends, Walter Cowan, once of the *Alexandra*, and Horace Hood, who, like Beatty, was to be given exceptionally early promotion. Hood and Beatty were in fact gazetted commanders in November 1898. Beatty was then twenty-seven, and had been a lieutenant for only six years. The average age spent in the rank was at that time over twelve years. The promotion took him over the heads of 395 officers, every one of whom must have gnashed his teeth in that Beatty seemed to be having all the luck.

What more natural than that when Colville was appointed captain of the *Barfleur*, which flew the flag of the second-in-command, China Station, he should ask for Beatty as his executive officer? Beatty went out to the Far East not, as had at one time seemed likely, as a junior 'snotty', but in a responsible rank. His ship was the successor to the famous vessel which had operational service ranging from the battle of the Saints in 1782 to Sir Robert Calder's action against Villeneuve in 1805. Her ship's company were not expecting anything other than routine duties in China. These they regarded as irksome, and there was envy of the men directly concerned with the war in South Africa, which was then engaging a high proportion of Britain's manpower.

Excitement was just round the corner. The British Ambassador at Peking suddenly requested that guards should be sent to the Legation, which was in danger from an anti-foreign organization called the 'Righteous Harmony Fists', colloquially known as the Boxers. The *Barfleur* was ordered to anchor off the Taku bar, at the mouth of Pei-ho River, the nearest point to Peking. A force of mixed nationalities was assembled. It included Russians, French, Germans, Americans, Austrians, Italians and Japanese. It was significant of the prestige then enjoyed by the British Navy that in spite of the unpopularity of the country almost throughout the world, owing to the current conflict with the Boer Republics, everyone agreed to serve under Admiral Sir Edward Seymour, the British Commander-in-Chief.

The fighting ashore in North China before the Boxer rising was suppressed was protracted and heavy, for the Chinese were better armed than the hordes of the Khalifa. Beatty, with a party from the *Barfleur*, was always to the fore, his courage and leadership being outstanding. Many officers who were later to play important parts in the First World War also distinguished themselves, among them Jellicoe, who was wounded in the chest; Cradock, who lost his life in 1914 off Coronel fighting von Spee; and Roger Keyes. Beatty himself was twice wounded, once seriously, but he carried on, his arm in a sling. A young midshipman who was acting as his ADC was mortally wounded at his side, and B. J. D. Guy, midshipman of the *Barfleur*, won the Victoria Cross for rescuing wounded under heavy fire. He was the first of his rank to have been so honoured since the Crimea.

Beatty did so well that, after only two years as a commander, he was promoted captain, with seniority dating from November 1900. This made him the youngest captain in the Navy, and put him ahead of 217 officers on the list of commanders. He was still under thirty, the average of a captain at that time being forty-two. He had been greatly liked in the *Barfleur*. 'We, his ship-mates,' wrote one of the lieutenants, 'were the losers by his promotion, as we were deprived of his company and leadership, under which the *Barfleur* was such an efficient and happy ship.'

Beatty had long been in love with a married woman. She was Ethel Tree, daughter of Marshall Field, a Chicago millionaire and a pioneer of the chain-store. Ethel Tree, like Beatty, was a fearless rider, and spent some of her happiest hours in the hunting-field, but she was inclined to be spoilt, a characteristic which did not diminish with time. There was no scandal. Ethel Tree was divorced in the United States on the ground of her desertion of her husband, and she and Beatty were married in London in May 1901, when Beatty was thirty and his wife twenty-seven. Both partners were strong-willed, but while Beatty was devoted to the Navy, in which he intended to remain in spite of his wife's wealth, she was mainly concerned with getting her own way. This included a house in London, a place in Leicestershire for hunting, a grouse moor in Scotland, and a steam yacht.

Beatty's wound took far longer to put right than anyone expected and left him with two fingers permanently crippled. He gave it no chance to recover through rest, for he actually hunted and even took part in point-to-point races long before the doctors certified him as fit for sea duty. When at last they did, in July 1902, he was appointed to the cruiser *Juno*, belonging to the Mediterranean Fleet. Although small, the ship was comparatively new and well armed. She had eleven 6-inch guns and three torpedo tubes. Beatty found her Commander was much older than himself, and the ship's drill and shooting were at first deplorable. The new captain changed that. Even the grimy toil of 'coaling ship' could be speeded up by vigorous methods. Beatty wrote to his wife in October:

> The wretched collier did not get alongside till 11 p.m. We started coaling at 11.30. and finished at 1 a.m. The men worked like Trojans, and got the 166 tons in at the rate of 110 tons an hour when they had never done more than 64 tons an hour before in the three years they have been in commission. Even the Commander was smiling, although at first he was much annoyed because I had torn up his arrangements and made him carry out mine, but the end justified the means, and the old dear doesn't bear any malice.

Command of two other cruisers followed, the *Arrogant* and *Suffolk*. Ethel Beatty followed her husband south to Malta, where their first child was born. Beatty got into trouble with the authorities on one occasion for driving the *Suffolk* too fast, against the advice of his Chief Engineer. This damaged her engines, a serious matter, for she was about twice the size of the *Juno* and brand-new. There was talk of a court martial, and Mrs Beatty was reported to have said: 'What!—court martial my David? I'll buy them a new ship!'

Beatty left the Mediterranean in September 1905 and spent a year on half pay. He was then given the job of Naval Adviser to the Army Council, which enabled them to live in London. At the end of two years he relinquished the post in favour of a sea-going command. She was the battleship *Queen*, a successor to the three-decker which had done such notable service with Gardner in the fleet of Lord Howe.

The *Queen*, like every other capital ship afloat, had just been made obsolescent by the launch of Fisher's turbine-driven, all big-gun *Dreadnought*, but Beatty soon turned her into one of the smartest battleships in the fleet. He insisted on speed, system and realism, encouraging his officers to perform their duties as if they were under war conditions, since he was sure that war was coming.

Circumstanced as he was, Beatty could afford to be critical of his superiors, not to their faces, but certainly in the way he sometimes handled his ships. An amusing instance had occurred in the modest *Juno* when, against all etiquette, he crossed the bows of the fleet flagship. The Commander-in-Chief was Sir Arthur Wilson—'Old 'ard 'eart' to the sailors. Wilson signalled for an explanation. The reply flashed back: 'It was the quickest way to my station.' Wilson was satisfied.

If Beatty was one of the few captains who did not risk everything worth living for by speaking his mind, at least he had a mind to speak. There were many flag officers he thought antiquated or muddle-headed, and few that he approved wholeheartedly. Foremost among the best was Prince Louis of Battenberg, soon to become First Sea Lord. 'Charming and simple,' Beatty called him, 'and yet all there.' Prince Louis was equally approving of Beatty, and when Beatty left the *Queen* he wrote: 'My wish was that the other ships might be as good.'

This was an age of naval expansion, chiefly due to the size of a German naval programme which had been the life work of von Tirpitz, aided by Kaiser Wilhelm II, who regarded the Imperial Navy as his particular toy. The Kaiser was a reader of Mahan on Sea Power, which might have made him realise that to build the second most powerful navy in the world, in addition to having the most powerful army in Europe, was inviting every sort of trouble. Whether it would have deterred him is doubtful.

Beatty was now likely to be closely concerned with the way in which the Navy was being run, for he had become the senior captain. When he got his flag, as he duly did in January 1910, he was, at thirty-nine, the youngest admiral since the era of Nelson. He was destined for high command unless his luck deserted him.

Although he could afford to take chances, he never took a bigger one than when he turned down an appointment offered him as Second-in-Command, Atlantic Fleet. He was at once put on half-pay. It happened to suit him, and Ethel too, and his two young sons also benefited from having their father at home, but he had incurred the displeasure of their Lordships. It would take a war, or a friend of exceptional influence, to set him on the right path once more. Sure enough, the friend came along. It was Winston Churchill.

At that time Churchill must have been one of the happiest men alive, if health, energy, copious ideas, absorption in a task which fascinated him, a happy marriage, a position of power, and the excitement of politics could make him so. He had exchanged the office of Home

Secretary for that of First Lord of the Admiralty and at the age of thirty-seven became responsible to the country for the world's largest maritime armament. What more could an ambitious man hope for at his time of life?

The answer was, someone nearer to his own generation than the grave and for the most part conservative admirals who sat with him in the famous Board Room with its wind vane and its portraits of William IV and Nelson. He found Beatty. The Sea Lords, or most of them, were against giving the silver-spooned prodigy employment, but there was no denying Churchill, who made Beatty his Naval Secretary. They had served together in the desert with good results. It would be so again. Churchill could pour out all his schemes, practical and otherwise, to Beatty.

The post of Naval Secretary could be made highly influential by an officer of drive. The Naval Secretary was responsible for captains' appointments; he acted as liaison between the Admiralty and the Palace; and in the days before a naval staff had been properly organized, he was the principal technical adviser to civilian First Lords. The duties were entirely different from those of the Permanent Secretary, the office once occupied by Pepys, who was head of the civilian staff. A Naval Secretary had the best possible opportunity to ensure that his own next post led towards the top.

With a First Lord as restless and dynamic as Churchill, it was inevitable that Beatty should be worked hard. This he welcomed. Most people other than regular naval officers would also have enjoyed the trips which Churchill made in the Admiralty yacht *Enchantress*, which was well equipped and could accommodate guests. Beatty was reserved about such excursions, which were apt to bore him, but they led to remarkable contacts.

He soon found himself preparing memoranda on all sorts of subjects, chiefly strategical, at Churchill's instigation. As he had always been keenly interested in the wider aspects of naval warfare this was no great strain, except for the actual writing. In general, Beatty could hold his own in any society, and indeed he often had to, for although he once shied at embarking with Churchill's colleague Lloyd George, whom he looked upon as a demagogue of a most unfortunate type, the Liberal Prime Minister, Asquith, was quite another matter, though Beatty found that even he could be tedious.

Many leading personalities were at one time or another aboard the *Enchantress*, and on one particular occasion, in June 1912, Beatty found himself dining with the Prime Minister, Prince Louis, Churchill and Lord Kitchener. As he told his wife, 'I must keep my wits about me.'

The conversation could hardly help being of extreme interest, for this group of men had interests far beyond the Navy.

Beatty served Churchill for a year, except for a short break in the summer of 1912 when, to test his capacity in sea-going command, he was given ten days to prepare a reserve cruiser squadron for manoeuvres, and was then ordered to take it to sea, his flag in the *Aboukir*. His performance was evidently held to be adequate, for in March 1913 he was appointed to the Battle Cruiser Squadron, with his flag in H.M.S. *Lion*. This was the most dazzling command in the Navy.

⚓   ⚓   ⚓

The idea of the battle cruiser, which students of war described as a hybrid term for a hybrid type of ship, derived from Admiral Sir John Fisher, the genius and disrupter of the Navy as Beatty knew it. As early as 1902 Fisher was considering a plan for a fast vessel which he playfully christened H.M.S. *Unapproachable*. The reality came about in 1908, when the *Invincible* was completed. This ship, and her sisters, combined speed with punch, protection coming a poor third. It was believed that they would be able to destroy inferior ships while themselves keeping out of range.

By the time Beatty took command of the battle cruisers seven had been completed, of which the *Lion* and her sister ship the *Princess Royal* were the largest. The *Queen Mary*, very slightly larger still, was nearly ready. Their function under war conditions was to expand, for the Germans were building them, and with good protection. It was laid down that the first task, when battle was joined, was the destruction of similar enemy vessels if present, and 'after their destruction, or in their absence, to attack the van of the enemy's battle fleet'.

Beatty chose Ernle Chatfield, a gunnery specialist, as his flag captain and the two men suited one another perfectly. The *Lion* was vast and impressive. Built at Devonport dockyard, she mounted eight 13.5-inch guns and twenty-eight smaller ones, had two torpedo tubes, and her turbines gave her a maximum speed of 28 knots, seven knots faster than any British battleship afloat. She displaced 26,350 tons, and her complement was well over a thousand.

Few works of man have presented such an awe-inspiring sight as a battle cruiser squadron at full power, every ship being reckoned the equivalent, in Churchill's view, of an army division. Steaming between 25 and 28 knots, with bow and stern waves piling and creaming fore and aft, funnels pouring smoke visibly lifted by the forced draught of the furnaces, the underside of the black cloud a dull red glow, they gave the impression of irresistible might.

When firing her guns, a ship would be momentarily obliterated by circles of dazzling orange flame. These would be followed by tremendous concussion, the mere blast causing a flurry of spray across the surface of the sea. Seconds later, a thick, sepia mass of burnt cordite whirled away astern. Then another salvo followed. When firing broadsides, the combined flash was sometimes so great as to give the impression that the ship had blown up. It is not surprising that deafness was common among naval gunners.

In a memorable passage in his *Harbours of England*, Ruskin once wrote:

> . . . it will always be said of us, with unabated reverence 'They built Ships of the Line.' Take it all in all, a Ship of the Line is the most honourable thing that man, as a gregarious animal, has ever produced. By himself, unhelped, he can do better things than Ships of the Line; he can make poems and pictures, and other such concentrations of what is best in him. But as a being living in flocks, and hammering out, with alternate strokes and mutual agreement, what is necessary for him in those flocks, to get or produce, the Ship of the Line is his first work. Into that he has put as much of his human patience, common sense, forethought, experimental philosophy, self-control, habits of order and obedience, thoroughly wrought handwork, defiance of brute elements, careless courage, careful patriotism, and calm expectation of the judgement of God as can well be put into a space of 300 feet long by 80 broad.

At a time when steam had replaced wind, steel replaced wood, guns extended their range beyond the horizon, and size expanded to more than twice the length of the largest man-of-war under sail, there was still some truth in Ruskin's passage. The big ships of Fisher's Navy did indeed represent 'might, majesty, dominion and power'. And they often had a beauty of line which could not have displeased the seamen of earlier years.

By the time Beatty took command of his squadron he had developed certain personal peculiarities which distinguished him from the more conventional flag officer and helped towards a popular image of a dashing hero. There was, for instance, his six-button monkey-jacket when eight was more usual, and his cap worn at a rakish angle. He had a disconcerting way, possibly the result of pain from his wound, of suddenly screwing up his face into a fearsome grimace and holding it there.

Beatty believed in letting his officers get on with it, and as his flagship was refitting when his appointment came through, he took himself off to Monte Carlo. On one occasion, in the earlier days of his command, he was expected to arrive at Weymouth about midnight as the ships had orders to sail in the morning. The barge crew waited for him until 3 a.m., when he suddenly appeared, saying to the officer of the watch, 'Let the barge crew have a lie-in: I'm sorry I'm late, but I hired a taxi in Piccadilly and told him to drive to Weymouth and the damned fellow lost his way twice!' Considering the taxis of those days, that would have been an epic journey.

Chatfield's early impression of Beatty, formed when he joined the armoured cruiser *Aboukir* for the Admiral's brief spell with the Reserve Fleet, was never modified. He wrote:

> I quickly realized that I was with a man of exacting character. Each ship Beatty had served in from the rank of Commander he had brought to a high state of efficiency. He had a love of doing everything at high pressure and high speed. This was not a pose: it was entirely characteristic: whether at sea or in the hunting field . . . yet he had a great power of restraint when he judged it to be necessary.

Although Chatfield was right in his main diagnosis, Beatty was not without pose, or he would not have allowed himself those idiosyncrasies which journalists seized upon. He sometimes spoke of himself as a victim of the Press. To some extent this was true, but to a greater degree it was his own fault. It also brought benefits. It kept his name before the public. Those he commanded felt themselves to be in the limelight. This was good for morale, and helped towards smartness, though it could lead to resentment on the part of others not so favoured.

There was less than a year and a half between the time when Beatty took charge of the battle cruisers and the opening of the First World War. A few optimists might have had doubts as to whether Armageddon would come. In the Royal Navy the question was not 'if' but 'when', for every sailor knew that in German ships the nightly toast, given with arrogant confidence, was '*Der Tag*'.

The months of preparation were strenuous. There were occasional diversions, such as a visit to Brest in February 1914, when the *Entente Cordiale* was well and truly celebrated, and another in June to Russia. Riga, Revel and Kronstadt were the ports of call, the Russians even excelling the French in the profusion of their hospitality. In the Gulf of Finland, the Tsar had the chance to see a fast, fully trained squadron undergoing manoeuvres in close order in an area to which, under conditions of modern war, they could never hope to penetrate with Germany hostile. It was significant that Beatty made a passage through the difficult waters of the Belt, once so familiar to Saumarez.

Beatty received the Knighthood of the Bath in the Birthday Honours of 1914, and Ethel thus became Lady Beatty. Her varied social life continued as long as possible, but after the late summer it would become, to her, almost intolerably circumscribed. Her husband's daily wartime letters, so far from being a solace, were all too often concerned with how best to soothe her. That remained his task until her death seventeen years later.

As for the war itself, it is hard, even after sixty years' hindsight, wholly to disagree with what Beatty wrote on the day it opened:

> . . . it is a cruel war, because there never has been any reason for it. We have been forced into it, entirely through the rapacity and thirst for power, and a large portion of the world, by Germany. Never in the history of the world has there been so little reason or so little cause.

Germany was so well prepared, so ready to regard solemn treaties she had signed herself as scraps of paper, that the earlier phases included many sharp shocks. The Navy felt them as well as the nation as a whole, and at the same time much of what was actually achieved at sea was unsensational, and in any case could not be trumpeted.

The German battle cruiser *Goeben*, accompanied by the light cruiser *Breslau*, was allowed to reach Turkey, a fact which was to alter the scheme of alliance adversely to Britain, France and Russia. Admiral Cradock, with whom Beatty had served in China, met with defeat and death off Chile, but was avenged a few weeks later by battle cruisers dispatched from home under Admiral Sturdee. The Germans showed themselves expert in mine-laying, sinking the new battleship *Audacious* by this means; whilst a single submarine accounted for three armoured cruisers in quick succession, the *Aboukir*, *Hogue* and *Cressy*, with heavy loss of life.

What was not apparent to the public at large was that the German merchant fleet, one of the best in the world, ceased to sail: that Germany herself was distantly blockaded: and that the British Expeditionary Force was transported to France without loss. It would be supplied by the Navy for the duration of the struggle.

There was one other matter for encouragement. On 28 August 1914, although there was no full-scale naval battle such as most people had expected, and looked forward to, a mêlée occurred in the Bight of Heligoland between British and German forces. Owing to poor liaison between the various naval Commands it was in some ways an unsatisfactory affair. Nevertheless, it was a clear-cut victory, and the credit was due to Beatty.

The operations were devised, without much thought, in the hope of provoking the Germans into risking some of their bigger ships. Submarines under Roger Keyes and destroyers from Harwich under Reginald Tyrwhitt were to be the spearhead of a raid on a very heavily defended area. Anything, so it was felt, was better than the tension of waiting for an enemy who showed no signs of eagerness to do battle.

Through a combination of inexperience and accident, the staff work at the Admiralty was atrocious. Jellicoe, away at Scapa with the Grand Fleet, was never properly put into the picture. In the course of the proceedings, British submarines attacked their own cruisers, luckily without success, mistaking them for the enemy. Tyrwhitt, flying his broad pendant in the *Arethusa*, entrusted himself to a ship only three days out of the builder's hands. Not surprisingly, considering how long most ships take to 'work up', all but one of her 6-inch guns jammed immediately after firing.

The German reaction was to support their local patrols with cruisers, which fought splendidly. They hit the *Arethusa* so hard that she had to summon destroyers, which were also soon hit. It was quickly apparent that it would need all Tyrwhitt's skill and luck to make a good retreat without serious loss.

Suddenly, shortly after noon on a day of mist, Beatty appeared from the north-west, leading his battle cruisers at full speed to the help of the flotillas, straight into an area of sea within a few miles of Heligoland itself. An officer in one of the destroyers wrote:

> There, straight ahead of us in lovely procession, like elephants walking through a pack of pi-dogs, came the *Lion*, *Queen Mary*, *Invincible* and *New Zealand*, great and grim as some antediluvian monsters. How solid they looked, how utterly earthquaking.

The reality did not belie the impression. Beatty had a hard decision to make in taking the battle cruisers into the Bight at all. He considered all the risks, and discounted them one by one. Even so, he was a little uneasy, and said to Chatfield, 'Am I justified in going into that hornets' nest with these great ships? If I lose one it will be a great blow to the country.' Chatfield was in no sort of doubt.

With the whole-hearted support of his staff, knowing his squadron to be trained to a hair and longing for action, Beatty felt as confident in action as he had ever done as a younger man.

His intervention was decisive, not to say eruptive. As a result, the Germans lost three cruisers, one destroyer and 1,200 men killed, wounded or taken prisoner, including two flag officers. All the British ships got home, and although material damage was serious, human loss was small, 35 killed and 40 wounded. The *Arethusa* arrived under tow, which she would never have done but for Beatty.

As a result of the fracas (through which so much faulty staff work was revealed on both sides, not all of it corrected), there was gloom in the German fleet and euphoria among the battle cruisers. One direct result was that the Kaiser declared that all sallies by his ships must be approved by himself.

The British had no monopoly of the habit of insulting enemy coasts, as the Germans soon proved. In past centuries the French had made many raids on Channel towns, sometimes with devastating results, but the general public knew no history to speak of and would not have been impressed if they had. So when, early in November, German battle cruisers bombarded Great Yarmouth, and in December, Scarborough, Hartlepool and Whitby, causing civilian casualties to the number of 122 killed and 343 wounded, indignation knew no bounds. The affair did not surprise the Admiralty, which had always expected such alarms. What was disappointing was that the raiders were not intercepted. This was partly due to bad luck, largely to weather conditions, bad signalling and too rigid adherence to the idea that you must 'wait till the Admiral says'. British officers had many forms of courage, but few possessed the kind that Nelson showed when he disobeyed orders at St Vincent and Copenhagen because he could see what was happening more clearly than his Commander-in-Chief.

When the Germans were making for home after the Scarborough raid, Commodore Goodenough in the cruiser *Southampton* actually made contact with the enemy's cruiser screen, and only broke off action because of a signal from Beatty which was not intended for ships engaged, of which there were two. The signal was drafted by Ralph Seymour, Beatty's flag lieutenant who, as was customary in those days, combined the duty of signal officer with attendance on the Admiral. This was one of a series of mischances deriving from this particular officer, but the blame really rested with a system under which, while communications grew ever more complex, they continued to be handled at sea in an unsatisfactory way.

As for too rigid obedience, Beatty wrote to Jellicoe after the episode:

I had in personal interviews previously impressed on him [Goodenough] that he might always use the freest discretion, and that if he, on the spot, considered any of my orders unsuitable to the existing situation he should never hesitate to vary them and report to me. This indeed is an elementary duty of cruiser officers.

Elementary or not, the principle that, when necessary, a senior officer should disobey, did not always get home, either then or later. Goodenough was not relieved, and later did splendidly in action, but it seemed that officers needed at least one lesson in enlightened initiative. Beatty was exceptionally loyal to his subordinates, sometimes excessively so, and it was also Churchill's view that men should be allowed at least one chance to redeem errors due to inexperience or misjudgement.

There was terrible frustration, even among the battle cruisers which had at least seen some action: it was worse in the Grand Fleet, away at Scapa Flow, which had not. What made it so difficult to bear was the continuous heavy fighting and appalling casualties occurring on the Western Front. In the North Sea, gales, snow, sleet, rain, mist, fog, continuous cold all too often made it a miserable place for sea campaigning against a foe who never appeared. Beatty wrote to his wife:

> Can't you understand the feeling of hopeless inutility which comes over one from time to time when we spend days doing nothing, when so many are doing so much? . . . My great barns of cabins are like vaults, I never get them warm . . . There is no joy in life under such conditions . . . It's a wonderful thing, hope. We live on it, month in and month out . . . My time *must* come!

These were exactly the feelings expressed by generations of commanders in the days of the blockade of Brest and Toulon. But at least men like Beatty could relieve their minds to those who they felt might understand them. For inarticulate men, the sense of impotent waiting, in conditions of perpetual discomfort, was like a deadweight.

Beatty's time *did* come, on 24 January 1915. The occasion could have been turned into a 'chase' victory such as would have rejoiced Lord Hawke. In the event, it was not so.

Intelligence had reached Beatty at noon the previous day that Admiral Hipper, who commanded the German battle cruisers, had been ordered on a reconnaissance in the direction of the Dogger Bank. Beatty sailed that evening with the *Lion*, *Tiger*, *Princess Royal*, *New Zealand* and *Indomitable*, together with a squadron of light cruisers under Goodenough. Tyrwhitt's flotillas from Harwich were also at sea, and it was the *Aurora*, one of the Harwich cruisers, which first gained touch with the enemy during the night.

At dawn on 24 January Goodenough, who was about five miles to eastward of the *Lion*, sighted Hipper right ahead. Hipper turned for home and Beatty ordered his ships to work up to maximum speed. The chase was on. By 8 a.m. the quarry was in sight of Beatty, fine on the *Lion*'s port bow, with at least 150 miles to traverse before shore defences could cover the German ships. Visibility was good, the sea was calm, and even a North Sea winter's day seemed to promise the necessary time to ensure the destruction of the enemy. By 9.20 a.m. all the heavy ships were in action except the *Indomitable* which, being older and slower than the rest, gradually dropped astern, though she was doing so well that Beatty signalled, 'Well done, *Indomitable*'s stokers'. At first, the British ships concentrated their fire on the German rear ship, the *Blücher*, which was scarcely a battle cruiser at all and had only eight 2-inch guns. The Germans made the *Lion* their target. Hipper had the *Seydlitz* as his flagship, then came the *Moltke*, *Derfflinger* and *Blücher*.

As the range closed, Beatty ordered a ship-to-ship distribution of fire, but the *Tiger*, which had never before fired her guns at a moving target, and was not yet fully worked up, mistakenly concentrated on the *Seydlitz*, leaving the *Moltke* unmarked. As a result, this powerful ship was able to give her undivided attention to the *Lion*.

Apart from the *Blücher*, which was clearly doomed unless Hipper reversed course, supported by a sortie from the main High Seas Fleet, the ship in most immediate danger was the *Seydlitz*. The British gunnery was not impressive, but one shell, landing in the vitals of the German flagship, would probably have blown her up but for the gallantry of a Chief Petty Officer, who managed to turn the red-hot wheels of the flooding valves of a magazine in the nick of time.

Soon after ten o'clock the *Lion* was hit three times by heavy shells, which later brought her port engines to a stop. At 10.50 a.m. another hit put her last remaining dynamo out of action. The *Tiger*, *Princess Royal* and *New Zealand* swept past her, but then came a submarine scare. Beatty himself believed he had caught sight of a periscope and suspected a trap. He ordered a turn to port which at once opened the range. By that time all but two of the *Lion*'s signal halyards had been shot away, and his succeeding message was wrongly understood as ordering a concentration on the sinking *Blücher*.

The chase was thereupon interrupted, and although Beatty ordered a destroyer alongside, directing her captain to take him at full speed towards the *Princess Royal*, critical time had been squandered, and further pursuit had become useless. By 12.45 p.m. the battle was over. The *Blücher*, fighting magnificently to the last, had saved her consorts, and the sole remaining task was to nurse the *Lion* back to Rosyth, whither she was towed by the *Indomitable*. Had Moore, Beatty's second-in-command, pursued the Germans in the *New Zealand* on his own initiative, a modest success might well have been turned into a considerable victory.

Fisher, who was then First Sea Lord, wrote afterwards to Beatty:

> I've quite made up my mind. Your conduct was glorious. *Beatty Beatus*. He [Moore] was a long way ahead, he ought to have gone on, had he the slightest Nelsonic temperament in him, regardless of signals . . . In war the first principle is to disobey orders. Half an hour would have finished the *Derfflinger* and *Seydlitz*.

This was a typical exaggeration, for the German ships could stand amazing punishment, and their gunnery was admirable. Nevertheless, there was something in what Fisher said, and Moore, though exonerated from blame, was given a less active command.

There was no doubt in the battle cruisers of their feeling for Beatty. Winston Churchill recorded its effect.

> When, in February 1915, I visited him on board the *Lion*, with the scars of victorious battle fresh upon her from the action at the Dogger Bank, I heard from his captains and his admirals the expression of their respectful but intense enthusiasm for their leader. Well do I remember how, as I was leaving the ship, the unusually imperturbable Admiral Pakenham caught me by the sleeve: 'First Lord, I wish to speak to you in private,' and the intense conviction in his voice as he said: 'Nelson has come again.'

The Nelsonic spirit was there, but not the Nelsonic conditions. Beatty's turn to port was unfortunate, in the light of hindsight, for there were no enemy submarines present, and there was no danger, as had been feared, that Hipper might lay mines in his wake to hamper or foil pursuit.

What was clear was that the enemy would concentrate on the *Lion* in any future big-ship action. It was also evident to the Germans that they must make better arrangements in the handling of shells. The matter had become crucial, and it was remedied in their dockyards.

The difference in casualties was as marked as at Heligoland. There were 950 Germans killed, 80 wounded and 189 were rescued as prisoners-of-war from the gallant *Blücher*. The British total was 15 killed and 32 wounded, and serious damage was done only to the *Lion* and *Tiger*. The *Tiger*, finest of the battle cruisers then built, but only recently completed, had workmen still on board, some of whom panicked, and her captain, Henry Pelly, was four years older than Beatty, with no battle experience.

⚓   ⚓   ⚓

It was well over a year after the Dogger Bank action before the Kaiser, eager to show that his fleet could strike a blow for the Fatherland at a time when the German Army was fiercely engaged at Verdun and elsewhere, authorized Scheer, his Commander-in-Chief, to plan a full-scale operation which would make use of two weapons with which the Germans, with some reason, felt themselves to be well equipped, in addition to the surface ships. Submarines would be employed against the British Grand Fleet, if it emerged. Zeppelin airships, which had successfully taken the place of battle cruisers in raiding the British Isles, would provide reconnaissance and perform other valuable duties.

The idea was that part of the British surface fleet, probably the battle cruisers, should be drawn into a trap. When this was brought about, the main weight of the High Seas Fleet would fall upon it before help could arrive, and thus the balance of strength at sea would be altered to German advantage. Hipper's battle cruisers and lighter units were to attack British shipping off the Norwegian coast and in the Skagerrak. Meanwhile, Scheer himself was to cruise about fifty miles away to the south, ready to deal with any detachment which might be sent to protect the merchantmen. Submarines took up positions through which the British Grand Fleet might be expected to pass, and indeed it was the discovery of their presence which gave the Admiralty the first indication that the Germans contemplated something on a large scale.

The date chosen by Scheer was 31 May 1916. By a strange chance, Jellicoe had also planned a movement designed to draw enemy forces into much the same area of sea. Although, therefore, both sides had the same end in view at the same time, neither realized that the main opposing fleet would be involved. Scheer was misled by reports that only detached ships were likely to be at sea, and his submarines had almost reached the limit of their endurance by the date pre-arranged. Zeppelin reconnaissance was severely restricted owing to poor visibility; in fact, aircraft had no effect on the operations.

At noon on 31 May the fleets were actually converging towards the entrance to the Skagerrak, Jellicoe from the north-west, Beatty from the west, Hipper from the south-east, with Scheer not far behind him.

Just after two o'clock, when Beatty was expecting to rendezvous with Jellicoe, the cruiser *Galatea*, whose position on the scouting screen was about thirty miles east of the *Lion*, sighted two ships which she reported as 'probably hostile'. Beatty at once set course to get between the enemy and his base, turning the battle cruisers south-south-east. The signal was not seen by Rear-Admiral Hugh Evan-Thomas and the

5th Battle Squadron, which had been sent to support Beatty in place of the battle cruisers *Invincible, Indomitable* and *Inflexible,* which were with Jellicoe. It was the first of many signal failures during the day, but Evan-Thomas, who had four of the fastest battleships then afloat, the *Barham, Warspite, Valiant* and *Malaya,* did not lose distance more than temporarily.

The ships seen by the *Galatea* were indeed from the larger German force, and shortly after 3.30 p.m. the British and German battle cruisers were within sight of one another. Beatty and Hipper at once informed their respective Commanders-in-Chief. Jellicoe was then about sixty miles to the north and Scheer about fifty to the south. Beatty had with him the *Lion, Princess Royal, Queen Mary, Tiger, New Zealand* (flying the flag of Rear-Admiral Pakenham, second-in-command) and *Indefatigable.* Hipper, with the *Lutzow, Derfflinger, Seydlitz, Moltke* and *von der Tann,* had one ship less, as at the Dogger Bank.

Action began at 3.48 p.m., Hipper steering towards Scheer, Beatty parallel with him. Ahead of Beatty was W. E. Goodenough, now a Rear-Admiral and commanding the 2nd Light Cruiser Squadron, which formed a screen to cover Beatty from surprise and to scan the southern horizon. Beatty did not wait to concentrate with Evan-Thomas. He had complete confidence that his six ships were more than a match for Hipper's five.

He was in for a rude shock. At first, visibility favoured the Germans, and their shooting was good, much better than that of the British battle cruisers. At 4 p.m., an event occurred which raises the biggest question in scores concerning the battle. Beatty and the *Lion* came within a second or two of disaster. The incident was a repetition of that on board the *Seydlitz* at the Dogger—the danger of explosion due to flash. Beatty's biographer, W. S. Chalmers, who was then on the Admiral's navigating staff, recorded it as follows:

> . . . a blood-stained sergeant of Marines appeared on the Admiral's bridge. He was hatless, his clothes were burnt, and he seemed to be somewhat dazed: on seeing me he approached and asked if I were the captain. While directing him to the compass-platform above my head, curiosity got the better of me, and I asked him what was the matter: in a tired voice he replied, 'Q turret has gone, Sir. All the crew are killed, and we have flooded the magazines.'
>
> I looked over the bridge. No further confirmation was necessary: the armoured roof of Q turret had been folded back like an open sardine tin, thick yellow smoke was rolling up in clouds from the gaping hole, and the guns were cocked up in the air awkwardly.

Strange that all this should have happened within a few yards of where Beatty was standing, and that none of us on the bridge should have heard the detonation.

The ship was saved by the dying action of Major F. J. W. Harvey of the Royal Marines, who ordered the turret's magazines to be flooded, and of those who obeyed that order before they themselves were killed, some died with their hands still on the door clips. Nearly a hundred officers and men died on board the *Lion*, and Churchill did not exaggerate when he wrote: 'In the long, rough, glorious history of the Royal Marines there is . . . no deed which in its character and consequences ranks above this.' Major Harvey was awarded the Victoria Cross posthumously and, had it not been for his action, it is doubtful—here is the 'if'—whether the battle cruisers, with the admiral and the *Lion* lost, could have led Hipper and Scheer to Jellicoe. Pakenham, in the *New Zealand*, was a long way to the rear of the *Lion*, and it would have been difficult for him to assume effective command in the middle of a fierce engagement, particularly in view of two further disasters. Both the *Queen Mary*, which was regarded as being as efficient as the *Lion*, and the older *Indefatigable*, were hit by salvoes and blown up. Beatty, when he learnt the news, remarked quietly to Chatfield: 'There seems to be something wrong with our bloody ships today'. It was indeed so, but there was nothing wrong with their fighting spirit, and this was soon to tell.

The shooting of the battleship squadron, which came into action later than was expedient, was better than that of the more experienced battle cruisers, and Hipper soon began to suffer. In fact, from the moment Evan-Thomas became engaged German gunnery began to deteriorate, and it was Hipper who turned away, speeded by a torpedo attack by Beatty's destroyers.

At 4.33 p.m., only seven minutes after the *Queen Mary* had been sunk, Admiral Goodenough reported by visual signal that he had sighted the German High Seas Fleet steering north. This was the supreme moment in Beatty's naval life. He had been lured towards what the enemy hoped was a trap, suffering cruelly in the process. Goodenough's alertness now enabled him to play the same game with Hipper. He steered towards Goodenough so as to sight the German fleet for himself, then swung his ships round in succession on a northerly course, settling down to close with Jellicoe by the quickest route. Once again, through bad signalling, Evan-Thomas's ships were late in turning. They came under heavy fire from the High Seas Fleet, but gave better than they got.

Beatty's task was now two-fold. He must lead Scheer on, but he must prevent Hipper and his advanced light cruisers from sighting Jellicoe. At 5.40, he set course in such a way as to bend back the head of the German line. His tactics enabled Jellicoe to deploy his squadrons between the Germans and their coast. Despite cumulative errors in navigational reckoning, a vast pall of smoke, and the inevitable confusion of 251 ships in so small an area of sea (150 British, 101 German), it seemed as if Beatty had delivered Scheer into Jellicoe's hands, for by 6.30 Scheer found himself facing an arc of fire stretching to the horizon. Jellicoe had 'crossed the T'; that is to say, he had put the Grand Fleet in such a position that his opponent was running full tilt into the greatest concentration of gunfire which could be brought to bear. The deployment from column to line formation had been carried out with perfect timing, and annihilation of the German fleet seemed possible.

Scheer had practised a manoeuvre against just such a dire emergency. This was the *Gefechtkehrtwendung*, or 'battle turn about', during which the entire line of battleships simultaneously reversed course. It was one which was thought almost impossible under heavy fire. Nevertheless, Scheer carried it out, at about 6.30, and again later, at about 7.12.

During the initial mêlée, one more serious British loss occurred. The original battle cruiser *Invincible*, flying the flag of Rear-Admiral Horace Hood, which was ahead of the Grand Fleet, suffered exactly the same fate as the *Queen Mary* and the *Indefatigable* by the explosion of her magazines. At the time she was firing splendidly, and her tragic loss suggests a second major 'if'. If Jellicoe had not supported Beatty's original force with Evan-Thomas's battleships, and had Hood's ships been in their place, it is possible that almost the entire British battle cruiser fleet would have been eliminated. The Germans would then have scored the victory they sought, and the two main fleets might never have met, and certainly not in the favourable circumstances in which Beatty delivered Scheer to his Commander-in-Chief.

Scheer's return was seen by ships of the Grand Fleet soon after seven o'clock, and it seemed that the great opportunity for the weight of battleship fire had come at last. Scheer's second 'turn about' was made in even more difficult circumstances than the first, so much so that he ordered his destroyers to attack behind a smoke screen, and the redoubtable Hipper, who had already endured so much, was ordered to 'Charge the enemy. Ram. Ships are to attack without regard to consequences.' Within two minutes of the signal the *Derfflinger* had two turrets blown to pieces, her decks were a shambles, and she was on fire fore and aft. It was a 'Death Ride' indeed, but so well were the German ships constructed that Scheer completed his turn within eight minutes, and once more he had escaped. Jellicoe had altered course away, to avoid torpedoes, and this order, established practice which had Admiralty approval, aided the Germans in their evasion.

At 7.45 Beatty was once more able to report the position of the enemy, and at 8.17 the German battle cruisers closed the range, and Beatty opened fire. Before Hipper could retire the *Derfflinger*'s last turret had been put out of action and the *Lutzow* was in such a condition that she never returned to port. The situation was again becoming critical for Scheer, but by 8.35 he was once more lost in the mists. Jellicoe asked Beatty to give him the enemy's bearing, but there was a hitch in transmission and the answer did not get through to the *Iron Duke*, the fleet flagship, until nine o'clock, by which time it was too dark to risk further fighting owing to difficulties of recognition.

Jellicoe's aim was now to get between the enemy and his base, and to fight it out in the morning, but at 9.30 Scheer made a thrust to break through the Grand Fleet. This time he succeeded in passing astern of it, making his way home by the Horns Reef passage. The Admiralty had known that this was his likeliest route, for a Zeppelin reconnaissance in that direction had been ordered and the signal had been intercepted. The message was never passed on to Jellicoe, and it proved to be the last and saddest failure in communication on a day which had been full of them. There was some fierce fighting during the night in which destroyer flotillas were involved, and in which the German battleship *Pommern* was sunk, but with darkness the main battle ended.

Nothing remained next day but a realization that Scheer had eluded Jellicoe. During the afternoon of the first of June, a day of proud memories for the Royal Navy, Beatty came into the *Lion*'s chartroom. 'Tired and depressed,' recalled his biographer, 'he sat down on the settee, and settling himself in a corner, he closed his eyes. Unable to hide his disappointment at the result of the battle, he repeated in a weary voice: "There is something wrong with our ships," then, opening his eyes and looking at the writer, he added: "and something wrong with our system." ' Having thus unburdened himself, he fell asleep. It was the sleep of a man who had fired the first and last salvoes in the only battle of the war in which the principal fleets were engaged.

⚓   ⚓   ⚓

The British lost three battle cruisers, three cruisers, eight destroyers and 6,097 men at Jutland. The Germans lost a battleship, a battle cruiser, four cruisers, five destroyers and 2,551 men. By the rule of arithmetic, they had won, but the strategical position was exactly as before. Jellicoe maintained surface supremacy, and Germany remained blockaded.

Five months after the battle, Beatty left the battle cruisers. He hauled down his flag on board the *Lion* and hoisted it as an Admiral in the *Iron Duke*, transferring to the *Queen Elizabeth* early the following year. As Commander-in-Chief, he had gone into fleet management, having under his charge the mightiest naval surface force ever assembled. After the entry of the United States into the war a squadron of their battleships formed an integral part.

Decision by that time had moved elsewhere. The Kaiser and his naval advisers had adopted unrestricted submarine warfare. They were acting on advice once offered to Napoleon by a privateer commander after Trafalgar: that the Emperor should lay up all his ships of the line and concentrate on the war on trade. Germany came within measure of success in this insidious form of warfare against which no answer was found until, belatedly, the time-honoured method of convoy was revived and losses decreased as if by magic.

Beatty accepted the surrender of the German fleet on 21 November 1918. It would have been a gracious gesture to have invited Jellicoe and Fisher, Churchill and Battenberg, but this was not done. He became an Admiral of the Fleet the following year, at the age of forty-five, and his activities were thereafter transferred to the Admiralty. As First Sea Lord and professional head of the Navy, a post which he held for nearly eight years, he worked continuously for the advantage of the Service to which he had given his life. Five years after the end of hostilities he prophesied that 'the Fleets of the future will be commanded by naval officers with as intimate a knowledge of the air as of the gun and submarine . . . and it may well be that in the future the Commander-in-Chief of a Fleet, with his Staff, will be quartered on board an aircraft carrier.'

Ironically enough, some of Beatty's sternest peacetime duels were with his old friend and former wartime chief, Winston Churchill, who, as Chancellor of the Exchequer, was constrained to assume the role of reluctant paymaster. The friendship held.

Beatty's aim was an adequate and balanced Navy, and it was no fault of his that the state of the world during the immediate post-war years appeared such as to allow Britain's relative strength to decline to what was in fact a dangerous level. Beatty resigned office in 1927 and lived the rest of his life in retirement, finding in hunting his most enjoyable relaxation, as it had been ever since his youth.

It is usually put down to his credit that Beatty took no part in the protracted and acidulated warfare of words which arose from the events of the battle of Jutland. It is true that he wrote no book, but his measures, while in authority at the Admiralty, to ensure that his own version of events prevailed, were energetic and not over-scrupulous or indeed fair to Jellicoe. Few eminent men submit to criticism readily, even if they think themselves capable of such humility. Beatty was certainly not among them. The truth was, surely, that all the commanders who fought at Jutland, British and German alike, did their jobs creditably, and that Hipper and Beatty did them superlatively. It was sheer ill luck that it was the Germans, not the British, who, after the Dogger Bank action, were forced to take strong measures to protect their ships from the effects of flash.

One of Beatty's last public appearances was in November 1935 when, although in very bad health, he insisted on paying his last respects to Jellicoe. It was against the advice of his doctor, for at the time he was still in bed with influenza. Indeed he would scarcely have managed the long, slow walk through the streets of London had not a journalist, shocked at how ill he looked, handed him a glass of brandy during a pause in the procession.

Two months later, George V died. Beatty again disregarded the advice of his doctor that he would not be able to stand the ordeal of another winter funeral, saying: 'He was not only my King, he was my friend.' Once more he accompanied the slow-moving gun carriage, drawn by sailors from the fleet. He himself died on 11 March 1936, within a few weeks of the King. He was buried near Nelson, Collingwood, Jellicoe and other sea officers in the crypt of St Paul's. 'I am one of your greatest admirers,' Churchill had written to him twelve years earlier. 'I never cease to proclaim you as inheritor of the grand tradition of Nelson.'

The words echoed those of Admiral Pakenham, spoken at sea in time of war.

12

The Greatest Command
of All: Nimitz

⚓   ⚓   ⚓

If Beatty commanded the largest fleet ever assembled until, consequent upon the Peace Treaties following the First World War, navies began to diminish, Admiral Chester W. Nimitz had overall charge of the most powerful naval force ever brought together for combat. This was the United States Pacific Fleet of the Second World War.

In scale, the strategy for which Nimitz was responsible, under the supreme direction of Admiral Ernest J. King, Chief of Naval Operations, dwarfed all maritime campaigning previously known. This was not surprising, seeing that the Pacific covers nearly half the world's surface and is more than twice the size of the Atlantic.

As for numbers of ships engaged, to set against the 251 combined total at Jutland—at the separate engagements which made up what is known as the battle of Leyte Gulf, fought between 24 and 26 October 1944, during which a large part of the Japanese Navy was destroyed, 282 ships were involved. There were 216 from the United States, two from the Australian Navy, and 64 Japanese. This takes no account of aircraft, which were numbered in hundreds and proved decisive.

No one ever took over a great command in stranger circumstances than Nimitz. It was in the aftermath of disaster at Pearl Harbor, where, in a surprise attack on 7 December 1941, the United States battleship fleet was decimated by the Japanese without declaration of war. Nimitz himself was without personal experience of combat, and so remained. It did not signify. His task was planning, fleet control and fleet management, like Beatty's after he had left the *Lion*. Those with a sense of history could have reflected that Lord Barham, who at the age of nearly eighty took charge of strategy at the time of Trafalgar, also had had no serious operational service, and was fully effective in the role his country required.

The fair-haired Chester William Nimitz had Nordic ancestors, and a Baltic background far removed from the part of the world where he was to make his name. One of his family had served the Swedish king, Gustavus Adolphus, and fell with him at the battle of Lützen in 1632. A son, and a grandson, were also among the 'Blue Boys' of an army famed in northern Europe.

The family later moved to Hanover. In the 1840s Karl Heinrich Nimitz, the admiral's great-grandfather, emigrated to South Carolina to escape harsh economic conditions in Germany. His son Charles Henry, who had a love for the sea, moved to Texas, which had recently been annexed by the United States. There, in 1852, he built an hotel shaped like a steamboat, which became a Texas landmark and is now a memorial museum. One of Charles Henry's twelve children married a local beauty, Anna Henke, but died five months later. Chester William Nimitz, a posthumous child, was born in February 1885.

The boy had an affectionate grandfather still living, and shortly after her first husband's death Anna married her brother-in-law, William Nimitz, by whom she had two children. The family were poor but most united, and Chester was willing to spend long hours at work about the hotel in addition to studying to enter the Naval Academy at Annapolis. In September 1901 he became a Naval Cadet, passing his examinations with credit.

At that time, the United States fleet was expanding so fast that Nimitz's class graduated ahead of schedule. In January 1905, after gaining seventh place in a class of 114, Midshipman Nimitz was sent to San Francisco to join the USS *Ohio*, flagship of the Asiatic Fleet. During the following summer, he was one of six midshipmen invited to a garden party given by the Emperor of Japan to celebrate the victory of his country in the war against Russia which had recently ended.

Nimitz was elected to approach the redoubtable Admiral Togo, victor at the battle of Tsushima, to ask him to their table. Togo smilingly agreed, sipped the captured Russian champagne being served, and chatted briefly, in English, to the young men. Togo made a deep impression on Nimitz, and many years later, when he was a captain of some standing, he was present at his funeral.

At the age of twenty-one, and in the rank of ensign, Nimitz was given his first command—a gunboat, together with a minute naval base at Mindanao in the Philippines. He was next assigned to an aged destroyer, the *Decatur*, which had long been laid up, and was ordered to commission her at Cavite. One dark night he ran the ship on to a mudbank. He got a steamer to tow him off next day, but all the same he was court martialled for 'hazarding a ship of the United States Navy'. He received a reprimand.

The incident did not affect his career in the slightest, although, to his disappointment, since he wanted to serve in battleships, he became a submariner. These were the days when submersibles were, in his own words, 'a cross between a Jules Verne fantasy and a hump-backed whale'. The life appealed to him. He commanded four submarines in succession, and made a special study of underwater tactics and diesel engines. In 1912, when he was a lieutenant and in charge of the *Skipjack*, he dived overboard to rescue a seaman, and was given a Life Saving Medal. He married the same year. His bride was Catherine Vance Freeman of Wollaston, Massachusetts, by whom he had four children, a boy and three girls. Catherine was a lady of great charm who shared her husband's love of sport and classical music, and who was of the greatest help to him in his career.

Just before the First World War Nimitz was sent to Europe to study diesel construction, particularly in Germany and Belgium. A few years later, when the United States entered the conflict, Nimitz, by then a lieutenant-commander, was appointed to the staff of the Submarine Force, U.S. Atlantic Fleet. Here, says his biographer, Professor E. B. Potter:

> ... he found relations between British and American officers breaking down under the stiff weight of protocol. This, he decided, was an outdated way of doing things. He believed that the British would respond to simple friendliness and good performance, and he drilled this point of view into his junior officers and men. The idea worked, and Nimitz quickly established amicable teamwork between the Allied commands in his area of operations.

It was in fact the rule rather than the exception that in the First World War the Navies co-operated admirably. They had a lead from the top. Admiral Sims, the senior United States admiral in European waters, was actually offered a seat on the Whitehall Board of Admiralty, but was ordered by his Government to decline it.

There followed routine appointments as Nimitz rose steadily in his profession—executive officer of the *South Carolina*, command of the *Chicago*, and then a period of staff or training duties including a spell at the University of California as the first Professor of Naval Science. When he went back to sea as a captain it was to the *Augusta*, flagship of the Asiatic Fleet.

Three years at the Bureau of Navigation—later and more aptly renamed the Bureau of Naval Personnel—gave Nimitz the chance of assessing the character or capabilities of every senior officer with whom he was likely to serve. Appointments with cruisers and battleships followed, and then in June 1939 Nimitz, by then a Rear-Admiral, returned to the Bureau of Navigation, this time as its head. It was in this appointment that he heard the news of Pearl Harbor. He was at once called into conference with Frank Knox, Secretary of the Navy, an Office corresponding to that of First Lord of the Admiralty, the Under-Secretary, James Forrestal, the Chief of Naval Operations, at that time Harold Stark, and other leading characters. Among these men Nimitz was rather junior, as Beatty had been when acting as Naval Secretary to Winston Churchill, but his knowledge of the Navy's leading officers proved invaluable, and everyone came to respect and to rely upon his judgement of character.

Shortly after the Japanese attack, Knox flew to Pearl Harbor to size up the situation for himself. On his return, he announced his belief that a new Commander-in-Chief must be appointed. Turning to Nimitz, he asked: 'How soon can you get ready to travel? You're going to command the Pacific Fleet.'

Nimitz was startled, for such an appointment had never occurred to him as being within the bounds of possibility. There were 28 flag officers senior to him, and in any case he had been hoping for a sea-going job. The task he had been given could only be exercised from a shore base, and Nimitz was not sure that he relished the idea. Then he settled down to accepting it, travelling to San Francisco by train, just as he had over thirty years before as a midshipman to join his first ship.

The journey itself was unusual. Nimitz wore civilian clothes in the interests of 'security', although all along the Altantic coast of America lights were blazing away, making the task of the U-boats assigned to sink unescorted merchant shipping ridiculously easy. The admiral travelled as 'Mr Wainwright', accompanied by Lieutenant La Marr of the Bureau of Navigation, whose duty it was to divert Nimitz from the stern realities ahead.

In fact, it was Nimitz who did the diverting. He was in boyish high spirits until, shortly after the train left Chicago, the lieutenant handed over the first full report of the Pearl Harbor disaster. That kept Nimitz quiet, and La Marr heard him murmur from time to time, 'It could have happened to anyone!' It was a typical Nimitz judgement—slow to blame.

At San Francisco, a four-engined flying-boat was waiting to take Nimitz to Hawaii, and to the greatest challenge any admiral could have had.

⚓   ⚓   ⚓

Nimitz arrived at Pearl Harbor on Christmas morning, 1941, in a steady downpour. Through the mist, he could make out the sides, hulls and fighting tops of the battleships sunk in the air attack less than three weeks before. Some would be raised and repaired, and would fight again. One, the *Arizona*, resting on the seabed, would in course of time become a permanent memorial to those who lost their lives on 7 December, 1,103 of whom were from this ship, out of a complement of 1,400. There had been a total loss of over 2,000 from the Navy, 327 from the Army and Marines, and 70 civilians.

Nimitz found no defeatism at Hawaii, only defiance and anger. Since the initial attack, Guam had fallen, so had Wake Island. Thailand had been overrun. Singapore was threatened, and the British had lost the

Prince of Wales and the *Repulse* to air attack in the Gulf of Siam. In the Philippines, the Japanese had eliminated American air power at Luzon and wrecked the naval base at Cavite. Invading forces were advancing on Manila. From the Marshall Islands the enemy had penetrated into the Gilberts, whence they would threaten the Ellice Islands and Samoa.

Although it was certain that there was worse to come, there was a feeling of hope as well as determination. The big aircraft carriers *Saratoga, Lexington, Enterprise, Yorktown, Wasp* and *Hornet* were intact, and they would replace the battleships as the core of the fleet. The fuel stores had received little damage, and the repair facilities could quickly be made usable.

Nimitz assumed command on 31 December, reading his orders from the deck of the submarine *Grayling*, appropriate for an old submariner. Then he called a meeting of the Staff. As the members filed into the conference room they faced a quiet, broad-shouldered man with grey eyes and with fair hair beginning to turn white. Nimitz was fifty-five, and in the pink of physical and mental condition. He had no peculiarities of manner, but had about him an air of courteous serenity.

He told the assembled officers that he needed the benefit of their experience. 'There will be no changes,' he added. 'I have complete confidence in you. We've taken a terrific wallop, but I have no doubts as to the ultimate outcome.' Everyone left the meeting with a renewed spring in their walk.

Nimitz had four immediate objectives: the first was to restore morale: the second was to try to divert Japanese strength away from the East Indies; the third was to safeguard communications with Midway and Australia, and the fourth was to hold the line against further Japanese expansion in the Pacific. All four purposes could be achieved through offensive operations, which meant aircraft carrier raids on Japanese bases.

Several officers, including some who had recently been his seniors, opposed such a policy as being too risky—a sure way to lose the precious carriers. Among those who agreed was Admiral William F. Halsey, who not only welcomed the idea but volunteered to carry out a strike against the Marshall Islands, the Japanese stronghold in the Central Pacific. Halsey thus endeared himself to Nimitz, and went on to become one of his two principal tactical commanders, the other being Raymond A. Spruance.

The raids, which began in February 1942, were spectacular rather than important. Halsey bombed the Marshalls with aircraft from the *Enterprise*, Frank J. Fletcher the Gilberts from the *Yorktown*. Halsey next struck at Wake Island and then at Marcus, only a thousand miles from Japan. Other forays followed, the culmination being in mid-April when the *Hornet*, with sixteen long-range army aircraft lashed to her flight deck, joined the *Enterprise* under Halsey's command and, approaching Japan, launched bombers for attacks on Tokyo and other cities.

Besides being morale-boosters, the raids electrified the public both in America and in Japan, just as the isolated raids by the Royal Air Force on Berlin had done when Britain stood alone. Savage treatment by the Japanese of captured flyers, in a war in which little mercy was shown and none expected, inflamed feeling, and had a marked effect on Halsey, who was under severe strain. So great was the impact of the offensives that Nimitz was given the additional title of Commander-in-Chief, Pacific Ocean Areas. This gave him authority over all United States and Allied naval and military forces in the Pacific theatre of war, except for those in General Douglas MacArthur's South-west Area.

The Japanese continued their conquests—the East Indies, Malaya, Burma, northern New Guinea, the Solomons, and the defence of what remained in the Philippines could not be maintained much longer. The enemy now had access to ample oil supplies, and could set up a huge perimeter of air bases to defend what they had won. The next target was Port Moresby on the southern coast of New Guinea, from which Allied bombers could reach the key Japanese base at Rabaul in the Bismarck Archipelago.

Nimitz knew this. His experts had possession of the Japanese signal code, just as the Germans had that of the British in the initial phases of the war in Europe. He was able, therefore, to assemble carrier groups in the Coral Sea. The battle which followed between 4 and 8 May 1942 was the first in history where the principal ships never sighted one another. The Americans lost the *Lexington*, and the *Yorktown* was badly damaged; the Japanese lost the light carrier *Shoho*. Although the enemy emerged with smaller losses, strategically the victory was with the Americans who, for the first time, had been able to halt the Japanese advance. They had also inflicted as many casualties on Japanese flyers as would keep two big carriers, the *Shokaku* and *Zuikaku*, out of action for some time.

There was no opportunity to assess results and assimilate lessons from the Coral Sea engagement before Nimitz was faced with a full-scale crisis. Evidence was building up that Admiral Yamamoto, the Japanese Commander-in-Chief, was about to attack the Aleutians and Midway with his main strength. To counter this offensive, Nimitz would have to rely on carrier forces, submarines and land-based aircraft. Resources were terribly limited and a major blunder could be disastrous. The *Wasp*, which had been loaned to the British to fly aircraft to Malta, was still in the Atlantic. The *Saratoga*, torpedoed the previous January, was repaired, but had no screen. This left only the *Enterprise*, the *Hornet* and the damaged *Yorktown*. Nimitz ordered them up from the South Pacific at top speed.

Yamamoto's idea in attacking Midway was to draw United States forces piecemeal to the defence of the island, fall upon them in strength, and complete the work begun at Pearl Harbor in the first assault of the war. He knew that the available American carriers were in the South Pacific, and counted on surprise to enable him to concentrate his own forces, which were scattered, before these or any other American ships could reach the Midway area. Once again, Nimitz's possession of the enemy code enabled him to prevent Yamamoto from surprising him.

Halsey, with the *Enterprise–Hornet* group, arrived at Pearl Harbor on 26 May. Halsey, who was clearly sick, went to hospital, and Nimitz turned the command over to Spruance, the cruiser admiral. Spruance had no experience of carriers, but Nimitz relied on his reputation for acumen and decisiveness. He briefed him with great care and then sent him to cruise north-east of Midway on the flank of what he expected to be the Japanese approach.

Admiral Fletcher's *Yorktown* group arrived the day after Halsey, and after a round-the-clock repair effort, the damaged carrier was made ready for a sortie by 30 May. Fletcher and Spruance met 350 miles north-west of Midway, and there Fletcher, as senior officer, assumed tactical charge. Nimitz himself retained overall command, enjoining radio silence on the carriers. He kept himself informed by reconnaissance aircraft sent from Midway and by submarine contacts.

The days immediately following the sailing of the three carriers were acutely anxious. Nimitz knew that the odds were much against him, and that defeat of the carriers would leave Pearl Harbor and all other Allied bases wide open to attack by the main Japanese fleet.

By the morning of 3 June, reports began to come in that Japanese carrier aircraft had raided Dutch Harbour in the Aleutians. Reconnaissance aircraft had also sighted a large enemy force approaching Midway from the south-west. Nimitz concluded that the Dutch Harbour operation was a diversion, and that the Midway force carried occupation troops. He was relieved that his carriers had not been drawn out of position, for he was convinced that the decisive encounter must take place in the Midway area.

Early on 4 June the Japanese launched a heavy air attack on Midway itself, although Yamamoto's battleship force, which had been expected to bombard installations as well as giving cover to the troops, was never sighted.

There were anxious hours at Nimitz's headquarters until, at 10.20 came a sortie which altered the course of the battle. By an amazing but unintended synchronization, *Hornet* bombers and *Yorktown* bombers, approaching the enemy carriers from different points of the compass, completely unaware of each other, attacked at the same moment. Bombs ripped open the decks of the *Kaga*, *Akagi* and *Soryu*, starting fires which destroyed these ships. The *Hiryu*, the one remaining carrier, escaped for the moment but was found by airmen from the *Enterprise*, and was set ablaze with four direct hits.

The ship had her revenge. Before her abandonment, *Hiryu*'s torpedo planes and bombers damaged the *Yorktown* so badly that Admiral Fletcher had to transfer his flag to a cruiser, turning over the carrier command to Spruance in the *Enterprise*. At 2.55 Yamamoto ordered a general retreat: he had had enough, and without air cover was likely to suffer more damage without adequate compensation. Spruance pursued him, but with caution, for he did not intend his precious carriers to become involved with battleships. On 6 June the Americans overtook two collision-damaged cruisers, the *Mogame* and the *Mikuma*, which had made a brief, face-saving bombardment of Midway, and had had to take violent evasive action from threats by submarines. The *Mikuma* was sunk, but the *Mogame* managed to struggle 2,000 miles to Truk Island, leaking oil all the way.

The Japanese got in the last blow with their submarine arm, in general the least successful of their fighting services. While the semi-derelict *Yorktown* was under tow, a spread of torpedoes sank a destroyer alongside her and damaged the carrier still further so that she sank on the morning of 7 June.

Midway was not only the highest point of Nimitz's career as a strategist, it was one of the decisive battles of the war. Japanese preponderance was so seriously reduced that something like equality at sea was achieved, and that within six months of initial disaster. Spruance, who handled his carriers with distinction, was summoned to Pearl Harbor to become Nimitz's Chief of Staff. He was to be groomed for a major command at sea when the new American fleet, building at furious speed, was ready.

Spruance found three questions pinned above Nimitz's desk which every subordinate was expected to answer if he had some project to put forward.

    1. Is the proposal likely to succeed?

2. What might the consequences be of failure?
3. Is it in the realm of practicability of material and supplies?

Although not expressed in the tersest of language, these were indeed the relevant questions, and as Nimitz was a good listener, they were often asked. Being accessible was of great value. People felt they could speak their minds freely—they would not be shot down. The admiral himself said 'Some of the best help and advice I've had comes from junior officers and enlisted men.' Although no remote figure, the final decisions were very much his own, subject always to the ruling of the Joint Chiefs of Staff at Washington, who intervened less and less, thanks to King's support. Sometimes decisions were made in the teeth of contrary advice.

Euphoria after Midway would have been totally out of place. What the victory did was to give the Americans the chance to seize the initiative. Their choice was Rabaul. General MacArthur would advance on the Japanese base by way of New Guinea and New Britain, Nimitz from the south-east by way of the Solomons. A separate South Pacific Area Command was set up, Admiral Robert L. Ghormley being in charge.

The Solomons campaign began on 7 August 1942, when the 1st Marine Division landed on Guadalcanal. The Japanese were taken by surprise but counter-attacked with vigour. They also inflicted a severe defeat on the Americans on the night of 9–10 August at the battle of Savo Island. A force of seven cruisers from Rabaul entered the sound north of Guadalcanal and ran through Allied amphibious forces, firing guns and torpedoes. When they retired, almost undamaged, they left three American and one Australian cruiser in a sinking condition, a third cruiser badly damaged, and a thousand dead. There was some talk of a court martial on the senior officer of the amphibious forces, but Nimitz agreed with an investigating committee appointed by the Secretary of the Navy that blame was too widely distributed for any one particular officer to be held responsible. This was another wise decision, for the Admiral concerned, Richmond K. Turner, went on from strength to strength at later stages in the war.

Towards the end of August came the almost inevitable carrier battle in which the *Enterprise* was badly damaged, but the Americans once again forced the Japanese to retire by sinking a light carrier and shooting down 90 aircraft. Japanese submarines had their other major success by fatally damaging the *Wasp*, also hitting the *Saratoga* and the battleship *North Carolina*. Things were going so badly in the Solomons that there was even talk of abandoning Guadalcanal to the Japanese. It was at this stage that Halsey was once more declared fit, and Nimitz decided to send him to replace Ghormley.

Ghormley, distressed at what amounted to public humiliation, called on Nimitz when he arrived at Pearl Harbor to ask for an explanation. Nimitz's way with his friend could scarcely have been bettered.

'Bob,' he said, 'I had to pick from the whole Navy the man best fitted to handle the situation. Were you that man?'

'No,' said Ghormley. 'If you put it that way, I guess I wasn't.'

Halsey was as aggressive as any admiral of his own or any other era. He raised morale by his very presence, and restored good relations between the various Commands. He sent his two carrier groups to tackle the most powerful Japanese force which had been assembled since Midway, but in the course of the battle of the Santa Cruz Islands, the *Hornet* was sunk, the *Enterprise* damaged once again, and at the end of it there was not a single serviceable American carrier left in the Pacific. Nevertheless, defeatism was overcome. By the autumn of 1942 the struggle for Guadalcanal reached its climax in a series of air and sea actions in which the Americans lost two cruisers and five destroyers, and the Japanese two battleships, a cruiser, a destroyer and nearly a dozen transports. They then wrote off Guadalcanal, merely holding on until they had built airfields in the Central Solomons. In January 1943 they withdrew their starving garrison.

A year later, Rabaul was surrounded by troops under General MacArthur and was bombed into impotence by aircraft supplied largely by Halsey. By that time, the American Pacific Fleet had been rebuilt, and what were known as Task Forces—strong independent squadrons ranged round carriers—supplied by a Fleet Train which enabled them to keep the sea for long periods, had made a series of raids on many strong enemy positions. Next came the formation of the Fifth Fleet, to which Spruance was appointed. 'The admiral thinks it's all right to send Raymond out now,' said a wag at Nimitz's headquarters. 'He's got him to the point where they think and talk alike.'

Now that adequate forces were available for full-scale strategic planning, Nimitz intended to assault the Japanese perimeter in the Central Pacific. He convinced the Chiefs of Staff that the Gilberts should first be seized before attempting an invasion of the Marshalls. Nimitz felt that land-based aircraft must be an essential supplement to those which could be provided by the carriers.

The 2nd Marine Division took four days to conquer Tarawa, the Japanese headquarters and strong-point in the Gilberts. Casualties amounted to over three thousand, including a thousand killed. This was felt to be an exorbitant price to pay for what appeared to be a small gain, but Nimitz knew that it would immeasurably ease the tasks ahead, and he was right.

His principal admirals, Spruance included, recommended caution in tackling the Marshalls, particularly in view of the losses at Tarawa. They favoured the outer islands first, then Kwajalein, the enemy head-quarters at the centre of the archipelago. To their surprise and concern, Nimitz proposed by-passing the outer islands altogether, assaulting Kwajalein straight away, leaving the American communications vulner-able. At a conference called to discuss the operations, the advice of every single officer was 'outer islands first'. After a pause, Nimitz quietly announced, 'Well, gentlemen, our next target will be Kwajalein.'

Later, Spruance, Turner and Major-General Holland M. Smith of the Marines called on Nimitz to ask him to reverse his decision. Nimitz heard them out patiently and then said: 'Sitting behind desks in the United States are able officers who would give their right arms to be out here fighting the war. If you gentlemen can't bring yourselves to carry out my orders, I can arrange an exchange of duty . . . make up your minds. You have five minutes.'

The assault was carried out as Nimitz intended. The Japanese were thinking in the same terms as Spruance. Believing that the Americans would not dare to drive straight for Kwajalein they had left their head-quarters relatively weak, their main strength being sent to the outer islands. These presented no serious problems, for first the carriers and then, when Kwajalein had been occupied, aircraft from that centre, and from the Gilberts, rendered them impotent.

Having convinced himself that carriers could if necessary support major assaults without the help of land-based aircraft, and carriers being no longer in short supply, Nimitz planned a leap of 1,000 miles to Saipan in the Marianas. The operation began in June 1944, the same month as the great Anglo-American invasion of Europe. It drew out the Japanese carrier fleet, equipped with new aircraft, but with inade-quately trained pilots. The naval forces met at the battle of the Philip-pine Sea on 19–20 June. Spruance, who was in command, refused to be drawn away from his primary task of covering the Saipan beach-head. The result was that the Japanese were forced to attack him and were shot down in droves in what became known as the 'Marianas Turkey Shoot' because, for almost the first time, enemy airmen proved easy victims. To add to Japanese discomfiture, American submarines sank two of their carriers, a third falling to Spruance's aircraft.

After the conquest of Saipan, and of nearby Guam and Tinian, Spruance returned to Pearl Harbor to rest and to plan further advances. Halsey replaced him in the Fifth Fleet, which thereupon changed its title to Third Fleet. The alteration in command, and resulting change in numbering, became common practice. It was not always satisfactory, because the methods of Spruance and Halsey were very different. Spruance was quiet and meticulous, refusing to create a public image. Halsey, nicknamed 'the Bull', was flamboyant and unexpected. Senior officers found Spruance easier to work with, and the general view in the Navy was that while Halsey was a 'sailor's admiral', Spruance was an 'admiral's admiral'.

Halsey probed the defences of the Philippines with his carriers and judged them to be so stretched that he advocated invading at Leyte, almost in the middle of the island group, rather than at Mindanao in the south. Both Nimitz and MacArthur agreed. As soon as practicable, Nimitz turned over as much as possible of his resources to the small Seventh Fleet, which was known as 'MacArthur's Navy', the senior officer being Admiral Thomas C. Kincaid.

The Japanese reaction to the threat to the Philippines brought about one of the more complex naval actions of the war, the battle of Leyte Gulf. On 20 October 1944, Kincaid began putting troops ashore, whilst Halsey's Third Fleet manoeuvred in distant support. The invasion started the enemy in motion, and by 24 October two powerful surface forces were threading their way though the islands, a southern group heading for Surigao Strait, south of Leyte Gulf, and a central group making for San Bernando Strait, to the north of the Gulf. Halsey's aircraft attacked the central force, temporarily causing it to retreat.

In mid-afternoon, Halsey learned from his airmen that there was a third Japanese force to the north of him, including carriers. There were in fact only 17 ships altogether, and the carriers were denuded of aircraft, but Halsey, to whom a Japanese carrier was like a red rag to a bull, believed this to be the main threat. He cancelled all his previous dispositions, which had been made for the protection of the San Bernando Strait, and gave chase with his entire force of 65 ships. This was exactly what the enemy wanted.

Kincaid, thinking that Halsey had left a strong force behind, sent all his available ships to repel the Japanese southern group. This was done in masterly fashion, making use of some of the veteran battleships which had been damaged at Pearl Harbor, and since repaired. Then Kincaid signalled to Halsey to ensure that the San Bernando Straits were guarded, only to be electrified by the answer that Halsey's entire force was with him.

The central enemy group now had a golden chance to decimate the invasion fleet, with only light carriers protecting it. Kincaid's messages grew urgent, but the day was saved by magnificent self-help directed by Admiral Clifton A. Sprague who, in an improvised defence against vastly superior forces, drove off the attack with the loss of only two carriers. The enemy received much damage from what were in fact desperate air attacks, and withdrew. The invasion proceeded, but it had been a very near thing.

Halsey's chase to the north had caused acute anxiety to Nimitz, and led to a signal which deserves remembrance. At the time when Kincaid's calls for help were becoming urgent, Nimitz asked Halsey to report the whereabouts of Task Force 34, which included his battleships.

For security reasons, U.S. cipher messages had 'padding' added to the beginning and end of the text, the padding being separated by double letters. The signal was enciphered at Pearl Harbor to read:

'(Turkey trots to water GG) Where is (Repeat)
where is Task Force 34 (RR The world wonders.)'

The padding, here inserted within brackets, should have been removed before the signal was delivered to Halsey, but through an error in his flagship the words 'the world wonders' were left in, thus contravening a rule that padding should have no possible connection with the text. Ironically, in this case, it had much.

Halsey was furious at what he considered to be a 'calculated insult' from his Commander-in-Chief. It was nearly an hour before he ordered the Task Force south. By then, Sprague had already beaten off a most formidable attack, in which the daring and self-sacrifice of his destroyer officers was a major factor.

The battle was the last in which the Japanese were able to use their fleet in full strength. They were short of oil, and their loss and damage at Leyte Gulf was crippling. Already short of trained airmen, they relied henceforward on suicide attacks, known as Kamikaze, the Divine Wind. The words related to a typhoon in the year 1281 which destroyed two fleets, one from Korea and the other from South China, sent by Kublai Khan against Japan. Kamikaze attacks were invariably spectacular and often damaging, but they showed the straits to which Japan was reduced. When British carriers later joined Halsey's fleet, although they experienced suicide attacks in some numbers, their armoured flight decks, a feature lacking in the American ships, kept them operational.

After the Philippines, Iwo Jima and Okinawa were the final island stages on the long sea road to Japan. On 25 January 1945, Spruance relieved Halsey for the Iwo Jima operation. Nimitz, who had recently been promoted to Fleet Admiral, the highest rank in the U.S. Navy, shifted his headquarters from Pearl Harbor to Guam in the Marianas, to be nearer the scenes of the final advance.

Just before the assault on Iwo Jima, Spruance led a task force to the shores of Japan itself, giving Tokyo its first naval bombing since the small-scale raid by Halsey's carriers in 1942. At Iwo Jima, the Japanese provided a surprise by the strength of their defence. Their navy and air forces were by this time weak, but their soldiers were as fanatical as ever. The cost of the assault, to the two Marine divisions employed, was high, but it was worthwhile in military terms, for the island provided airfields where the big B.29s could refuel, and be accompanied by fighters for the final stage in bombing Japan.

Nimitz was reluctant to consent to a British fleet taking part in the later phases of the naval war, for his supply arrangements were stretched. He was overruled, and the contingent, small by comparison with the Americans, received a welcome, particularly when Halsey was in charge of operations. The British took part at Okinawa, the conquest of which proved unexpectedly swift and easy in spite of a sticky start, and of some success by the suicide bombers.

At one stage, when operations appeared likely to be bogged down, Nimitz arrived for a personal inspection. The senior general, Simon B. Buckner, received him politely, but the relationship between the U.S. Navy and Army was not easy, and Buckner told Nimitz that this was ground, and therefore Army, business. 'Yes,' replied Nimitz, 'but ground though it may be, I'm losing a ship and a half a day. So if this line isn't moving within five days, we'll get someone here to move it so we can all get out from under these stupid air attacks.' Nimitz had by that time been an observer of what suicide bombers could do.

The line got moving, and by 21 June 1945 Okinawa was secured. Afterwards, Halsey, with the combined American and British forces, paraded up and down the east coast of Japan, striking almost at will. In August, the Soviet Union declared war on Japan and invaded Korea, while B.29s dropped atomic bombs on Hiroshima and Nagasaki. Nimitz ordered Halsey to cease fire on 15 August 1945.

⚓   ⚓   ⚓

The rest was honour and glory. On 2 September, in Tokyo Bay, Nimitz embarked on board the battleship *Missouri*. Half an hour later General MacArthur arrived, his personal standard being broken alongside that of Nimitz. The Instrument of Surrender was signed by MacArthur on behalf of the Allied Powers. Nimitz signed for the United States.

The following month, Nimitz visited Washington and called on James V. Forrestal, who had succeeded Knox as Secretary of the Navy. Forrestal offered Nimitz honourable semi-retired advisory status, but Nimitz said he would prefer a spell as Chief of Naval Operations. 'But,' protested Forrestal, 'you should now step out of the limelight while your fame is greatest. As CNO you risk your laurels.'

In point of fact, there had been considerable disagreement between the two men, and in any case, the question of 'limelight' did not arise, for of all Supreme Allied Commanders, Nimitz was the most self-effacing. Somewhat grudgingly the Secretary agreed to the admiral's request, but insisted that the appointment could be for two years only. 'That suits me exactly,' Nimitz replied.

On 24 November 1945, at Pearl Harbor, and on the deck of the submarine *Menhadon*, Nimitz relinquished the command he had held in an unbroken spell for almost four years. He had seen the United States Pacific Fleet grow from the half-shattered opening phase to becoming the strongest maritime force the world had ever seen.

Once at work together, Nimitz and Forrestal proved to be an unexpectedly successful pair. All the same, Nimitz did not exceed his two-year span. When he retired, in 1947, he could have gone into business and made his fortune, so successful had he proved as an administrator. Instead, he took up residence in California, near the ocean where he had spent so much of his life. Later on, he gave time to the preparation of a work on Sea Power, which he prepared in collaboration with Professor E. B. Potter. He refused to write his memoirs, or even to authorize a biography, being one of the few senior commanders to forgo this luxury. His later years were spent at special quarters put at his disposal at the Naval Station on Treasure Island in San Francisco Bay.

Nimitz died on 20 February 1966, a few days before his 81st birthday. At his own request, he was buried without the ceremony of a State funeral. His body rests at Golden Gate National Cemetery, near the Pacific, among thousands of men who served with him in the greatest of all naval wars.

Epilogue:
'Valour and Sufferance'

When George Monck, with a remarkable record both as soldier and sailor in the time of the Stuarts and the Commonwealth, spoke of the 'chief parts of a soldier' as being Valour and Sufferance, he was thinking of the run-of-the-mill man-at-arms. But the idea has a general truth for the tactician, whether by sea or land. If bravery in battle follows patience in awaiting it, the practitioner will have done a large part of his duty.

Strategy, fleet control and administration, are matters requiring different qualities. Of the personalities touched upon herein, Hawke, endlessly patient, yet fearless in taking justifiable risks when the chance arose, was not called upon to exercise strategical judgement on the highest levels, but that he was a highly capable fleet administrator is shown by his record in the work of close blockade, than which no task could be more gruelling. His friend, Saunders, besides having outstanding luck all through his life, had both strategical and tactical flair. This was seen in his encouragement of Wolfe to assault Quebec from above the town, bringing success after weeks of failure and frustration.

Bougainville and Suffren were typical Frenchmen in their intelligence and originality. Bougainville would have succeeded brilliantly in any line he undertook. His opportunities as a flag officer were limited, but his success in leading an expedition into the Pacific (and his skill in writing its story) indicates how good he was in the matter of control of his men, how determined in the pursuit of an object. As for Suffren, the strategist in him was largely stultified by ineptitude in his captains. Had he had subordinates as skilled and as experienced as his rival Hughes, there is no doubt that his successes would have been achieved at far less cost.

Howe, Collingwood and Saumarez combined the qualities of 'Valour and Sufferance' with the art of fleet management. Howe was familiar with the inner corridors of power in a way which few other admirals have ever been, Anson excepted. Collingwood and Saumarez were called upon for diplomatic duties far beyond what could have been expected from professional sailors. Both experienced the purgatory of blockade, in the pattern set by Hawke; both excelled in action.

The Gardners and the Rowleys were men who could rise to an occasion. That they have been forgotten is no fault of their own. It arises from the fact that in every nation's history, only a handful can ever hope to become 'household names'.

David Farragut, given the wider opportunities which his quality deserved, could have been a trans-Atlantic version of Hawke, although his personality was more simple. Beatty and Nimitz seem in almost direct contrast, Beatty often in the limelight, not always by his own wish, yet not, perhaps, resenting it too keenly, Nimitz unalterably quiet.

Admiral Spruance, one of Nimitz's two stars, had wise words to say on the subject of an admiral projecting an image:

> Personal publicity in war can be a drawback because it may affect a man's thinking. A commander may not have sought it; it may have been forced upon him by zealous subordinates or imaginative war correspondents. Once started, however, it is hard to keep in check. In the early days of a war, when little about the various commanders is known to the public, and some general or admiral does a good and perhaps spectacular job, he gets a head start in publicity. Anything he does thereafter tends towards greater headline value than the same thing done by others, following the journalistic rule that 'names make news'. Thus his reputation snowballs, and soon, probably against his will, he has become a colourful figure, credited with fabulous characteristics over and above the competence in war command for which he has been conditioning himself all his life.
>
> His fame may not have gone to his head, but there is nevertheless danger of this. Should he get to identifying himself with the figure as publicised, he may subconsciously start thinking in terms of what his reputation calls for, rather than of how best to meet the actual problems confronting him. A man's judgement is best when he can forget himself and any reputation he may have acquired, and can concentrate on making the right decision.

It was thus that Spruance explained why he avoided personal publicity, 'not through ungraciousness, but rather to keep his thinking impersonal and realistic'. It was a matter in which he was the direct opposite of Halsey. By his attitude he sacrificed panache, some of which would have rubbed off on his command, stimulating morale in circumstances where this would often have been valuable.

Spruance was his chief's idea of a tactical model. What of Nimitz the prototype? Professor Potter conveys a gracious image, but an important consideration should be taken into account. Nimitz was determined that, when the war was over, there should be no acrimony such as had occurred between leading American admirals after the nineteenth-century war between the United States and Spain. So far as lay within his power, which was considerable, he succeeded.

Nevertheless, Nimitz could be tough. For one thing, he had to rule a tough team. He also had to carry his point of view with the single-minded and ruthless Fleet Admiral Ernest J. King, ruler of an American two-ocean Navy. Nimitz usually got his way. In his later years he was notably gentle, but no one can attain to his rank seated remotely on a cloud. Occasionally he must hurl thunderbolts, and an Olympian simile is surely appropriate to such a commander, removed in distance, if never in feeling, from the actual scenes of combat.

The sailor needs an image of his leaders, both immediate and more distant, to which he can respond, and which will help to stiffen his fibre and quicken his thought in the testing, nerve-racking and some-times protracted ordeal of warfare. Over the centuries, the standard of leadership at sea in time of war has been high, sometimes outstandingly so.

Out of the countless hours of high drama, upon the outcome of which so much depended, the historically-minded may well recall Hawke's thunderous swoop into Quiberon Bay on that dark November afternoon in 1759; Saunders's convincing feint directed upon Mont-calm's lines at Beauport while, away above Quebec, Wolfe's infantry climbed the steep path to the Heights of Abraham; Bougainville, his great world voyage behind him, in the van of the French Fleet at the critical encounter off the Chesapeake; Suffren's unbroken resolution in pitting himself again and again in opposition to a fighter as stubborn as himself; Howe's feat in bringing supplies to beleaguered Gibraltar where, nineteen summers later, Saumarez made his astonishing re-covery from disaster; Farragut 'damning the torpedoes' on his way to triumph at Mobile; Beatty, undeterred by the sudden destruction of two of his great battle cruisers, leading the German Commander-in-Chief towards Jellicoe; the cool and scientific Nimitz, nurturing the strength of the American Pacific Fleet from its time of trial after Pearl Harbor to complete predominance over the Imperial Navy of Japan.

Surely these illustrate high qualities in command at sea.

Sources and
Acknowledgements

1 'The Great Lord Hawke.' There is at last a wholly satisfactory biography: *Admiral Hawke* by Ruddock Mackay. O.U.P., 1965.

2 'Admiral Saunders and the Capture of Quebec'. The *Naval Chronicle* Vol. VIII (1802) is fairly full. The best modern account of the St Lawrence campaign is *Quebec 1759: The Siege and the Battle* by C. P. Stacey. Toronto, 1959. The staff officer's notes referred to are in the Public Record Office of Northern Ireland (D/162/77B). The definitive work on Cook is *The Life of Captain James Cook* by J. C. Beaglehole. London, 1974.

3 'Louis-Antoine de Bougainville'. The standard life is *Bougainville Navigateur et les Découvertes de son Temps*, by Jean-Etienne Martin-Allanic. 2 vols. Paris, 1964. The second edition of Bougainville's *Voyage Autour du Monde* (2 vols, Paris) and Forster's English translation appeared in 1772. A study of the impact of the early Pacific voyages is to be found in *European Vision and the South Pacific* 1768–1850 by Bernard Smith. O.U.P., 1960.

4 'Suffren's Great Adventure'. The standard life is the *Histoire du Bailli de Suffren* by Charles Cunat. Paris 1852. An account of Sir Edward Hughes appears in the *Naval Chronicle* Vol. IX (1803). A summary of the Suffren–Hughes campaign appeared in a booklet published by the Ipswich Corporation: *The Maritime Struggle for India* 1781–1783, by Edward H. H. Archibald. Ipswich, 1972.

5 'Howe and the Relief of Gibraltar'. There is no biography of Howe later than Sir John Barrow's *Life* (London, 1838), but there are fascinating glimpses in Lady Bouchier's annotated copy of her *Memoir of Admiral Codrington* (London, 1865): British Museum C.45 f. 12. *The Glorious First of June* (London, 1961) by the present writer contains an account of the battle of 1794.

6 'Children of the Service: the Gardners'. The life of the first Lord Gardner is sketched in the *Naval Chronicle* Vol. VIII (1802), and of the second Lord in the *Naval Chronicle* Vol. XXI (1809).

7 'Children of the Service: the Rowleys'. An account of Admiral Sir William Rowley is to be found in the *Naval Chronicle* Vol. XXIV (1810). I am indebted to Sir Charles Rowley for information about his forebears and for kindly allowing the reproduction of his portrait of Admiral Sir Charles Rowley by Daniel Gardner.

8 'Nelson's Collingwood'. In *Nelson* (London, 1975), and *The Life and Letters of Vice-Admiral Lord Collingwood* (London, 1968) the present writer has summarized recent research, and made use of an important series of letters, now British Museum Add. MSS 52780.

9 'Lord de Saumarez'. The only biography of Saumarez is the *Memoirs and Correspondence of Admiral Lord de Saumarez*, by Sir John Ross. 2 vols. London, 1838. The *Saumarez Papers* edited by A. N. Ryan for the Navy Records Society (London, 1968), is of great value, and there is an outline of Saumarez's earlier career in the *Naval Chronicle* Vol. VI (1801).

10 'Farragut: The American Paragon': *Admiral Farragut* by A. T. Mahan (London, 1892) is still the best biography.

11 'Beatty of the *Lion*'. *The Life and Letters of David Beatty, Admiral of the Fleet*, by Rear-Admiral W. S. Chalmers. (London, 1951.)

12 'The Greatest Command of All: Nimitz'. I am very deeply in the debt of Professor E. B. Potter of the Naval Institute, Annapolis, for kindly allowing me to use articles of his which appeared in the Institute's *Proceedings*: viz 'Chester W. Nimitz' (July 1966) and 'The Command Personality' (January 1969). Nimitz is far too little known outside the United States; for instance, when he died, London papers did not carry an obituary.

Index

Aboukir, HMS, 152, 154, 155
Abu Klea, HM gunboat, 146, 147
Active, HMS, 31
Adam, Robert, 13
Akagi, Japanese ship, 178
Alabama, Confederate ship, 132
Aleutians, 176
Alexander, HMS, 111
Alexandra, HMS, 145, 146
Algeciras, action off, 113–16
Alms, Captain James, 50, 51, 105
American Civil War, 131–41
Amherst, General, 20
Andromeda, HMS, 85
Anholt, 118
Annibal, French ship, 49
Arethusa, HMS, 156, 157
Arizona, US ship, 174
Arkansas, Confederate ship, 135
Arrogant, HMS, 149
Artésian, French ship, 49
Audacious, HMS, 144, 155
Augusta, US ship, 173
Auguste, French ship, 41

Badger, HMS, 93
Baird, General Sir David, 84
Ball, Captain, 111
Ballard, Lieut. Samuel, 74
Baltic, control of the, 117–22
Barfleur, HMS, 81, 97, 98, 107, 108, 147
Barham, HMS, 162
Barham, Lord, 78, 81
Battenberg, Prince Louis of, 150, 151, 166
Battle cruiser, type, 152, 153
Baudin, Admiral, 130, 134
Beatty, Admiral of the Fleet Earl, xi, 145–67, 188
Bedford, Lieut. William, 73
Belle Isle, 13
Bellona, HMS, 70
Beresford, Lord Charles, 145
Bernadotte, Marshal, 120

Berwick, HMS, 6, 81
Bickerton, Sir Richard, 53
Bideford, HMS, 81
Birt, Sarah, 7
Bizarre, French ship, 53
Blackwood, Captain, 102
Bladen, Martin, 5, 6
Blücher, German ship, 159, 160
Boadicea, HMS, 95
Bomanjee, Jamsetjee, 53
Boreas, HMS, 95
Boscawen, Admiral, 6, 10, 13, 20, 47
Boudeuse, French ship, 38
Bougainville, Louis-Antoine de, 22, 27, 29, 31, 35–43, 186
Bowen, Captain John, 74, 75
Boxer Rising, 148, 149
Brandywine, US ship, 130
Brenton, Captain Jahleel, 113, 117
Brest, 10, 73, 112
Bridport, Lord, 76, 77, 109
Brilliant, French ship, 51, 52
Britannia, training ship, 145
Brooklyn, US ship, 131, 139, 141
Brosses, Charles des, 37
Buchanan, Commodore Franklin, 140, 141
Buckner, General Simon B., 184
Bureau of Navigation, 173
Burford, HMS, 77
Bushnell, David, 77
Byng, Admiral John, 8, 47
Byron, Admiral John, 37, 48, 71, 83

Caesar, HMS, 73, 112, 114, 115
Calder, Admiral Sir Robert, 77, 78, 84
Caldwell, Admiral Benjamin, 75
Camperdown, HMS, 146
Captain, HMS, 110
Carteret, Captain Philip, 38
Cato, HMS, 106
Cavite, 175
Centaur, HMS, 119
Centurion, HMS, 19, 21, 26, 29

Chads, Commander James, 28–30
Chalmers, Rear-Admiral W. S., 162
Charles XIII of Sweden, 120
Chatfield, Admiral, 152, 156, 163
Cherub, HMS, 128
Chesapeake, battle of, 42
Chicasan, US ship, 137, 141
Choiseul, Duc de, 36
Churchill, Sir Winston, 145–7, 150, 151, 158, 160, 163, 166, 167
Circe, HMS, 76
Cleopatra, French ship, 57
Codrington, Edward, 74
Collingwood, Vice-Admiral Lord, 75, 76, 78, 86, 91–102, 110, 113, 186
Collingwood, Edward, 97
Collingwood, Commander Wilfred, 95
Colville, Admiral, 147
Commerson, Philip, 38
Conflans, Marshal, 10–12
Conqueror, HMS, 83
Conway, General, 8
Cook, Captain James, 15, 22, 26, 30, 38–40, 69, 81, 96
Coral Sea, battle of the, 176
Cornwallis, Admiral Sir William, 76
Cornwallis, General, 3
Cotes, Francis, 14
Cotton, Admiral Sir Charles, 84–6
Courageux, French ship, 70, 72
Cowan, Admiral Sir Walter, 146, 147
Cowper, William, 61
Cradock, Admiral Sir Christopher, 148
Crescent, HMS, 109
Cressy, HMS, 155
Culloden, HMS, 110
Curtis, Sir Roger, 74, 75

D'Ache, Admiral, 48, 77
D'Alembert, J., 35
Danae, HMS, 83
Daphne, HMS, 76
Darby, Admiral, 61
Dardanelles, The, 100
Davys, John, 36
Decatur, US ship, 72
De Cordoba, Admiral, 64, 110
Defence, HMS, 75, 121
De Grasse, Comte de, 3, 42, 43, 84, 119
De Guichen, Comte de, 41, 62
Denis, Captain Peter, 19, 70
Denmark, 118–22
Derfflinger, German ship, 159, 160, 162, 164, 165
D'Estaing, Admiral, 41, 48, 71, 83
Des Barres, J. F. W., 22
Diana, HMS, 26
Diderot, D., 35, 40
Dogger Bank, battles off, 106, 158–60
Dolphin, HMS, 37, 38
Dominica, 5
Dongola, 147
Dorsetshire, HMS, 70

Douglas, Sir Andrew, 75
Douglas, Sir Charles, 71
Drayton, Captain Perceval, 136, 137, 139, 140, 141
Dreadnought, HMS, 149
Duchess of Richmond, transport, 63
Duckworth, Admiral, 100
Duff, Commodore Robert, 11
Duke, HMS, 71
Dumaresq, Captain Philip, 113, 118
Durell, Rear-Admiral Philip, 21, 22, 24

Eagle, HMS, 20, 69, 85, 138
El Teb, HM gunboat, 147
Enchantress, Admiralty yacht, 151
Endeavour, HMS, 15
Enterprise, US ship, 175–9, 180
Ericsson, John, 137
Erie, US ship, 130
Essex, HMS, 12, 81
Essex, US ship, 127–9
Essex Junior, US prize, 128, 129
Europa, HMS, 71
Euryalus, HMS, 102
Evan-Thomas, Rear-Admiral Sir Hugh, 161–4
Excellent, HMS, 97, 110
Exeter, HMS, 51

Falkland Islands, 36–8
Fantasque, French ship, 48
Farragut, David, xi, 127–42, 187, 188
Fateh, HM gunboat, 147
Favourite, HMS, 31
Field, Marshall, 148
Fighting Instructions, The, 6
Finisterre, battles off, 7, 20, 27
Fisher, Lord, xii, 149, 153, 160, 166
Fletcher, Admiral Frank J., 175, 177
Fletcher, John, 107
Florida, store ship, 37
Folsom, Rev. Charles, 129
Formidable, French ship, 12
Formidable, HMS, 71
Forrestal, James V., 173, 185
Fort Morgan, 139, 140
Fortitude, HMS, 106
Fox, G. A., 132
Foudroyant, French ship, 82
Franklin, US ship, 142
Fremantle, Admiral Thomas, 86

Galatea, HMS, 161, 162
Gambier, Admiral, 75, 118
Ganteaume, Admiral, 101
Gardner, Daniel, 86
Gardner, 1st Baron, 69–76
Gardner, 2nd Baron, 76–8
Garter, Order of the, 65
Geary, Sir Francis, 15, 16, 22
George II, King, 6, 9, 14, 69
George III, King, 14, 39, 65, 72, 99, 106, 109

George V, King, 145, 167
Ghormley, Admiral Robert L., 179, 180
Gibraltar, 61–4, 82, 111
Gilbert Islands, 175, 180
Glorious First of June, battle of, 65, 69, 72–6, 97, 98
Goeben, German ship, 155
Gold, Joyce, 92
Goliath, HMS, 111
Goodenough, Commodore W. E., 157, 158, 162, 163
Gordon, General, 146
Gosport, HMS, 83
Göteberg, 119
Granger, General, 138, 140
Grant, General, 135, 142
Graves, Admiral Thomas, 3, 42, 92
Gray, Thomas, 30
Grayling, US ship, 175
Greyhound, US ship, 130
Guadalcanal, 179, 180
Guam, 174, 181, 184
Guerrier, French ship, 41
Gustavus II Adolphus, King of Sweden, 171
Gustavus IV Adolphus, King of Sweden, 119, 120
Guy, Midshipman B. J. D., 148

Halsey, Admiral William F., 175, 177, 180–3, 188
Hannibal, HMS, 113
Hardy, Admiral Sir Charles, 20, 62, 106
Hartford, US ship, 133–42
Harvey, Major F. J. W., 113
Haswell, Commander Robert, 93
Hatchlands, 13
Hawaii, 174, 175
Hawke, Admiral Lord, xii, 3–15, 19, 20, 31, 47, 81, 82, 93, 186
Hawke, 2nd Baron, 3, 4, 7, 8
Hawkins, Richard, 36
Heligoland, 118
Hermione, Spanish ship, 31
Hero, HMS, 77, 78, 121
Heroine, HMS, 72, 76
Héros, French ship, 12, 48, 51, 53, 55, 57
Hickey, William, 53–6
Hillyer, Captain James, 127–9
Hinchinbrook, HMS, 93, 94
Hipper, Admiral von, 158–66
Hiroshima, 184
Hiryu, Japanese ship, 178
Hogue, HMS, 155
Holland, Samuel Jan, 22
Holmes, Rear-Admiral Charles, 21, 27–30
Hood, family of, 69
Hood, Rear-Admiral Horace, 147, 164
Hood, Admiral Lord, 107, 108
Hope, Captain George, 118
Hornet, HMS, 93
Hornet, US ship, 175–8, 180

Hoste, Sir William, 86
Howe, Admiral Earl, 9, 11, 15, 28, 61–5, 72, 74, 75, 82, 98, 186
Howe, General, 28
Hughes, Sir Edward, 21, 32. 50, 57
Hughes, Sir Richard, 95
Hunter, HMS, 29
Hutt, Captain John, 72
Hyder Ali, 48, 50, 52, 56

Implacable, HMS, 119
Indefatigable, HMS, 162, 163
Indomitable, HMS, 158, 159, 162
Inflexible, French ship, 6, 20
Inflexible, HMS, 162
Intrépide, French ship, 6, 20
Invincible, HMS, 156, 162, 164
Iron Duke, HMS, 165, 166
Iwo Jima, 183, 184

Jackson, President Andrew, 130
James, Admiral Sir William, xii
Jellicoe, Admiral Earl, 156, 157, 161–6
Jenkins, Captain Thornton A., 135
Jervis, Admiral Sir John (later Earl of St Vincent), 28, 72, 83, 97, 98, 101, 110, 112, 113, 117
Johnson, Samuel, xi, 4, 13, 138
Johnstone, Commodore George, 48, 49, 128
Jones, Paul, 127
Jonquière, La, Admiral, 7
Jouett, Captain, 139, 140
Juno, HMS, 149, 150
Jutland, battle of, 161–6

Kaga, Japanese ship, 178
Kamikaze, 183
Keats, Captain Richard, 114, 115, 119
Kempenfelt, Rear-Admiral Richard, 61, 106, 107
Keppel, Admiral Lord, 11, 12, 32
Keyes, Admiral Lord, 148, 156
Khartoum, 146
Killick, Mr, 24
Kincaid, Admiral Thomas C., 182
King, Fleet Admiral Ernest J., 171, 179, 188
King, Sir Richard, 50, 51, 56, 57, 86
Kitchener, Lord, 146, 181
Knapton, George, 14
Knox, Frank, 173
Knox, Captain John, 24
Kwajalein, 181

Lafayette, Marie-Joseph, 130
La Marr, Lieut., 174
Latona, HMS, 63
Launay, M., 54
L'Etanduère, Admiral, 6, 47
Leon, French ship, 70
L'Etoile, French ship, 38
Levant, HMS, 70

Lexington, US ship, 175, 176
Leyte Gulf, 182–3
Lincoln, President Abraham, 131
Lind, James, 121
Linois, Admiral, 113
Lion, HMS, 145, 152–66
Lively, HMS, 81
Locker, Captain, 93
Louis XV, King, 36
Louis XVI, King, 43, 50
Louisbourg, 10, 20, 22
Lowestoffe, HMS, 27, 30, 93
Lutzow, German ship, 162, 165
Luzon, 175

MacArthur, General Douglas, 176, 179, 180, 184
Macclesfield, Lord, 35
Magnanime, HMS, 9, 12, 28, 51
Mahan, A. T., 131, 132, 150
Maidstone, HMS, 70
Malaya, HMS, 162
Malouines, Les, 36, 38
Malta, Knights of, 47
Manhadon, US ship, 185
Manhattan, US ship, 137
Marianas, 181, 182
Marlborough, HMS, 109
Martin, Captain Byam, 119
Martin, Captain Henry, 83
Mathews, Admiral Thomas, 5, 81
Mauritius, 85
Mediator, HMS, 95
Medway, HMS. 69
Mermaid, HMS, 95, 96
Merrimac, Confederate ship, 133
Metacomet, US ship, 139
Midway, 175–8
Mikuma, Japanese ship, 178
Minorca, 127, 142
Minotaur, HMS, 121
Mississippi, US ship, 133
Missouri, US ship, 184
Mitchell, Captain, 56
Mobile, attack on, 135–41
Mogame, Japanese ship, 178
Molloy, Captain Anthony, 159, 160
Moltke, German ship, 159, 162
Monarch, HMS, 83
Monarque, French ship, 6
Monck, George, 186
Monckton, Brigadier, 21, 25
Monitor, US ship, 133
Monmouth, HMS, 51, 105
Montague, HMS, 82, 83
Montcalm, Marquis de, 22–31, 35
Montreal, HMS, 103
Moore, Admiral, 159, 160
Moore, John Francis, 3
Morant Keys, 94
Mordaunt, General, 8
Motte-Picquet, La, 42
Murion, French ship, 113

Murray, Admiral George, 85
Murray, Brigadier, 21, 27
Mutine, HMS, 111

Nagasaki, 184
Nantucket, 41
Napoleon I, xi, 43, 77, 100, 102. 113, 117, 119
Naval Chronicle, The, 14, 78, 92, 94
Naval Secretary, duties of, 151
Nelson, Lord, 65, 85, 91–9, 110, 111, 116, 127
Neptune, HMS, 21
New Orleans, attack on, 133–5
New Zealand, HMS, 156, 158, 159, 162, 163
Nicaragua, 94
Nile, battle of the, 111, 112
Nimitz, Fleet Admiral, xi, 171–85, 188
Norris, Captain Richard, 81, 82
Norris, Admiral Sir John, 81
Nootka Sound, 71, 95
North Carolina, US ship, 179
North Stoneham, 3
Nottingham, HMS, 20
Nuestra Senora de Cavadonga, Spanish ship, 19

Ohio, US ship, 172
Okinawa, 183
Omdurman, battle of, 147
Orient, French ship, 111
Oriflamme, French ship, 82
Orion, HMS, 110, 111
Orphée, French ship, 47, 82
Osborne, Admiral Henry, 82

Page, Rear-Admiral Benjamin, 78
Pakenham, Rear-Admiral, 160, 162, 163, 167
Palliser, Admiral Sir Hugh, 31, 32, 69
Palmer, Surgeon, 140
Pantheon, The, 44
Parker, Sir Hyde (the Elder), 106
Parker, Sir Hyde (the Younger), 118
Parker, Sir Peter, 93, 106
Parry, Rear-Admiral, 70
Paul I, Tsar of Russia, 119
Pearl Harbor, 171–5, 177, 180
Pegasus, HMS, 75, 85
Pelican, HMS, 94
Pelly, Captain Henry, 160
Pembroke, HMS, 22, 23, 46
Perkins, George H., 140
Peuple Souverain, French ship, 111
Phips, Sir William, 23
Phoebe, HMS, 127–9
Piggott, Captain W. A., 146
Pitt, William (the Elder), 8, 14
Pitt, William (the Younger), 65
Pocock, Admiral Sir George, 6, 16, 48, 77
Poder, Spanish ship, 6

Pommern, German ship, 165
Pompadour, Madame de, 35
Popham, Sir Home, 84
Porter, David, 127–33
Porter, John, 130
Port Moresby, 176
Potter, Prof. E. B., 173, 185, 188, 190
Preston, HMS, 70
Prince, HMS, 97
Prince George, HMS, 85
Prince of Wales, HMS, 78, 117
Princess Royal, HMS, 152, 158, 159, 162
Providien, 51, 52
Pym, Captain Samuel, 85

Quebec, 20–31
Queen, HMS, 72–5, 149
Queen Charlotte, HMS, 65, 74, 75
Queen Elizabeth, HMS, 166
Queen Mary, HMS, 152, 156, 160, 163
Quiberon Bay, battle of, 4, 10–12, 31, 83

Rabaul, 176, 179, 180
Rainier, Admiral Peter, 50, 77, 84
Raisonnable, French ship, 70, 84
Rattler, HMS, 95
Raven, HMS, 70
Real Carlos, Spanish ship, 115
Red River campaign, 135, 136
Resolution, HMS, 12, 70, 77, 85
Réunion, French ship, 109
Richmond, US ship, 138
Robespierre, M. de, 43
Rochefort, 4, 8
Roddam, Admiral, 96
Rodney, Admiral Lord, xii, 5, 6, 9, 20,
   42, 61, 71, 83, 103, 119
Rousseau, J. J., 40
Rowley, Sir Charles, 81, 85–7
Rowley, Sir Joshua, 81, 82–3
Rowley, Sir Josias, 81, 84, 85
Rowley, Sir William, 81, 82
Royal George, HMS, 4, 12, 61, 62, 121
Royal Society, 35
Royal Sovereign, HMS, 102
Royal William, HMS, 31
Ruby, HMS, 77, 146
Ruskin, John, 153
Russell, HMS, 107, 108

Sadras, 50, 51
St André, Jean-Bon, 73
St Antoine, French ship, 115
St George, HMS, 121
St Vincent, battle of, 97, 98, 110
St Vincent, Lord (*see* Jervis, Sir John)
Saipan, 181
San Hermenegildo, Spanish ship, 115
San Josef, Spanish ship, 98, 110, 117
Santa Cruz Islands, 180
Santissima Trinidada, Spanish ship, 98,
   110

Saratoga, US ship, 175, 177, 179
Saumarez, Lord de, 105–23, 186, 187
Saumarez, Captain Philip, 6, 19, 20, 105
Saunders, Sir Charles, 6, 8, 13, 14, 19–32,
   50, 186
Savo Island, battle of, 179
Scheer, Admiral, 161–5
Seven Years War, The, 8, 13
Sérieuse, French ship, 111
Sevelod, Russian ship, 119
Sévère, French ship, 52
Seydlitz, German ship, 159, 160, 162
Seymour, Admiral Sir Edward, 148
Shannon, HMS, 91
Shirley, Governor, 95
Shoho, Japanese ship, 176
Shokaku, Japanese ship, 176
Simcoe, Admiral, 22
Sims, Admiral, 173
Singapore, 174
Skipjack, US ship, 172
Smith, Major General Holland M., 181
Smith, Sir Sidney, 85
Soleil Royal, French ship, 11, 12
Solide, French ship, 47
Solomons campaign, 179, 180
Somerset, HMS, 21, 32
Soryu, Japanese ship, 178
South Carolina, US ship, 173
Speke, Captain, 70
Sphinx, French ship, 49
Sprague, Admiral Clifton A., 183
Spruance, Admiral Raymond A., 175,
   177, 178, 180, 181, 188
Squirrel, HMS, 26
Stanhope, Captain, 108
Stark, Admiral Harold, 173
Strachan, Sir Richard, 78
Suckling, Captain Maurice, 93
Suffolk, HMS, 83, 149
Suffren, Bailli de, xii, 6, 47–57, 186
Sultan, HMS, 51, 55, 71
Superb, HMS, 50, 51, 55, 83, 114
Superbe, French ship, 12
Sutherland, HMS, 38, 39
Swaythling, 7
Sweden, 118–22

Tahiti, 38–40
Tallapoosa, US ship, 142
Tecumseh, US ship, 137–9, 141
Tennessee, Confederate ship, 137–40
Thackeray, W. M., 102
Thames, HMS, 114
Thesée, French ship, 12
Tiger, HMS, 158–60, 162
Tinian, 181
Tippoo, Sultan, 56, 84
Tisiphone, HMS, 106, 107
Tokyo, 176
Torbay, HMS, 12
Townshend, Brigadier, 21, 27, 29, 30–1
Trafalgar, HMS, 146

Trincomalee, 51–3, 57, 77
Troubridge, Captain T., 110, 112
Truk, 178
Tryal, HMS, 19
Turner, Admiral Richmond K., 179
Tyrwhitt, Admiral Sir Reginald, 146, 156

Valiant, HMS, 71, 162
Vanguard, HMS, 111
Vaudreuil, Comte de, 6
Venerable, HMS, 114, 115
Vengeur, French ship, 74
Verron, M., 38
Vesuvius, HMS, 28
Vicksburg, 135, 136
Victoria, HMS, 146
Victoria, Queen, 142, 145
Victoria and Albert, Royal yacht, 146
Victory, HMS, 61, 64, 75, 106, 118, 121
Villaret-Joyeuse, Admiral, 73
Ville de Paris, French ship, 108
Ville de Paris, HMS, 101
Villeneuve, Admiral, 77, 99
Voltaire, 8
von der Tann, German ship, 162
von Platen, Baron, 120, 122

Wake Island, 174
Wallis, Captain Samuel, 38, 39
Walpole, Horace, 3, 9, 19
Walpole, Sir Robert, 5
Warren, Sir John, 112
Warrior, HMS, 71
Warspite, HMS, 162
Washington, George, 3
Wasp, US ship, 175, 177, 179
Watson, Seaman, 139
Wellington, Duke of, 102
Whitehead, Robert, 146
Wilhelm II, Kaiser, 150, 160, 161
William IV, King, 85, 86, 95, 114, 116, 122, 151
Wilson, Admiral Sir Arthur, 150
Winnebago, US ship, 137
Wolfe, Major General James, xii, 9, 20–31, 186

Yamamoto, Admiral, 176–8
Yarmouth, HMS, 20
Yorktown, 3
Yorktown, US ship, 175–8

Zoutman, Admiral, 106
Zuikaku, Japanese ship, 176